BBBBBBBBB
BBBBBBBBBOO
OOOOOOOOOOOOO
OOOOOOONNNNN
NNNNNNNNNNNN
GGGGGGGGGGGG
GGGGGGGGGGGGG
G G G G G G G G G G G G

THE CULT OF MAC

LEANDER KAHNEY

**NO STARCH
PRESS**

Printed by Craft Print International Limited in Singapore
2 3 4 5 6 7 8 9 10—07 06 05 04

No Starch Press and the No Starch Press logo are registered trademarks of No Starch Press, Inc. Other product and company names mentioned herein may be the trademarks of their respective owners. Rather than use a trademark symbol with every occurrence of a trademarked name, we are using the names only in an editorial fashion and to the benefit of the trademark owner, with no intention of infringement of the trademark.

Publisher: William Pollock
Managing Editor: Karol Jurado
Cover and Interior Design and Composition: Octopod Studios
Copyeditor: Andy Carroll
Proofreader: Stephanie Provines
Indexer: Kevin Broccoli

For information on translations or book distributors, please contact No Starch Press, Inc. directly:

No Starch Press, Inc.
555 De Haro Street, Suite 250, San Francisco, CA 94107
phone: 415-863-9900; fax: 415-863-9950; info@nostarch.com; http://www.nostarch.com

Articles reprinted from Wired News, www.wired.com. Copyright © 2004 Wired Digital Inc., a Lycos Network Company. All rights reserved. Photographs and illustrations on pages 15–17, 43, 51, and 221 used with permission of Geek Culture®. Photograph on page 104 used with permission of AP/World Wide Photos.

Library of Congress Cataloging-in-Publication Data
Kahney, Leander.
   The cult of Macintosh / Leander Kahney.-- 1st ed.
        p. cm.
Includes index.
   ISBN 1-886411-83-2
 1. Macintosh (Computer)--Anecdotes. 2. Computers--Social aspects.
I.
Title.
   QA76.8.M3 K35 2004
   004.165--dc22

                                        2003021938

DEDICATION

To my wife, Traci, and children, Nadine, Milo, Olin, and Lyle.

ACKNOWLEDGMENTS

The biggest thanks go to the Mac community. Thanks to everyone interviewed and who sent pictures, comments, story tips, feedback, criticism and encouragement. I'd also like to thank colleagues and former colleagues from Wired News, especially Jeremy Barna, Frank Leahy, Alison Macondray, David Miller, and Jon Rochmis.

Thanks to Boris Anthony for his design work on the Cult of Mac Web site, Frank Leahy for setting it up, and John Mahoney for donating the domain.

I must also thank Raines Cohen, Marty Cortinas, Bruce Damer, Nobuyuki Hayashi, Jeffy Milstead, David Morgenstern, Snaggy and Nitrozak, and Alex Wipperfurth.

Leander Kahney
San Francisco, CA

BRIEF CONTENTS

THE CULT OF MAC

Loading

CONTENTS IN DETAIL

THE CULT OF MAC

Loading

THE CULT OF MAC

Loading

THE CULT OF MAC

Welcome!

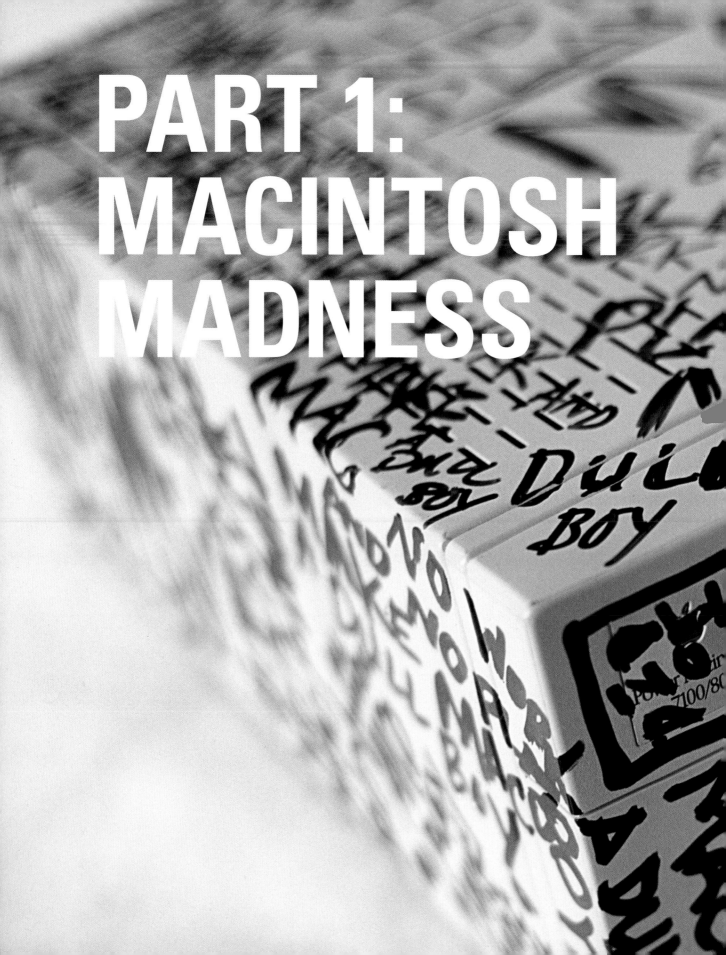

PART 1: MACINTOSH MADNESS

TECHNO FETISHISM

Chap

Chapte

Cha

ter 2

apter 6

Chapter 15

(TOP) MAC POWER: MAC USERS
ARE NOT MERELY AN AD HOC GROUP
OF PEOPLE WHO HAPPEN TO USE
THE SAME KIND OF COMPUTER.
THEY REPRESENT A DISTINCT SUB-
CULTURE, WITH ITS OWN RITUALS,
TRADITIONS, AND MINDSET.
CREDIT: ROBERLAN BORGES

(BOTTOM) ADDICTIVE: "APPLE IS
LIKE A STRANGE DRUG THAT YOU
JUST CAN'T QUITE GET ENOUGH
OF," MUSICIAN BARRY ADAMSON
TOLD THE *GUARDIAN* NEWSPAPER.
"THEY SHOULDN'T CALL IT MAC.
THEY SHOULD CALL IT CRACK!"
CREDIT: MACADDICT

5

MAC LOYALTY

There are 25 million people around the world who use Macintosh computers, according to Apple. But unlike ordinary personal computers, people don't simply use Macs—they become fans. They develop a passion for the machines, which can sometimes turn into an obsession. "Apple is like a strange drug that you just can't quite get enough of," musician Barry Adamson told the *Guardian* newspaper. "They shouldn't call it Mac. They should call it crack!"

Mac loyalty is so well known, it's a cliché. Mac users are routinely referred to as Apple's faithful, Mac zealots, members of the cult of Mac, Appleholics, Macheads, Maccies, Macolytes, and Mac addicts. The biannual Macworld conference is often compared to a religious revival meeting, where Steve Jobs is worshipped like a rock star or a charismatic cult leader.

The Mac community is arguably the largest subculture in computing. Mac enthu-siasts—as a group—are probably more loyal, more dedicated, than users of any other computer platform, perhaps even Linux. Linux and Unix users are, in fact, switching to Macs in droves thanks to the Unix-based Mac OS X. What other computer inspires fans to get tattoos and personalized license plates, amass huge collections of ancient machines, build Mac aquariums, or proudly describe them-selves as Mac fans, Mac freaks, or Mac nuts? The Amiga, perhaps, but certainly not Dell, Compaq, or Microsoft.

What makes Mac users so loyal? The answer, of course, depends on who is asked: Marketers say it's the brand; psychologists say it's a social relationship; and Apple loyalists say it's the merits of the machine, its friendliness, its simplicity. But some common themes emerge: community, the alternative to Microsoft, and the brand, which connotes nonconformity, liberty, and creativity. Mac users are not merely an ad hoc group of people who happen to use the same kind of computer. They represent a distinct subculture, with its own rituals, traditions, and mindset.

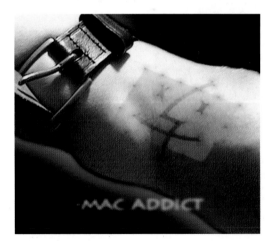

"If you see somebody in an airport in London, or someplace down in Peru or something, and you see an Apple tag on their bag, or an Apple T-shirt, it's like the Deadheads…you have an instant friend," Chris Espinosa, one of Apple's earliest employees, told Stanford Library. "Most likely, you share something very core to your being with this person, which is a life outlook, a special vision."

THE MAC COMMUNITY IS ARGUABLY THE LARGEST SUBCULTURE IN COMPUTING.

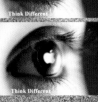

HEY, I'M A LOYAL MAC USER, TOO

Why are Macintosh users so doggedly loyal to Apple? Ask the experts (see Chapter 19), and they'll say Mac users have a psychosexual bond with their machines, or that the community resembles a new-age religion. They may also suggest that users treat their Macs more like babies or friends than like computers, and that the community itself and Apple's brand may be more important than the company's products. But like most other Mac users, I believe the Mac is the best computer out there. I do not think of myself as part of a cult, a quasi-religious community, or a weird techno-fetish ring.

A few years ago I bought an iMac. I didn't need it. I already had three good computers. I just wanted it. I didn't tell my wife until it was too late for her to nix it. I was in the doghouse for weeks. A year later, I bought another, newer iMac. Then I bought an iBook. That brought my computer tally to six. I didn't need more than one—and I couldn't really afford them—but I was unable to resist.

I am obsessed with Macs. Every time Apple comes out with something new, I want it. My god, I want it bad. Why? It's not easy to say. I'm not obsessive about anything else. Cars, clothes, power tools—they leave me cold. But with Macintosh, I can't get enough.

Part of it is design: Apple's products look great. You want to touch them, feel them, caress them. It's not sexual, but it is sensual.

Part of it is innovation: Apple comes out with some cool stuff. The company makes things easy that were once a pain—putting pictures on the Web, connecting to a wireless network, loading thousands of songs onto a portable music player.

Part of it is familiarity: I grew up using Macs. I know my way around. I still remember the magic of playing with MacPaint for the first time.

But a big part of it is subconscious: Somehow, Apple's products stimulate desire. Perhaps the machines tap into some primeval, magpie-like attraction to bright shiny objects, a universal, time-less urge to own nice things.

It's not unlike sex: You're smitten, and you've got to have it. Once you do, the ardor fades. But never mind—regular as clockwork, the next thing out of Apple reignites the yearning.

The desire is subconscious, but it is rationalized. You say to yourself: "My wife will go bananas, but a new iBook would be perfect for taking the kids to the park. Yeah, if I could work at the park, I could earn the extra money to cover the computer."

There are lots of advantages to using a Mac, most of which Mac users already know about. They're better built, better designed. They last longer. They rarely fall prey to viruses. But perhaps the biggest advantage is one that's rarely acknowledged: You get to join a highly creative, knowledgeable, and supportive community.

Mac users can be extremely cool. It's a lifestyle thing. Mac users tend to be liberal, free-thinking, counterculture. They dress well, look good, and have discerning taste (in New York, anyway). Take a Mac out in public and people want to look at it. Mac users have a sense of humor. They also help each other. Myriad Web sites help you find solutions to problems, pointers to the best deals, and great freeware or shareware.

Mac users are creative. What else would you expect from all the musicians, artists, designers, and filmmakers who make up

(ABOVE) THE CLASSIC APPLE
DECAL: WRITER SHANNON OKEY
HAD ONE IN HER CAR, UNTIL SOME-
ONE BROKE IN TO STEAL IT.
CREDIT: REDLIGHTRUNNER

(RIGHT) APPLE STICKERS: ON JUST
ABOUT EVERY BLOCK IN EVERY
CITY, THERE'S A VEHICLE WITH
AN APPLE STICKER.
CREDIT: MATTHEW MULLENWEG

Apple's core constituency? It's not unreasonable to say that a lot of the world's mass media—books, magazines, movies, music, Web sites—is made on Macs. A lot of highly creative people fire up their Macs every day to shape our culture.

Most of the stories in this book aren't about the clever things people create with their Macs—Apple covers that in its marketing. The stories are about grassroots Mac culture—the kind of thing Mac users do to show their loyalty to Apple and the Mac platform. They are about Apple tattoos, paper Macs, Mac aquariums, interface tweakers, songs about Macs, and people who spend their weekends visiting Apple's stores. They are about the culture surrounding the Macintosh: the Cult of Mac.

Some of the people in these stories are extremely devoted to the Mac. However, I suspect a lot of Mac users are like me: You think you're not as zealous, but you recognize and understand the devotion.

This chapter tells some tales of fellow Mac users who are just like you and me. Except, well, they're nothing like you or me. But maybe you'll recognize the devotion.

APPLE'S STICKIEST MARKETING PLOY

Car thieves break into vehicles for all sorts of reasons. In some inner-city neighborhoods, a thief will smash a window for a dime. But Shannon Okey has one of the more off-the-wall vehicle theft stories: Someone broke into her car to steal her Apple window sticker.

Okey, a writer who lives in the trendy district of Somerville, Massachusetts, near Harvard Square, awoke one morning in May to find that her car had been broken into. "Some maladjusted subhuman broke into my car last night," she wrote in her Weblog. "Did they take the little case of CDs? Nooo. Did they take anything of value? Nooo. That scoundrel broke my window to steal my Apple sticker!"

Okey's sticker was an older window-cling decal, the classic rainbow-striped kind. It was stuck on a rear quarter-window. A Gap shoulder bag was also stolen, containing a copy of *The Boston Dog Lover's Companion*, among other things, but Okey found it later in a trash can up the street. The only thing she never recovered was the decal.

Okey has a replacement but dares not put it in the car. "I don't want to risk losing my last 1980s Apple decal," she said. "It broke my heart because it isn't something I can replace."

That's not quite true. Apple decals as old-school as the one stolen from Okey's car can be found for a few dollars on eBay or on collectors' sites like RedLightRunner. So why would anyone steal an Apple sticker? It's not as if they're rare. Apple provides a couple of free decals with every new machine. The company started the practice in the late 1970s with the Apple II and continued it through the Apple III and the Macintosh line. During the mid-1990s, Apple provided boxfuls of decals to anyone who asked. It later dropped the rainbow motif when it changed its corporate logo to a solid color, which was red first and is now white.

Fred Davis, former editor in chief of *MacUser* magazine, said the idea of putting a window decal (as opposed to a solid sticker) in every computer box was very clever, because it encouraged people to stick it somewhere public. It was also, at least in the early days, an emblem of cool.

"Like the VW, the Apple II was the 'Volks-computer,'" Davis said. "The early Apple users were the hippies and freaks, as opposed to businesspeople, who were in the IBM PC or CP/M camps. So the rainbow sticker became a badge of hipness honor, signifying that you were smart enough and cool enough to have a personal computer. Now that they're ubiquitous and they cost a lot less, it's hard to imagine a time when it was as much of a big deal, but to Apple users it wasn't just a big deal, it was a social-political-cultural statement."

The decals were so attractive, in fact, that one independent software developer asked customers to send him Apple stickers instead of money. Australian programmer Gary Drury released his MacChange utility a few years ago under a "StickerWare" license, a variation on shareware that requested stickers instead of cash.

"Apple stickers looked cool at the time and were extremely hard to come by here in Australia," he explained. "I thought that it would be a fairly simple thing for users to put one in an envelope and send over." Drury, now a software director at Digital Voodoo, added that the utility was only worth $5, and Australian banks charged $6 to cash overseas checks.

He received a few decals, but not many. "Several people wrote their names and addresses on them, which was nice because it was a more personal thank you that I'd remember," he said. Naturally, he stuck a couple of them on his car.

Over the years, the stickers have been a marketing coup for Apple. It's almost guaranteed that proud owners of brand-new Macs will affix a decal on their car, boat, bike, skateboard, or storefront window. In fact, an Apple sticker is often the first thing people stick on a new car. Owners often peel stickers from their old vehicles and transfer them to new ones.

John Springer said it was the embellishment he made to the new VW Beetle he bought in 1998. "I got my new Bug a few days before the iMac went on sale," he reported in a Usenet post. "The first thing I did to it was put a big old seven-color Apple sticker in the rear window. And then I drove it to CompUSA on Aug. 15, parked opposite the front door so everyone would have to look, and went in and got my iMac."

There is also a surprising number of people who use Windows PCs but put Apple stickers on them. Jennifer Ozawa reported in her online journal that the first thing her husband did with his new Sony Vaio (which runs Windows) was stick an Apple decal on it. There are similar reports of people putting Apple stickers on PalmPilots, Windows desktops, and all kinds of electronic gear, from TVs and stereos to electric guitars. The stylish Apple logo lends gadgets an air of geek chic, even if they aren't Apple products.

A designer from Chicago who used a Windows PC, Paul McAleer, decorated his car with an Apple sticker before he even bought a Mac. "The big thing for me, though, was putting an Apple sticker on my car even though I still owned a PC," he wrote in his Weblog. "I'm a geek; I thought that was the coolest thing. It still kinda is."

CREATIVE STREAK: "BOB" FROM GERMANY (HE DECLINED TO GIVE HIS LAST NAME) WANTED AN ORIGINAL STICKER FOR HIS NEW CAR, SO HE CREATED A COPY OF THE DOCK IN MAC OS X AND STUCK IT IN HIS REAR WINDOW. "THE SIMPLE WHITE APPLE IS NICE, BUT EVERYBODY HAS THAT. SO I THOUGHT, WHY NOT GO A LITTLE STEP FURTHER?" HE SAID. "ORIGINALLY I WANTED TO RECREATE A COMPLETE DESKTOP, BUT I'M PRETTY LAZY." HIS LAST CAR HAD A STICKER SHOWING THE OLD FINDER ICON AND ANOTHER THAT READ "I WON'T BRAKE FOR WINDOWS USERS." HIS NEW DOCK STICKER HAS DRAWN LOTS OF PRAISE FROM APPLE FANS SINCE HE POSTED PICTURES ON THE WEB, BUT NO ONE KNOWS WHAT IT IS WHERE HE LIVES. "I LIVE RIGHT IN THE MIDDLE OF NOWHERE AND NOBODY KNOWS WHAT THE DOCK IS," HE SAID.
CREDIT: BOB

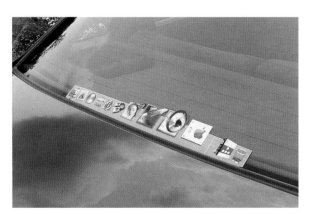

DID I MENTION I'M A MAC GEEK? JASON WOOD OF ONTARIO, CANADA HAS TAKEN THE STICKER PHENOMENON ONE STEP FURTHER BY PUTTING A "MAC GEEK" VANITY LICENSE PLATE ON HIS VW BEETLE, WHICH IS ALSO COVERED IN CUSTOM-MADE APPLE LOGOS. WOOD, WHO WORKS PART-TIME AT AN APPLE STORE AND OFTEN WEARS A "MAC GEEK" T-SHIRT, HAD A COUPLE OF LARGE VINYL APPLE STICKERS MADE BY A LOCAL PRINTER, WHICH HE STUCK TO THE DOORS OF HIS "MACMOBILE." "I ALWAYS GET A FEW FUNNY LOOKS," HE SAID. "USUALLY WHEN I'M PULLING OUT OF A PARKING SPOT, I NOTICE PEOPLE'S LIPS READING THE PLATES. SOME PEOPLE GIVE ME DIRTY LOOKS. I THINK IT'S FUNNY."
CREDIT: JASON WOOD

IT RUNS IN THE FAMILY: ROBERT MCANDREW GOT HIS MAC MAC ILLINOIS LICENSE PLATE BECAUSE OF HIS SURNAME (EVERYONE CALLS HIM MAC); THE PLATE HAS A PICTURE OF THE MIGHTY MACKINAW BRIDGE IN NORTHERN MICHIGAN, OFTEN REFERRED TO AS THE BIG MAC; AND HE'S A MAC NUT.
CREDIT: ROBERT MCANDREW

Apple stickers can even be found at rival computer manufacturers. An Atari employee reported on Usenet that there were Apple decals at Atari's headquarters—in the urinals.

Another form of declaring automotive allegiance to Apple are Mac-related vanity license plates, of which there are a surprising number, including things like MACGEEK, MACUSER, MACMYDAY, PWRMAC1, PWRMAC, and so on.

Robert McAndrew got his MAC MAC Illinois license plate because of his surname (everyone calls him Mac); the plate has a picture of the Mighty Mackinaw Bridge in northern Michigan, often referred to as the Big Mac; and he's a Mac nut. He was rear-ended once because the other driver was so interested in the plate, he reported in an online post. "Maybe I should have put WATCH OUT on the plate," he wrote.

Tim Flaskamp, a student from Germany, launched a Web site in January 2002 to track Apple stickers on cars. As of March 2003, his Apfelautos site (found at http://www.apfelautos.com/) had a gallery of 197 photos, and the site is still growing.

According to Flaskamp, every Mac user with a car puts a sticker on it. Flaskamp, a 27-year-old print technician from Bielefeld, Germany, got the idea for his site after moving to a new apartment. He always liked to spot other Mac users while out driving and was delighted to notice there were half a dozen Apple cars (or Apfel autos) in his new neighborhood. "I was very happy about the good surroundings," he said. He decided to honor this automotive bonding with a dedicated Web site.

The site is set up to let people submit pictures of their Apple-branded vehicles. The selection includes cars and motorbikes of every kind, all proudly displaying an Apple sticker in the back window or stuck somewhere to the vehicle's rear.

Though most of the contributors hail from Germany ("Cars might be a German obsession," Flaskamp noted), he's received pictures of Apple cars from all over the world. Some people send some unusual images. "People often send trash," he complained, "Photoshop trash—horses with Apple logos—or cars without stickers or hidden stickers, or crashed cars. One guy sent me a picture of his wife!"

MUSIC ABOUT MACS

Lots of music is made on the Macintosh, but there's not a lot of music made about the Macintosh. John Swerdan's music is a notable exception: He has recorded an entire album of songs inspired by his Mac.

Swerdan, an elementary school teacher from Lafayette, California, cut an album of pop-folk songs called StartupSounds. The themes are life, love, art, and, naturally, Macintosh computers. "In the early '60s, groups like the Beach Boys sang passionately about surfing and hot rods," he said. "I feel just as strongly about computers."

Swerdan felt so strongly that he wrote and recorded nine songs about Macs over a period of three years. The songs include "Startup/Hard Drive," "Quickdraw Bill," and "Poor Sad Mac."

"Poor sad Mac, born in a plastic age," Swerdan sings. "A time when the world still thought in beige. Crafted and molded just like a piece of art. An orphan, abandoned. It's enough to break your heart."

Swerdan, who plays all the instruments, recorded most of the album at his school's computer lab—on Macs, of course. He even used an iMac box as a kick drum. He couldn't afford a real drum.

The album is the melding of three passions, Swerdan explained: songwriting, Macintoshes, and an ardor for oddball vinyl. "I've been collecting strange LPs for several years," he said. "Things like William Shatner 'singing,' or dog-training LPs; records by hypnotists, taxi drivers, and folk songs about outer space. I was thinking it would be fun to throw together a collection of folk songs about computers."

(LEFT) ODE TO A MAC: NOT ONLY WERE SWERDAN'S SONGS INSPIRED BY THE MAC, THEY WERE RECORDED ON THEM TOO—AND THE CDS HE'S SELLING ARE BURNED ON THEM TOO.
CREDIT: JOHN SWERDAN

(ABOVE) HE WRITES THE SONGS— MAC SONGS: ELEMENTARY SCHOOL TEACHER JOHN SWERDAN WAS SO ENAMORED WITH HIS MAC, HE WROTE AN ENTIRE ALBUM OF SONGS ABOUT IT.
CREDIT: JOHN SWERDAN

MACHEAD: RADIOHEAD'S THOM YORKE IS ANOTHER BIG FAN OF THE MACINTOSH. LIKE JOHN SWERDAN, YORKE'S SONGS ARE ALSO MAC INSPIRED, BUT THEY ARE A BIT MORE TORTURED.
CREDIT: UNKNOWN

"IN THE EARLY '60s, GROUPS LIKE THE BEACH BOYS SANG PASSIONATELY ABOUT SURFING AND HOT RODS...I FEEL JUST AS STRONGLY ABOUT COMPUTERS."

The CD is on sale at Swerdan's Web site for $15, postage included. He's sold a few copies, has appeared on TechTV, and is starting to play live at local venues. "It's pretty good, very folksy," said Bruce Evans, who runs the Macintosh-devoted Geek Culture Web site. "I think he does a fine job at capturing the love between a boy and his Mac. Reminded me of a band called the Circle from the '60s. I like the song about Quickdraw Bill. Thought it was a great idea for a song."

Swerdan may be alone in recording an entire album inspired by Macs, but there are other Mac-inspired musicians. Andrew Tokuda, aka Digital Droo, cut an album of house music called The MacAddict Years.

Famous musicians who are also Mac fans include Trent Reznor, Björk, and De La Soul, who used an Apple startup chime at the beginning of a recent album. Janet Jackson also used a Mac startup sound in one of her songs.

Most mentions of "Macs" in rap music are to Big Macs, Mac Daddies, and the MAC-10, a submachine gun favored in drive-bys. But a lot of rappers are also Macintosh users, and their favorite computer often gets a shout-out in the lyrics of rap songs. The rap übergroup Hieroglyphics, Method Man, Lil' Zane, the Beastie Boys, and the Wu-Tang Clan have all referenced Macs in their music.

Rap musicians The Coup have included multiple "shout-outs" to Macs on their albums. The group's song "Me and Jesus the Pimp in a '79 Granada Last Night" from Steal This Album includes the lyric: "Microsoft motherfuckers let bygones be bygones, but since I'm Macintosh, I'm gonna double-click your icon."

The British rock band Radiohead are big fans of the Macintosh, as well. The band's lead singer, Thom Yorke, used to have a guitar emblazoned with a big Apple sticker. Radiohead's 1997 album OK Computer features an entire song sung by the Macintosh's text-to-speech software. Various Mac-generated voices and beeps can be heard throughout the album.

Even the album's title may be Mac-inspired: The Mac's built-in speech recognition software responds to the command "OK computer" as an alternative to clicking an OK button onscreen. However, the music is all about technological alienation and paranoia. Maybe Radiohead members aren't such big Mac fans after all.

(BELOW LEFT) THE IBROTHA: BROTHER COPLAND, PLAYED BY NEIL RAYMENT FROM THE *MATRIX* SEQUEL, PAYS HOMAGE TO HIS MACINTOSH.
CREDIT: JAKE BARNES

(BELOW RIGHT) FIGHTING FOR THE MAC, BY ANY MEANS NECESSARY: THE IBROTHAS FROM JAKE BARNES' SHORT ABOUT MAC FANATICISM.
CREDIT: JAKE BARNES

13

FILM: MAC FERVOR, MALCOLM X STYLE

Mac fanaticism is coming to the movies. A short film called *iBrotha*, starring Neil Rayment from the *Matrix* sequel, was shot in London in the summer of 2002. The independent production is about a young man so obsessed with Apple Macs, he becomes a Malcolm X–like revolutionary, fighting computer bigotry—by any means necessary.

"It's about that whole religious fervor that grabs Mac users the way it doesn't with users of other platforms," said writer/ director Jake Barnes, who described himself as a "recovering Mac addict." Brother Copland emulates Malcolm X—in a way. (Copeland was the name of Apple's aborted operating system in development before Mac OS X.)

Rayment, 30, and his twin brother Adrian feature in *Matrix Reloaded* as a pair of kung fu fighting villains. The menacing twins play rogue viruses, roaming the Matrix in all-white attire and silver dreadlocks.

iBrotha features a multicultural cast of characters, including Brother Ive (after Apple's lead designer, Jonathan Ive) and Brother Newton (Apple's discontinued handheld computer). It also stars an early Macintosh, the 512K.

The movie was shot during the summer in West and Central London. Some of the action takes place at the "Temple of Mac," a Nation of Islam–like place of worship. It features a lot of hats, dark suits, bow ties, and a cricket bat.

The movie is the first by Barnes, a 31-year-old ex-music journalist, and it has already attracted the attention of London's movie industry. Barnes has shown the eight-minute film to a number of producers and heads of movie studios, who gave it a warm reception. "I thought it had a great premise and it was great fun," said Richard Holmes, producer of *Waking Ned Devine* and *Shooting Fish*. "He's got great energy and definitely has a future." With the backing of the British Council, the movie will soon start making the rounds at film festivals. Barnes plans to submit it to the Turner, Bafta, and Cannes festivals.

Barnes said the movie explores the passion Macs inspire, but also shows how obsessive that passion can become. "I love Macs, but the film's about the fanatics," Barnes said. "Those who go a step too far. The premise is: 'What if Malcolm X evangelized Macs? Would he really?' Some think he would." The movie is a humorous way to look at race and class through the metaphor of competing computer platforms, Barnes added.

The movie's Web site is dedicated to the memory of Rodney O. Lain, a popular online Mac columnist who wrote under the iBrotha moniker. Lain committed suicide in June. "Rodney was a good writer and decided to take his own life halfway through the production," Barnes said. "It's a mark of respect and a way of showing we're not taking advantage of his infamous passing away."

Like Brother Copland, Lain was committed to promoting the Mac. Although he had a full-time job, he worked nights and weekends selling Macs at computer superstores, just to get the word out.

MAC O'LANTERNS LIGHT UP HALLOWEEN

Halloween has gone high tech. Is that Ellen Feiss, the teenage star of Apple's Switch campaign, or a 10-pound jack-o'-lantern? These amazing, photorealistic pumpkin portraits were created by Snaggy and Nitrozac, the pair who runs the popular, Mac-oriented Geek Culture Web site.

In addition to a likeness of Feiss, the pair's Mac O'Lanterns feature Apple cofounder Steve Wozniak, *New York Times* technology columnist David Pogue, and the ghost of the "Happy Mac," the beloved Mac startup screen recently murdered by Apple. The bogeyman of the bunch is Microsoft CEO Steve Ballmer.

"What would a collection of jack-o'-lanterns be without at least one super-scary face?" said Nitrozac. "The obvious choice was Steve Ballmer. It's derived from a screen grab from his screaming 'developers' video."

Inspired by Keith Colman's Pumpkin Portrait Page, Snaggy and Nitrozac created the likenesses by tracing high-contrast print-outs of the subjects' faces onto the surface of each pumpkin. The highlighted areas of the face were cut out entirely, the gray areas scooped out halfway and the black areas left alone. The result is a reverse bas-relief sculpture that emits light from the highlighted areas. The effect can be strikingly photographic, especially in Feiss's case.

"The reaction has been phenomenal, especially to the Ellen Feiss portrait," said Snaggy." People are amazed that a carved pumpkin can look so good, and some don't believe they aren't retouched photos. It is really quite freaky and a little disturbing!"

Instead of candles, the pair used white Christmas lights to illuminate their jack-o'-lanterns. For people interested in creating their own Mac O'Lanterns, Nitrozac has posted a tutorial on the site.

(TOP ROW LEFT) MAC O'LANTERNS: THE GENIUSES BEHIND THE GEEK CULTURE WEB SITE CELEBRATED HALLOWEEN WITH PUMPKINS CARVED TO RESEMBLE ICONS OF MAC CULTURE. FROM LEFT TO RIGHT: APPLE COFOUNDER STEVE WOZNIAK; SWITCH STAR ELLEN FEISS; A HAPPY MAC STARTUP ICON; AND THE BOGEYMAN OF THE BUNCH, MICROSOFT'S STEVE BALLMER. SPOOOKY!

ALL IMAGES FROM COURTESY OF GEEK CULTURE (HTTP://WWW. GEEKCULTURE.COM/)

(TOP ROW RIGHT) SCARY: MICROSOFT'S STEVE BALLMER IS ONE SCARY BOGEYMAN. THE PORTRAIT WAS INSPIRED BY HIS INFAMOUS "DEVELOPERS" VIDEO, WIDELY AVAILABLE ON THE WEB, WHERE HE CAVORTS AROUND A CONFERENCE STAGE LIKE AN APE ON AMPHETAMINES, SWEATING PROFUSELY.

(MIDDLE ROW LEFT) IMMORTALITY, KINDA: "NEW YORK TIMES" TECHNOLOGY COLUMNIST DAVID POGUE, A VETERAN MAC ADVO- CATE, WAS DELIGHTED WITH HIS VEGETATIVE LIKENESS. "NOW, I'VE TRULY ACHIEVED IMMORTALITY," HE WROTE IN AN EMAIL TO GEEK CULTURE. "WELL, OF THE SORT THAT ROTS AFTER A WEEK."

(MIDDLE ROW RIGHT) PUMPKIN PORTRAIT: UNBELIEVABLY, THIS IS A CARVED PUMPKIN, NOT A RETOUCHED PHOTO.

(BOTTOM ROW) DETAIL, DETAIL: THE EFFECT WAS CREATED BY PASTING A GRAYSCALE PHOTO ONTO THE PUMPKIN AND CUTTING OUT THE LIGHTED AREAS OF THE FACE ENTIRELY. THE GRAY AREAS WERE SCOOPED OUT HALFWAY, AND THE BLACK AREAS LEFT ALONE. THE RESULT IS A REVERSE BAS-RELIEF SCULPTURE THAT EMITS LIGHT FROM THE HIGHLIGHTED AREAS. THE FOLLOWING PICTURE SHOWS HOW IT WAS DONE.

MAC OS X BIRTHDAY PARTIES, OR BLOWING OUT A CANDLE FOR OS X

In an odd case of life imitating art, a number of Mac fans held birthday parties for Apple's Mac OS X operating system: a scenario satirized by the popular Joy of Tech cartoon. When the operating system turned one year old in March 2002, Apple didn't make a peep about it, and the occasion passed largely unnoticed, except for the long-running Joy of Tech cartoon at the Geek Culture Web site, which published a strip picturing the unlikely event of a riotous birthday party for Mac OS X. Little did the cartoonists know that real parties were being held to mark the event.

In Hong Kong, an Apple dealer threw a well-attended party in honor of the anniversary. The party drew quite a crowd. There was even a birthday cake, decorated with fresh strawberries and a single candle.

A similar party was held in Toronto, Canada, by Mac Solutions, an Apple dealer. "It was standing room only, and the cake was delicious," said one attendee.

The general meeting of Washington Apple Pi, a Mac user group, coincided with the operating system's birthday. To celebrate, a giant blue "X" cake was devoured.

In Belpre, Ohio, Arlen Owens brought a cake to work to celebrate the birthday. "Today is the first anniversary of the release of Mac OS X," Owens said in an email he sent to about 25 coworkers at the wall-covering plant. "Please come to the engineering department and help celebrate."

Owens had decorated the cake with "Happy Birthday Mac OS X" in blue icing. He also put up a happy birthday poster in the plant's engineering office, along with some printouts of his Mac's computer screen.

As usual, Crazy Arlo, as he is known online, used the occasion to evangelize the Mac: He hoped to persuade his coworkers to switch from their humdrum Windows PCs to the magnificent Technicolor world of the Mac. He is constantly bending the ears of coworkers with talk about wonderful Macintosh computers. He even uses his family Web site as a soapbox for describing the benefits of Macs. Next to the Web pages of his wife and

(TOP ROW LEFT) HONG KONG STYLE: THE IMAC GURU PARTY IN HONG KONG TO CELEBRATE THE FIRST BIRTHDAY OF MAC OS X ATTRACTED A SIZABLE CROWD. PERHAPS IT WAS FOR THE CAKE? CREDIT: IMAC GURU

(TOP ROW RIGHT) HAVE YOUR CAKE AND EAT IT: MAC SOLUTIONS, AN APPLE DEALER BASED IN TORONTO, CELEBRATED MAC OS X'S FIRST BIRTHDAY WITH A STANDING-ROOM-ONLY PARTY AND THIS LAVISH CAKE. CREDIT: MAC SOLUTIONS

(BOTTOM ROW FIRST) YUMMY: WASHINGTON APPLE PI, A MAC USER GROUP, CELEBRATED MAC OS X'S BIRTHDAY WITH A BIG "X" CAKE, WHICH DIDN'T LAST LONG. CREDITS: LOU PASTURA AND LAWRENCE CHARTERS

(BOTTOM ROW SECOND) HAPPY BIRTHDAY, MAC OS X: ENGINEER ARLEN OWENS CELEBRATED MAC OS X'S FIRST BIRTHDAY BY BRINGING A CAKE TO WORK. CREDIT: ARLEN OWENS

(BOTTOM ROW THIRD) ONE FOR THE ALBUM: ENGINEER ARLEN OWENS IS A COMMITTED MAC EVANGELIST. HE USED THE OCCASION OF MAC OS X'S FIRST BIRTHDAY TO EXTOL THE VIRTUES OF THE MAC TO HIS COWORKERS. HE OFTEN TRUCKS HIS FAMILY TO THE LOCAL APPLE STORE ON WEEKENDS, A FOUR-HOUR DRIVE EACH WAY. HERE HE IS WITH ONE OF THE EMPLOYEES OF THE STORE, WHOM HE GRABBED FOR A SNAPSHOT AS A MEMENTO OF HIS VISIT. CREDIT: ARLEN OWENS

(BOTTOM ROW LAST) SNAGGY AND NITROZAC CELEBRATED OS X'S BIRTHDAY BY ORDERING A PIZZA WITH THE CHEESE ARRANGED IN A BIG X. CREDIT: GEEK CULTURE

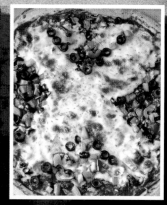

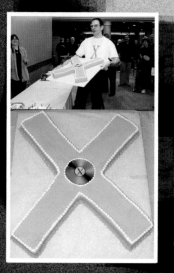

kids, who talk about softball or kittens, Arlo urges people to "Get a Mac."

Dawn Urchasko, the plant's nurse, recalled the gathering. "Yeah, he had that for Microsoft 10," she said, garbling the name of the operating system. "He led us to believe he made the cake. We were thinking it was a homemade cake, but it was a store cake he had bought and decorated. We were like, 'Aaaarlen. This is a store cake.' But it was fun."

Snaggy, who runs the Geek Culture site with his partner, Nitrozac, said: "I would have loved to see his coworkers' faces." Snaggy and Nitrozac celebrated OS X's birthday by ordering a pizza with the cheese arranged in a big X.

Snaggy also heard of a couple of other celebrations. Someone took a dozen blue-frosted cupcakes with big white Xs on them to their office, and a group of Canadian geeks went out for rounds of Labatt's "Blue" beer. "They toasted each new major app that has been ported over to X," Snaggy said.

NEW APPLE STORES MAKE FAST MAC FRIENDS

About once a month, Tadd and Nancy Torborg of Orlando, Florida, load their two kids into the car and drive halfway across the eastern seaboard to attend the grand opening of a new Apple Store. In the last year, the family has graced a dozen openings of Apple's new stores. They'll drive up to five hours through the night. Then they'll wait in line for hours with hundreds of other Mac fans for the store to open.

That, in fact, is the point: They like hanging out in the queue with like-minded Macintosh users. "The biggest reason for going is camaraderie with the other people who go," explained Tadd. "The group that Apple attracts is very appealing to me— they are creative technophiles. It's fun talking to them. I have yet to go to a user group meeting that attracts as impressive a group of people as that found in a grand opening line."

Nancy estimated there are at least a couple dozen people who regularly attend Apple Store openings on the East Coast. One of them recorded a video from a dozen visits on the store's machines and posted them to his Web site.

Allen Olivio, Apple's director of retail marketing, who has overseen a number of grand openings, said he, too, regularly meets

the same people over and over. "Isn't it astounding?" he said. "My jaw dropped. It's a great testament to the Apple brand and the Apple Store experience."

Apple has been opening stores in upscale shopping malls at a rate of one or two a month throughout 2002. The company has opened 50 to date, and it is planning to open 70 stores total, according to reports.

The grand openings attract huge crowds. Lines start forming outside the store in the wee hours and often persist all day. But unlike lines at, say, the DMV or post office, these aren't sullen affairs. People socialize. Many compete to see who has the oldest Apple T-shirt or one from the farthest-flung Apple Store.

(OPPOSITE PAGE) GRAND OPENING:
THE LINE OUTSIDE THE NEW APPLE
STORE IN ORLANDO, FLORIDA, TWO
HOURS BEFORE THE STORE FIRST
OPENED FOR BUSINESS.
CREDIT: VERN SEWARD

(BELOW LEFT) LIKE FATHER, LIKE
SON: TADD TORBORG AND HIS SON
JACK AT AN APPLE STORE OPENING.
THE TORBORGS HAVE ATTENDED
A DOZEN STORE OPENINGS, OFTEN
DRIVING HALFWAY ACROSS THE
COUNTRY TO GET TO THEM.
CREDIT: VERN SEWARD

(BELOW RIGHT) PRISTINE: INSIDE
THE BRAND-NEW APPLE STORE IN
ORLANDO, FLORIDA, ALL IS QUIET.
OUTSIDE, MASSES OF MAC FANS
GATHER FOR THE HONOR OF BEING
THE FIRST FEW HUNDRED THROUGH
THE DOOR.
CREDIT: VERN SEWARD

"I HAVE YET TO GO TO A USER GROUP MEETING THAT ATTRACTS AS IMPRESSIVE A GROUP OF PEOPLE AS THAT FOUND IN A GRAND OPENING LINE."

Wireless messaging with others in the queue is popular. A lot of people bring along AirPort-equipped laptops, and thanks to Rendezvous—Apple's networking technology that automatically detects similarly equipped computers—people can instant message each other all the way down the line. "People try to out-geek each other, showing off their old T-shirts or tech toys," Nancy Torborg said.

At first, Nancy was skeptical of her husband's plan to drag the family to an Apple Store opening. "The first time, I was highly suspicious," she said. "The idea of driving huge distances to go to a store opening sounded so silly. But people are so nice. It's been great. It's a hoot."

One day, an Apple Store employee showed her some "crazy guy's" Web page with photographs taken at a dozen opening events. Nancy sheepishly admitted it was her husband's Web page. "This is just something we do on Saturdays," she said. "We're kind of hard-core, but it's fun. It's like potato chips. We can't stop going." The Torborgs' 15-year-old daughter Laura likens them to Deadheads, without the cool microbus.

"Why would anyone drive all night to get into a store? It's such a blast. It's a lot of fun. They're the most benign people on the planet," Nancy said.

Vern Seward, a contributing editor for the Mac Observer, likened the store openings to the biannual Macworld trade show. "Hands were shaken, backs were patted, laughs were exchanged in an electric-charged atmosphere that could have reminded some of being at a keynote at a Macworld," he wrote. "It was a blast to watch."

Whereas Macworld gives Mac fans the opportunity to gather in numbers only twice a year, the store openings provide the same companionship once a month. At the first Apple Store opening in a suburban Washington, D.C., mall in May 2001, the line broke into a chant of "Apple, Apple," according to people who were there.

In August 2002, Apple held special late-night sales events to promote the launch of Jaguar, an update to Mac OS X. There were lines thousands strong at Apple

(ABOVE LEFT) OPEN FOR BUSINESS: THE STORE MANAGER THROWS THE DOORS WIDE OPEN TO A CHORUS OF RAUCOUS CHEERS. WELCOME ONE AND ALL!
CREDIT: VERN SEWARD

(ABOVE RIGHT) HIGH FIVES ALL AROUND: AS CUSTOMERS FILE IN THROUGH THE DOORS, THEY RUN A GAUNTLET OF HIGH FIVES FROM STORE EMPLOYEES.
CREDIT: VERN SEWARD

Stores across the country. In Palo Alto, a queue of 2,000 to 3,000 people formed. The cops showed up to oversee crowd control, and the store didn't close until 2:30 a.m. when the crowds finally thinned out. Apple estimated that 4,000 people visited the store that night.

TEKSERVE: NEW YORK'S MOM-AND-POP APPLE SHOP

Many cities have a friendly Mac computer store where Mac fans can find like-minded compatriots in the often lonely world of Windows PCs. The stores—often mom-and-pop shops—are the physical equivalent of online user groups—a place to solve problems, get advice, and chat about the machines. Before Apple opened a string of 50 stores in big city malls, these hometown Mac shops were often the only places Mac users could physically meet Mac fans like themselves.

I talked to one guy who lived in the rural Midwest. He was the only Mac user for miles around. Every other weekend, he drove his family to a newly opened Apple Store, four hours each way, just to hang out with other Mac users.

New York's mom-and-pop store is Tekserve, a giant Mac-only sales and repair shop in Manhattan's bustling Chelsea District. Tekserve has a dime soda machine and a folksy sign, but this is New York, so there's also Eric Huggins, a big security guard who walks the floor. Huggins is a big guy with a gentle manner, and he seems perfectly suited to his job of firmly calming down frantic customers who've lost irreplaceable files when their computers go belly up. "I'm here for when people wig out," he said. "That's my main purpose."

About 300 or 400 people visit Tekserve (http://www.tekserve.com/) every day for repairs to their Macs, and Huggins often sees someone crying or angry. They're not necessarily angry at Tekserve, but losing years' worth of files can turn a Buddhist monk into a crazed psycho. Luckily, crazed monks are rare.

The loftlike store is enormous: 20,000 square feet, running the entire length of a city block from front to back. It's located at 119 West 23rd Street, just down the street from the Hotel Chelsea, where Sid Vicious murdered his girlfriend. The *New York Daily News* called Tekserve "the epicenter of Mac culture in New York" (http://www.tekserve.com/nydaily3.html), and it is.

There's a very congenial atmosphere. The attractive wood floor is crowded with customers who chat or peruse new equipment while they wait for their number to be called, deli style. A vintage Coke machine dispenses the classic curvy bottles of Coke for a dime.

A lot of people outside New York know Tekserve from HBO's *Sex and the City*. Sarah Jessica Parker's character visited the store when her PowerBook broke down. She was visibly upset. The filmmakers used the real store (at an older location) but employed an actor to play a surly technician. "We like to think we're

TAKE A TICKET: TEKSERVE CUSTOMERS WAITING FOR SERVICE TAKE A NUMBERED TICKET, DELI STYLE. THE NUMBERS ARE CALLED ON OLD CLASSIC MACS MOUNTED ON THE WALLS. THERE ARE A NUMBER OF THEM DOTTED AROUND THE GIANT STORE. THERE'S ALSO A WALL OF OLD ALL-IN-ONE MACS BY THE FRONT DOOR, FENCING OFF A DISPLAY AREA. TEKSERVE'S FIX-IT PHILOSOPHY PUTS EVERYTHING TO USE.
CREDIT: LEANDER KAHNEY

HERE TO SERVE: NEW YORK'S TEKSERVE IS THE BIG APPLE'S MOM-AND-POP MAC STORE. HERE, COFOUNDER DAVID LERNER STANDS ABOVE THE STORE'S GIANT, 20,000-SQUARE-FOOT FLOOR SPACE.
CREDIT: LEANDER KAHNEY

not that rude," said cofounder David Lerner, a taciturn bearded fellow wearing an open-collar shirt and suspenders.

Lerner said a lot of celebrities visit the store, but showed characteristic New York contempt when asked who. "We have lots of famous customers, but we don't talk about it," he said sharply. "That's for the Apple Store," he added, referring to Apple's newly opened store in downtown Soho.

Conscientious service is a big part of Tekserve's philosophy, said Lerner. Technicians take time with customers, causing other customers to wait. When it comes to their turn, customers expect to get their share of attention. "It's kind of an unvirtuous circle," Lerner said. "We're trying to fix it."

Tekserve has seen every kind of computer calamity, from over-heated motherboards to mice nesting inside a machine. "We've had computers with all kinds of animals inside," Lerner said. Tekserve only charges for data recovered. It's a somewhat risky strategy, Lerner admitted, but he said they are able to recover files 85 percent of the time. Tekserve employs about 100 tech-nicians and salespeople. Repairs are made at the back of the brightly lit space.

As well as making repairs, Tekserve sells a wide range of new Apple machines. The store seemed to be doing a healthy trade in Apple's flat-screen iMacs. A couple were seen being carried out the door in the arms of Chelsea's well-heeled customers.

The store is full of old Macs on shelves and displays. The other cofounder, Dick Demenus, is a collector and claims to have almost the entire line of vintage Macs, including some rare machines. Part of his collection of vintage radios, TVs, and typewriters is also dotted around the store.

Business at the store is booming. It moved to its new location in the summer of 2002, from a fourth-floor walkup on the same block. In the last eight years, the store has moved four times to bigger locations on the same block. The prospect of competing with Apple's new flagship store (http://www.apple.com/retail/soho/) doesn't overly alarm Lerner. "It's worrisome, of course," he said. "The Apple Store tends to showcase products, but we do a lot of solution sales. We sell the whole package."

UNPACKING THE iMAC

When Apple's new flat-panel iMac starting showing up at people's homes in large numbers, its arrival prompted a strange manifestation of techno fetishism: People held iMac unpacking ceremonies for friends and family.

Like a tea ceremony, the unpacking of a new iMac took on some distinctly ritualistic touches: The iMac arrives in the mail. People are invited over. They gather around the boxed computer in the center of the room. Drinks are poured, lights lowered, candles lit. And while the new machine is unwrapped, someone takes pictures to post on the Web.

Philip Torrone, who documented his unpacking ceremony on his Web site with dozens of murky pictures and three badly lit movies, invited his fiancée and a friend (a psychologist) to his Minneapolis apartment to experience the unwrapping of his new iMac. He likened the occasion to Christmas morning.

"You savor every moment," he wrote in an email. "You don't open it like an ordinary box. This is something magical. Perhaps it was the two glasses of wine or the new iMac smell—a cross between Styrofoam and newly molded plastic—but it was

(BELOW) FOR POSTERITY: PEOPLE WERE SO EXCITED ABOUT GETTING THE FLAT-PANEL IMAC, A LOT OF THEM DOCUMENTED UNPACKING THE MACHINE AND SETTING IT UP.
CREDIT: JOHN BYRNE

23

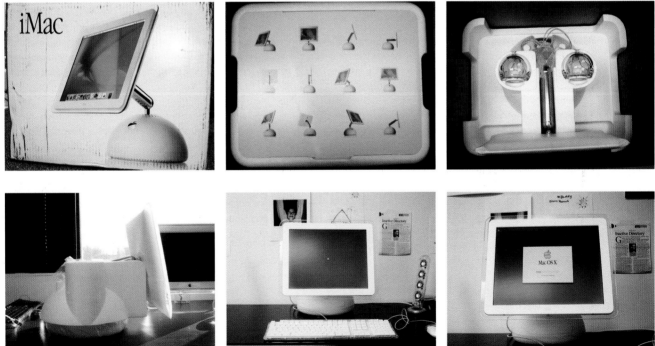

amazing. Each piece carefully wrapped, the DVDs, the special gray rag for the screen. It's as if Steve Jobs packed it himself. We wanted to wear rubber gloves when we unpacked it.

"Like all new Apple gear, it belongs in a museum and shouldn't be touched (fingerprints). I'm pretty sure it's as close to sex as you can get with a machine. I mean look at this photo."

Torrone, director of product development for Minneapolis advertising agency Fallon Worldwide, ordered his new iMac from Apple's Web store. Before it arrived, he checked the status of his order every day. He haunted rumor sites and chat forums to see if other people had received their machines. He even visited a local Apple store just to look at the new iMacs on display. When his iMac finally arrived, he took the day off work. "It's like 'senioritis,'" he said. "I couldn't do anything or even think when I knew the box was sitting there waiting."

There are at least a half-dozen Web pages documenting every stage of the unpacking and setting up of a new iMac.

The pictures, like amateurish porn, are badly lit and blurry. And they follow a predictable sequence: the unopened box, the opened box, unpacking the mouse....And they always end with the same climactic shot: the new iMac sitting on a desk.

The porn analogy is appropriate. In a recent forum thread at MacNN, one poster admitted he'd rather look at pictures of a partially unpacked iBook than pictures of partially unclothed women.

Dean Browell, a Web designer from Virginia, was invited with his wife to a setting-up ceremony at the home of friends Andrea and David Zuschin. "It was just us, a beer or two, and the attention totally focused on the new machine," Browell said. "It was truly neat. There is no way a PC user invites friends over just to see their new computer. That kind of excitement is wholly unique to Mac culture, and with an item glowing with personality like the new iMac, it's easy to fall in love."

Andrea and David Zuschin said they felt like "proud parents" when they took the iMac out of its box. "We weren't sure what to do with it; we just wanted to stare at it," said David Zuschin.

"Do we put a light cloth over it and be very quiet? I felt like we should get a baby monitor or something." Before it had even arrived, the Zuschins had named their new iMac "Bootsie."

Browell said he and his wife were as keen to see the new iMac as the Zuschins. "We were invited because we were as excited as they were," he said. The Zuschins had kept the Browells informed of the new iMac's progress as it was built and shipped from Taiwan.

The Zuschins didn't document the birth of Bootsie for posterity, but many others have. The unpacking photo essay was probably started by Andy Gore, former editor in chief of *Macworld* magazine. In the last couple of years, Gore wrote a series of salivating and slightly eccentric reviews of Apple hardware, accompanied by pictures of the box that just arrived in the mail, the box with the flaps open, and so on.

Even Slashdot, which normally adopts a cool stance toward Mac users, is getting into the spirit of things. The site recently posted a link to an unpacking site. Slashdot editor Timothy Lord, who posted the link, said he shares the technolust; he takes pleasure in seeing other people feverishly unwrap their new toys. "It's much more frugal to experience these things vicariously," he wrote in an email. "When the new iMac is under $1,000, I'd like one, too."

Lord said the new iMac is not the first piece of hardware to be honored with unpacking pages. He'd seen similar photo series for game consoles like the PlayStation 2 and the Xbox, and for expensive gadgets like digital cameras. Lord said unpacking pictures are often posted right after the gadget's release, when it's in short supply and still pricey. "Sometimes these unpacking sites are the only way to see what the systems look like from a user perspective, or to know what to really expect in the box," he said.

Sometimes the goods barely arrive at all: Tatsuaki Ryu's iMac unpacking page shows what happens when a computer is shipped at the bottom of a partially submerged container. But despite arriving soaking wet and covered in mud, Ryu's iMac still worked. "BTW, the machine is simply amazing," Ryu noted.

ALL ABOARD! (BUT NO PCS ALLOWED)

Doug Humphrey is a successful tech entrepreneur who owns a very big boat. It's neither a yacht nor a pleasure cruiser, but a gun-gray warship. An ex-British Navy warship.

Humphrey is a big, friendly guy. He does a lot of entertaining on his warship. He hosts parties and often takes friends out on the Chesapeake Bay, which is not too far from his home in Laurel, Maryland, an upscale Washington, D.C., suburb. Humphrey imposes a few rules, of course; seafaring wouldn't be safe without them. But one of the strictest, and most idiosyncratic, involves computers. He allows only Macs on board.

Humphrey is the founder of Digex, an early Internet service provider. He made out like a bandit when the ISP was sold and went on to launch a number of other companies, including Core Location, a kind of Web hosting service for large telecom companies, and Cidera, a broadband-via-satellite service.

Humphrey, a 42-year-old multimillionaire, is still president and CEO of Cidera. When the firm underwent a drastic downsizing recently, he moved his entire staff to Macs because it was too expensive keeping a fleet of Windows machines shipshape.

"We forced everyone to go to Macs for the desktops," he said. "The support load dropped to almost nothing, and the only complaints were from people who couldn't play games on their machines any longer. So sorry, no games at work. We are so mean."

The company uses Unix behind the curtains. But on the boat, it's Macs only. Humphrey insists the regulation is not Mac zealotry. "We avoid the Windows operating system since it is such a huge security risk," he explained. "We didn't want to have viruses blowing up systems that we depend on for navigation and monitoring engines and other systems. And since nothing seems to be able to stop all of these Windows viruses, the best way to win is to just stop using Windows."

Humphrey navigates the ship with the help of a Mac installed on the bridge. The boat has a built-in network, hooked to the Internet through a satellite link-up. Humphrey connects the ship's network to a DSL when it's in port.

Humphrey bought the 170-ton boat from a ship broker he found on Lycos' Yacht Server, who in turn had bought it from Britain's Ministry of Defence. The guns had been removed—Humphrey said the boat is strictly BYOG.

PLEASURE CRAFT: ENTREPRENEUR DOUG HUMPHREY'S WEEKEND PLEASURE CRUISER—AN EX-BRITISH NAVY WARSHIP. HUMPHREY HAS A LOT OF GUESTS ABOARD, BUT NO ONE CAN BRING A WINDOWS PC. ONLY MACS SAIL THE HIGH SEAS ON HUMPHREY'S CRAFT.
CREDIT: DOUG HUMPHREY

(LEFT) BYOG: HUMPHREY WON'T LET ANYONE BRING DANGEROUS COMPUTERS ABOARD, BUT HE DOES ALLOW GUNS. THE BRITISH NAVY REMOVED ALL THE BIG GUNS FROM THE BOAT BEFORE HUMPHREY BOUGHT IT, SO THE SHIP IS STRICTLY BYOG (BRING YOUR OWN GUN).
CREDIT: DOUG HUMPHREY

(RIGHT) WHO'S A PRETTY BOY THEN? A CAMERA-SHY DOUG HUMPHREY, HIDING BEHIND HIS DAUGHTER AND PET PARROTS.
CREDIT: DOUG HUMPHREY

Before Humphrey bought it, the ship was HMS Redpole, a coastal patrol vessel. Built in 1970, it's 120 feet long and can go up to 4,500 miles on one tank of gas (it holds 14,000 gallons of diesel).

Humphrey christened the ship the Badtz Maru, after a mischievous penguin from Sanrio, the company behind Hello Kitty. The ship has a full-time crew, and Humphrey uses it, on average, every other weekend.

Humphrey lives in the small town of Laurel with his wife and daughter. The house has eight Mac and Unix computers. He said the machines are loaded with copies of Microsoft Office for word processing and the like, "but never Exchange, of course, since it is one of the big security holes."

"I've used Macs for the last six years," he said. "I had a PC before that, but Macs were fun and more reliable. I don't play computer games, so that might help explain why I don't miss the Windows box."

APPLE'S PRODUCTS STIMULATE DESIRE

APPLE FETISH: SAUCY DESKTOP PICTURES FEATURING THE APPLE LOGO OR SOME APPLE HARDWARE ARE UNIQUE TO THE MAC PLATFORM. WINDOWS USERS JUST DON'T FETISHIZE THEIR MACHINES IN THE SAME WAY. HERE IS ONE OF MANY ITERATIONS OF THE IMAC GIRL FOUND AT THE APPLE COLLECTION WEB SITE.
CREDIT: SUBLIME ESSENCE

(THIS PAGE) THINK SEXY: THE
CLOTHING ON THIS SCANTILY CLAD
MODEL HAS BEEN DONE IN THE
STYLE OF A POWERMAC G4.
CREDIT: PRAVIN MENON/RICK LYON

(OPPOSITE PAGE LEFT) PUMPED UP:
THE APPLE COLLECTION, A WEB
SITE DEVOTED TO MAC CULTURE,
HAS A 33-PAGE ARCHIVE OF SOFT
PORN DESKTOPS; MOST OF THEM
HAVE BEEN "PHOTOSHOPPED" TO
FEATURE SOMETHING RELATED TO
APPLE—A LOGO, AN IMAC, OR A
G4 CHIP.
CREDIT: GUILLERMO

(OPPOSITE PAGE RIGHT) IMAC BOY:
WOMEN ARE NOT THE ONLY ONES
TO APPEAR AS DESKTOP IMAGES IN
SKIMPY MACINTOSH CLOTHING.
CREDIT: YVON ROY

SEXY DESKTOPS

The most popular way to customize a Mac is to change the desktop picture. Customizing the desktop isn't unique to the Mac platform, but some of the ways it's done, are. A lot of horny teenagers, for example, make soft porn desktop pictures for their computers, but many Mac fans adorn their saucy pictures with the Apple logo or some Apple hardware. Fetishizing the hardware by associating it with a sexy woman is something that doesn't happen on other platforms.

Take Mark Allen, a gay man living in New York. For about a year, Allen conducted an online relationship with a man living in Austin, Texas. But as the relationship matured, Allen realized it wasn't his cyberboyfriend he was falling in love with, it was his PowerMac G3.

Mark met Bryan online. Their first date was a romantic candle-light dinner, via webcam. In New York, Mark lit a candle and ate Chinese takeout while Bryan did the same 1,700 miles away in Texas. Soon they started sleeping together: Mark put his monitor and webcam next to his bed so he could watch Bryan sleeping, and vice versa. When they eventually met in person, about a year later, the relationship fizzled out. That's when Mark realized it wasn't Bryan he fancied, it was his Mac.

"Bryan, my cyberboyfriend, was in a lot of ways, my PowerMac G3, webcam, and telephone," Mark wrote on his Web site. "He literally lived inside of this machine ... that I myself could control like a light switch. The perfect boyfriend."

Mark diagnosed himself with a minor case of "objectum sexuality," a fetishistic attraction to inanimate objects—in this case, his Mac. "You may find the line between your attraction to your lover's face and your computer monitor starting to blur," he wrote.

The concept of objectum sexuality appears to have originated with Eija-Riitta Eklöf-Berliner-Mauer, a Swedish woman who "married" herself to the Berlin Wall in 1979 (Berliner Mauer is German for Berlin Wall). Eklöf-Berliner-Mauer started the Objectum-Sexuality chat group (age-restricted login required), where a number of like-minded individuals gather. There's a similar forum in German.

Objects people have become attracted to include toy trains, organs (the electronic kind), drilling rigs, and various buildings. The most common expression is the love of cars. There's a FAQ for having sex with cars (the tailpipe is involved) and sites devoted to car porn.

Objectum sexuality is not a recognized paraphilia in the American Psychiatric Association's manual of psychiatry, the Diagnostic and Statistical Manual of Mental Disorders. However, psychologist and cybersex expert Al Cooper said such fetishes exist, and nothing surprises him. "It's phenomenal the kind of things people fetishize," he said. "The world is a big place with a lot of people. There's somebody somewhere in the world with a fetish for anything."

Cooper, editor of Sex and the Internet and director of the San Jose Marital and Sexuality Centre, said he hasn't treated anyone with a Mac fetish, but thought Macs could become objects of sexual attraction. "It's not surprising people will fetishize the computer, because you can get a lot of sexual stuff off them," he said. "Part of [Apple's] campaign is to make them sexy. They are sleek and colorful....It makes it more likely people will fetishize it."

Mark Allen seems to be one of the few Mac fetish cases documented on the Web, but there are clues that he's far from alone. "Erotic" desktop pictures featuring half-naked models and starlets are common, but many available for download on Mac-oriented sites have been decorated with the Apple logo or some Apple hardware. The Apple Collection (found at http://

www.theapplecollection.com), a Web site devoted to Mac culture, for example, has a 33-page archive of soft porn desktops; most of them have been "Photoshopped" to feature something related to Apple: a logo, an iMac, or a G4 chip, and so on.

The people who make and consume these images certainly seem to be eroticizing the Mac. "If [the hardware] has a naked woman draped over it, it doesn't take someone with a couple of degrees to figure out the connection," Cooper said. The fetish connection is clearly illustrated by anime-inspired images of iMac girls and boys, which meld flesh and plastic into techno sex toys. And of course, there's the iBrator parody.

The Apple Collection's archive features work by scores of different Mac fans. "All you have to do is look at the products themselves, the lines, the curves," said John Jacobson, who created an erotic desktop. "The lines and smoothness are very erotic in a way...the lines flow...they are all pleasing to the eye."

Fetishistic Mac imagery appears consistently throughout the work of its creators: John Crose, Anna Zisa, and John Nascimento are examples. "I find the Mac to be sexy," said Nascimento, a 40-year-old carpenter who lives in California.

"I have an affinity toward beauty and elegance, coupled with function and stability."

There are archives of similar images at Mac OS Resources; AldeaMac, an Argentine site; and other Mac desktop archives like Spymac, which doesn't have a dedicated soft-porn archive. By contrast, similar images on Windows PC-related wallpaper sites are unadorned. Desktopgirls, Desktopia, and ChilaX's Wallpaper Outpost have large archives of soft-porn desktops, but none have been doctored with Dell, IBM, or Microsoft logos, or anything else for that matter. There are, however, a few Linux-related erotic images at Themes.org.

It's not just the fans. Apple uses sex in its advertising, but subtly. In one of Apple's TV ads from 1999, Jeff Goldblum asked if it was possible to fall in love with a computer. As an iBook twirled across the screen, he answered with a sexy, breathless, "Oh yes."

Just ask Mark Allen.

(LEFT) SEX OBJECT: IS IT POSSIBLE TO FALL IN LOVE WITH A COMPUTER? "OH YES."
CREDIT: GIRL: TOYBOX ARTS/STYLING: KEEKEEREE

(RIGHT) SAUCY SILHOUETTE: UNLIKE MOST, THIS DESKTOP BY JOHN NASCIMENTO LEAVES SOME OF THE DETAILS TO THE IMAGINATION. "I FIND THE MAC TO BE SEXY," SAID NASCIMENTO.
CREDIT: JOHN NASCIMENTO

Chapter 2

MACS AND THE COUNTERCULTURE

Chapter 3

Chapter 14

Chapter 1

Chapter 6

Chapter 12

Chapter 11

Chapter 13

Chapter 15

MACS AND POT

The Mac's roots in America's counterculture of the 1960s and 1970s is well documented. One of the most exhaustive essays on the subject, *From Satori to Silicon Valley*, was penned by Theodore Roszak, a professor of history at California State University at Hayward. Available at Stanford Library's "Making the Macintosh" online archive (http://library.stanford.edu/mac/primary/docs/satori/index.html), Roszak's essay argues that four major movements germinated in the 1960s counterculture: political protest, drugs, music, and the personal computer.

According to Roszak, the invention of the microprocessor was the enabling technology, but the desire to make "personal" computers sprang from the counterculture's yearning to defy authority, epitomized at the time by IBM, with its big corporate and government mainframes. Roszak's thesis enjoys wide acceptance, especially among personal computer pioneers. As Jim Warren, inventor and founder of the legendary West Coast Computer Faire, told *The Industry Standard* magazine: the personal computer revolution "had its genetic coding in the 1960s'... antiestablishment, antiwar, profreedom, antidiscipline attitudes."

Apple, the first major manufacturer of mass-market computers, was a counterculture company through and through. Its founders, Steve Wozniak and Steve Jobs, were a pair of long-haired college dropouts. Jobs was especially bohemian, having lived on an Oregon commune, traveled to India, and adopted a vegetarian diet. Even the company's name screams counterculture: "Stephen Wozniak...came up with a quaintly soft, organic identity that significantly changed the hard-edged image of high tech: the Apple," Roszak wrote. "One story has it that the name was chosen by Steven Jobs in honor of the fruitarian diet he had brought back from his journey to the mystic East. The name also carried with it an echo of the Beatles spirit."

Apple—at least in its marketing—has always espoused counterculture values: the Mac was touted as the computer "for the rest of us," a spin on the famous 1960s slogan "power to the people." Apple has used counterculture leaders, especially musicians like Bob Dylan and Joan Baez, in its advertising. And what other computer manufacturer would sell a psychedelic computer, as Apple did in 2001 with a flower-powered iMac?

Mac users especially have celebrated the idea of the Mac as a computer for counterculturalists: independent thinkers, free spirits, and creative types. Some early Mac user groups were overtly political. The Berkeley Macintosh Users Group, for example, "has its roots in The Hacker Ethic and Berkeley Radicalism," wrote Stephen Howard and Raines Cohen in a 1987 *BMUG Newsletter*. "We're in the business of giving away information. Help us keep this spirit alive and kicking, as long as we can."

(THIS PAGE) THINK STONED: APPLE HAS ALWAYS BEEN A COUNTERCULTURAL COMPUTER COMPANY.
CREDIT: UNKNOWN

(OPPOSITE PAGE) ROCK AND POT: TWO BIG DRIVERS OF THE COUNTERCULTURE—MUSIC AND MARIJUANA—WERE ALSO KEY TO THE DEVELOPMENT OF THE MAC, INSIDERS CLAIM.
CREDIT: UNKNOWN

Think Different.

Mac OS9

Chris Espinosa, Apple employee number eight, told Stanford Library's Mac archive project: "There were people thinking that if they could master personal computing technology, they could fight back against the Machine. And so while there were lawyers who just wanted to use them to automate their offices, a lot of people in the users' groups were really using personal computers as a tool against The Man."

It is unsurprising, then, that there is a strong connection between Macs and pot. Both are countercultures, in the loosest sense of the word, appealing to people who are creative or artistic, people who "think different."

"The entire personal computer revolution came out of the San Francisco Bay Area and was pioneered by pot-smoking members of the counterculture," said Steven Hager, editor in chief of *High Times* (http://www.hightimes.com/). "Because these people tend to be highly creative—pot enhances creativity—and because Macs are the choice of most art and video professionals, I guess that's your story."

A couple of veteran journalists who covered the creation of the Macintosh in the early eighties claim pot had a profound influence on the design of the machine: a claim denied by others, including Jef Raskin, the head of the Mac's design team.

"The Mac building was a very loose outfit," said one journalist, who asked to remain anonymous. "The building was permeated with a certain odor." Another journalist—the former editor of a well-known Macintosh magazine—said the Mac's engineers and programmers were always smoking weed. "There were people out the back in the parking lot smoking pot all the time," said the editor, who also asked to remain anonymous. "The IBM PC was created by people who drank alcohol. The Mac was created by people who smoked pot."

The editor noted that a lot of the Mac's original development team were fairly young; the average age was about 25, he said. "The personal computer industry was an outgrowth of the sixties counterculture," the editor said. "It was a rock-and-roll business in those days. Look at [Apple's famous] 1984 ad. It symbolized a generation shift. The IBM PC was the computer of the establishment. The Mac's purpose in life was to be the computer of the anti-establishment. I mean, it had the psychedelic interface. 'Wow man, good visuals.'"

The editor said that if the Mac development team hadn't been smoking pot, it might not have come up with a small, compact computer with a radical, graphical interface. "If they hadn't been smoking pot, maybe they wouldn't have invented the Mac," he said. "It would have been another Apple II, or an IBM PC; it would not have been the Mac. Who would have thought they wanted a computer to be cute?"

Half joking, the editor suggested further evidence of pot's influence could be found in the Mac's stoned, smiley startup face, the rainbow colors of the Apple logo, and early software like MacPaint, a drawing program perfect for drug-induced doodling. Nothing like it existed on the PC platform, despite the fact that a lot of Windows programmers—some now very rich and famous—were also dopers, according to the editor.

"We all noticed this when we were covering this stuff," he said. "At PC Expo, people smell like booze. At Macworld, people smell like marijuana." The editor said there's even a special pot-smoking area around the back of San Francisco's Moscone Center, the longtime venue of Macworld Expo, known as "the office." "Ten or 20 people are there all day long," the editor said. "CEOs, programmers, authors. People say, 'I'm just going to the office for a couple of minutes.'"

One early Apple employee confirmed the editor's pot-smoking claims among Apple employees. "I was there; we were all high," said the employee, who asked not to be identified.

Another source made the outrageous claim that one of Apple's team leaders, working on Mac OS System 7, purchased a vial of liquid LSD and shared it with his programmers to help them "break through creative blocks." "The Mac people were focused on getting into the heads of normal users," the source said. "[They] used psychedelics to break down their own preconceptions." The source said psychedelics were taken by the "troops," and few, if anyone, in management knew about it. The claim couldn't be verified and should be taken with a grain of salt.

The drug-taking claims were strongly disputed by Jef Raskin, the "father" of the Macintosh. "As the creator of the Macintosh project, and the guy who named it 'Macintosh' after his beloved McIntosh apples, I can firmly say that pot had nothing to do with it," Raskin wrote in an email. "Unlike our previous president, I have never even brought a reefer to lip, much less inhaled it. I also do not use alcohol, tobacco, or any other recreational drugs, and never have."

Raskin said to the best of his knowledge, there was no pot smoking at Apple by the Mac team during his tenure, and no other drug use. "I never saw Steve Jobs or Steve Wozniak use pot," he wrote. "What people did at home or after I left Apple is, of course, beyond my knowledge, but even at our social occasions, drugs were not a part of the scene. Pizza, yes. Puns, yes. Play, yes. Pot, no...I even prefer my apples unfermented."

Raskin was backed up by David Bunnell, the founding editor of *Macworld* magazine (http://www.macworld.com/), who saw no pot smoking at Apple. "I never saw any evidence of that among the people who created the Mac," he said. "And I was there. I was intimately involved with the Mac development team. I had free access to the Mac building. I don't recall seeing any evidence of people smoking pot while they were developing the machine."

Bunnell conceded that any pot smoking may have been witnessed only by those who were sympathetic to it. "They didn't invite me," he said. "Maybe I was too straight." Another former Apple employee, who requested anonymity, concurred: "If there was a drug culture at Apple, I would have found it, and I didn't," he said.

Marc Canter, founder of MacroMind (now Macromedia) and well connected in the Mac development community, said of course there was drug use at Apple—just like the rest of the PC industry, then and now. Canter said drug use certainly wasn't sanctioned at the workplace, and is no more widespread at Apple than any other company or industry. There were some who indulged, but most didn't, at least not at work. Over the years, Canter said, he has seen a lot of the PC industry's moguls toking pot at parties, including the industry's top dogs.

Pot smoking is an integral part of the culture of Northern California. It is the state's biggest crash crop. Pot is particularly prevalent in the high-tech sector. A survey by U.K. software provider TongueWag of 1,000 18-to-35-year-olds, revealed that one in three marijuana smokers is employed in the high-tech sector: a proportion far higher than for the population as a whole. "Tech is the only field I've known where marijuana is almost a sacrament," said one source. "The pseudo-autism it induces allows you to focus on mind-numbing detail for hours at a time."

Allan Lundell, a journalist at *InfoWorld* and West Coast editor of *Byte Magazine*, said early Mac culture was permeated with pot. "Most religions have rituals," he said. "For the first Macheads, a popular ritual was getting together to pass a joint, often at Macworld parties. Many programmers I knew loved to get high before writing code. This seemed to be more the norm than the exception, leading me to believe that software production in Silicon Valley would grind to a halt it wasn't for good sensimilla."

HE IBM PC WAS CREATED E
EOPLE WHO DRANK ALCOHO
HE MAC WAS CREATED BY
EOPLE WHO SMOKED POT."

HAPPY WEED: HAPPY WEED WAS A POPULAR GAME
IN THE EARLY 1990S. A VERSION OF PAC-MAN,
THE IDEA WAS TO RUN AROUND GOBBLING UP
GANGA LEAVES AND JOINTS WHILE AVOIDING THE
CAMPUS POLICE. IT WAS MAC-ONLY, OF COURSE.
CREDIT: CHRISTOPHER COUNCIL

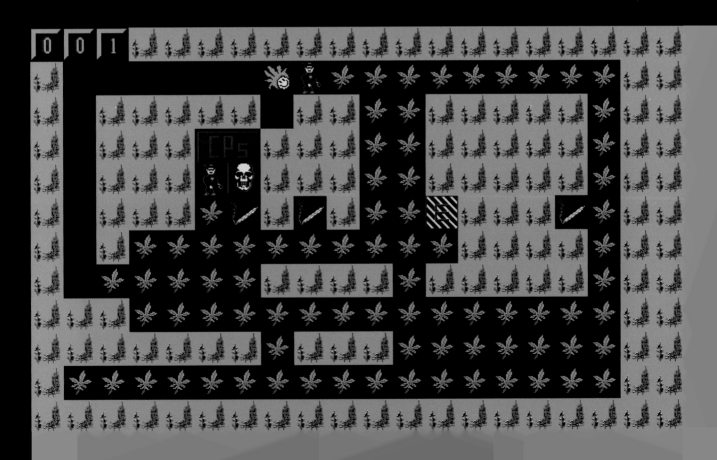

The Mac's graphical user interface really appealed to stoners, Lundell said, much more so than the cryptic codes of DOS. "It makes it possible to use the computer at 3 in the morning when you're stoned," he said. "But it's not just about getting high. It's about doing stuff when you get there."

Douglas Rushkoff, author of numerous books about technology and cyberspace, is one of the few writers to comment on the connection between Macs and pot. "Conceived on the bongwater-stained rugs of Reed College dorm rooms, the Apple personal computer bent over backwards to bring even the most stoned of us into the mix," he wrote in an online column. "It is no coincidence that the first shots of the computer revolution were fired from the same Bay Area that brought us Haight-Ashbury in the 1960s. The very conception of the almost hallucinatory realm we call 'cyberspace' required the imaginative capacities of people who were familiar with navigating hallucinatory headspace. This is why so many Silicon Valley firms eschew the employee drug testing of their counterparts in other industries. If high-tech companies weeded out weed users, they'd have few employees left."

The iBong

Giving new meaning to the term "high" tech, a couple of stoners have turned an old Macintosh into a bong. Agapornis and Prozac, a pair of 29-year-old computer nerds from Austin, Texas, traded chips for hits when they transformed an old all-in-one Mac into a device for smoking marijuana. "It has a lilting touch of deathlike intoxication," said Prozac. "It's treated us well."

The Mac bong, or iBong, is made from a water-filled bong mounted inside an old Mac SE 30. The bowl of the bong protrudes from the front of the computer, just below the screen. The mouthpiece sticks out the back. "It looks like any other dingy Mac," said Prozac. "But it doesn't draw as much suspicion [as a normal bong] if you do have to take it outside the house. We haven't taken it to Macworld, but it has been to a couple of computer swap meets. People like it. They laugh. It gets the usual, 'Woah dude, that's crazy' reaction. Everyone wants to try it."

The iBong delivers a "killer hit," according to the pair. After smoking the iBong one evening, Prozac wrote about the experience and posted it online (http://www.anus.com/tuc/tuc2/5.html). "My bong burnt bright," he wrote, "electrifiying fractals dancing in the raging embers, smoke curling like a halo around my bowed and fatal head.... The restlessness of a millennium's solitude soared through my rushing blood, the roar of being alive skipping like a jumping spark through my brain."

The iBong was inspired by the MacQuarium, a famous modification of Apple's old one-piece Macintosh computers that turns them into fish tanks. "We saw the MacQuarium and said, 'Let's put a bong inside one instead,'" said Agapornis. "We were probably stoned."

HIGH TECH: A PAIR OF STONERS TURNED AN OLD MAC SE/30 INTO A BONG. IT DELIVERS A "KILLER HIT," THEY SAY.
CREDIT: PROZAC

THE iBONG: PUTTING OBSOLETE TECHNOLOGY TO GOOD USE.
CREDIT: PROZAC

The pair has actually made three iBongs to date. The first was made in 1992, and it attempted to incorporate both a fish tank and a bong within the casing of the old computer. "We were working on a way to make an aquarium with the bong inside it so that the person taking the hit could watch the fish," explained Agapornis, "but the aquarium took up too much room." The pair also found the stem was too long, which made it difficult to take a hit; it required drawing in too much air.

The second model, which had a shorter stem, was too harsh. "It was like a pickle-jar bong," said Agapornis. "It was pretty painful." The third and final attempt got it just right. "It's not bad," said Agapornis. "It's pretty easy hitting."

But after ten years of perfecting the design, the two have discovered that they are smoking less and less pot; they've gone from chronic to occasional smokers. "We're not going through four quarter bags in a weekend—each—like we used to," said Agapornis. "We're not into a void like we used to be 10 years ago." Still, "the Mac bong is the best thing to have around when you're listening to the first four Burzum albums," he added. Burzum is a Norwegian black metal band.

FREE LOVE AND SELLING MACS

During the late 1980s, the biggest dealer of Apple computers in Northern California wasn't a computer megastore. It was a free-love commune in San Francisco's hippie Haight-Ashbury

District. Founded in the 1970s, the Kerista commune had about 30 members who practiced "polyfidelity." Members would sleep with a different person each night, but only with someone in their group. Every day, the sleeping schedule was drawn up on a Mac.

The Kerista commune was not just promiscuous; it was extremely industrious. In the span of about five years, the commune transformed a modest house-cleaning business into the biggest Macintosh dealership and consulting firm in Northern California. For three years in a row, the company, called Abacus, was featured in *Inc.* magazine's annual list of the fastest-growing enterprises in America. The company ran a pair of plush training centers in San Francisco's financial district and in Santa Clara. It operated three big repair facilities and a giant warehouse. It had consulting divisions for networking and publishing and even ran a computer temp agency.

"It was a fascinating company that people couldn't put their fingers on, for good reason," said a former commune member who asked to be referred to by his commune name, Love. "It was run by flamboyant, hippie types, who tended to be young and good-looking. But they were very good at evangelizing the Mac."

Kerista was founded as a scientific utopian community, according to another former member, Sun, who was attracted by, among other things, the commune's sexual freedom. "There were lots of guys who were into polyfidelity. That sounded

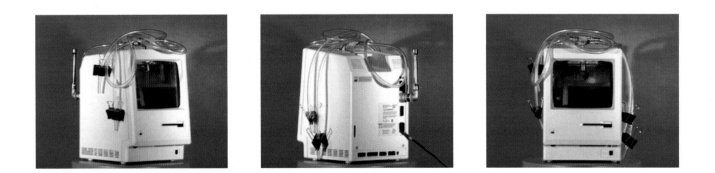

APPLE'S CORPORATE BONG? THIS MAC BONG APPEARS TO HAVE RESIDED AT APPLE'S CORPORATE HEADQUARTERS FOR MANY YEARS. THREE DIFFERENT SOURCES SAY THE BONG WAS STORED AT BUILDING 2 AT APPLE'S CAMPUS IN CUPERTINO, CALIFORNIA. THE PERSON WHO SENT THE PICTURE DID SO ANONYMOUSLY AND DECLINED TO SAY WHERE IT CAME FROM, BUT INQUIRIES TRACED IT BACK TO ENGINEERS AT APPLE. THE BONG IS MADE FROM A MAC SE AND IS A MULTIUSER DEVICE, WITH FOUR "DRAW" TUBES.
CREDIT: ANONYMOUS

good to me," she said, laughing. Now in her 40s, Sun is an attractive woman with long, brown hair. She lives in Boulder Creek, California, a rural enclave of Silicon Valley and home to a lot of "redwood nerds." She was disinherited from her wealthy family for joining Kerista.

The commune had four "families," or "Best Friend Identity Clusters." Commune members could sleep only with the six or seven other people in their cluster. There were equal numbers of men and women in each cluster. Everyone was in their 20s or 30s, except for the founder, known as Bro Jud, who was in his 60s.

There was also a "seduction squad": attractive girls who recruited new members at parties. Men were invited to sleep with them, but only if they first joined the commune, which meant having a vasectomy. "The commune already had two kids," Sun said. "Like any family, we decided two is enough and no more kids. Too many diapers. The favorable form of contraception was vasectomy. You had to be really committed."

The commune rented about half a dozen buildings and apartments in the Haight. Everyone had a key to each apartment. "Everyone had a giant key ring," Sun said. "One woman had a two-pound key ring."

"No one worried about money at all," Sun said. "It was all being accounted for on the community level. It seemed like an inexhaustible bank account. You made $15,000 a year, but you lived like you made $50,000. But we weren't extravagant. We lived comfortable middle-class lifestyles."

When Sun joined the commune, members were cleaning houses, fixing up gardens, and publishing a free advertising newsletter. Sun introduced them to Macintosh computers. The reception was very enthusiastic, and people immediately started small desktop-publishing sideline businesses. Soon, the commune was offering publishing services and advice to other small businesses, and it opened a computer-rental store on Frederick Street called Utopian Technology.

The commune's big break was getting a dealer's license from Apple, then the biggest personal computer maker in the world. Demonstrating its commitment to feminism, the commune had incorporated Abacus in the names of four female commune members: on paper, it was a women-owned business. The head of sales, known as EvaWay, approached then-CEO John Sculley and told him Apple looked bad because it didn't have any women-owned dealers in its reseller network. Sculley agreed and lobbied to get them a license.

The commune bought about 10 Macs and quickly sold them. Business took off like a rocket. First-year revenues were $1 million, and they quadrupled every year. The women-owned status of the company was a big bonus, helping to land so-called "preference" contracts with big corporations and government agencies. "Not bad for a bunch of hippies," said EvaWay, who is now an executive at a Bay Area startup. "All we wanted to do was change the world."

Love attributed Abacus' success to its hippie business ethic: The commune wanted to help create a utopian technological society, so they made sure people knew how to use their new machines. The company had a motto: "Abacus: A vision with a business."

"All of our competitors were just dropping off boxes," said Love. "We had everything: training, support, repairs. We were a one-stop shop for business folks." Love, now in his early 40s, still lives communally with three other adults in a house on the San Francisco peninsula. He works as an investment banker. "We were total nerds," added Sun. "We were very cool nerds."

Eventually, Abacus also started selling Compaq computers. Ironically, the success of the business took its toll on the commune, which folded under the pressure of running such a fast-growing enterprise. "We weren't professional managers," said Love. "There were many, many mistakes we made that created a business that did not run very efficiently." While computer prices plummeted, Abacus found itself sitting on a huge inventory no one wanted.

The commune disbanded in 1991, and a year later Abacus merged with Ciber, a Denver corporation that was going around the country consolidating failing dealers. The merger allowed 50 people to keep their jobs; some are still employed by Ciber. But there was no money—all the proceeds went to pay off debt.

"We went from being an artist community to a computer business," Sun said. "The whole culture changed. It became workaholic, yuppie cyberculture." "[We were] like a mom-and-pop computer shop, but with 30 people as the mom and pop. There was no real management, and the majority of people wanted to do something else with the affluence the business bought them. It allowed them to do something else, like moving to Hawaii."

"It brought huge amounts of wealth into a tribal community, which had never been seen before," said Allan Lundell, Sun's partner and, with her, the cofounder of Virtual World Studio. "This allowed them to build their dreams of a functional utopian culture and live in it."

TECHNO CHICK: "SUN" IS A FORMER MEMBER OF SAN FRANCISCO'S KERISTA COMMUNE, WHICH PRACTICED "POLYFIDELITY"—EVERY NIGHT MEMBERS OF THE COMMUNE SLEPT WITH A DIFFERENT PARTNER, BUT NEVER OUTSIDE A SMALL GROUP OF DESIGNATED MATES. SUN INTRODUCED THE COMMUNE TO MACS. IN A FEW SHORT YEARS, THE COMMUNE WENT FROM CLEANING HOUSES TO BEING THE BIGGEST APPLE DEALER IN NORTHERN CALIFORNIA, A MULTIMILLION-DOLLAR CORPORATION. CREDIT: SUN

LIFE ON THE COMMUNE: KERISTA'S FAR OUT WEST COMIC BOOK DETAILED LIFE AT THE COMMUNE, WHICH QUICKLY GREW INTO THE BIGGEST APPLE DEALER IN NORTHERN CALIFORNIA DURING THE LATE 1980S. THE COMIC BOOK WAS PUBLISHED ON AN IRREGULAR SCHEDULE AND GIVEN AWAY FREE. SUN IS SHOWN IN THE THIRD PANEL—THE DARK-HAIRED WOMAN WEARING A SCARF. CREDIT: EVEN EVE, FAR OUT WEST COMICS, PUBLISHED BY KERISTA COMMUNE CIRCA 1987

ELLEN FEISS: STONER CELEBRITY

The emergent star of Apple's Switch advertising campaign is Ellen Feiss, a young student who appears to many people to be stoned. After the Switch ad debuted in the summer of 2002, Feiss quickly shot to Net celebrity, largely because many people thought she had been smoking pot. She became the subject of numerous newspaper stories, fan sites, icons, desktop wallpaper, and merchandise like T-shirts and Frisbees bearing her image. Talk show hosts David Letterman and Jay Leno requested interviews, and Hollywood called with talk of TV shows and movie roles. Feiss declined all offers, but, of course, in true Hollywood style, she retained an agent.

Very little is known about Feiss, except she's a teenager and a student; Apple isn't revealing any details. In her only interview with the *Brown Daily Herald*, a student newspaper, Feiss revealed she was under the influence of drugs, but it was allergy medication, not marijuana.

Feiss is part of Apple's Switch campaign, which features testimonials from dozens of real people explaining why they switched from a Windows PC to the Mac. The high-profile campaign has been widely imitated, from a ham-fisted attempt by Microsoft to portray a member of its PR team as a Mac-to-PC switcher, to a gubernatorial primary in Baltimore.

Feiss's appeal is multifaceted: she's young, attractive, and endearing. To some, though, what counts is Apple's tacit acknowledgement that some of its customers use controlled substances. "Dudes just look at the photo—she looks so baked!" someone wrote on the message board at EllenFeiss.net, one of her fan sites. "LOL. It's just too funny. I think Macs are a great fit for stoners."

Feiss's celebrity started with Mac users, but soon grew to include marijuana advocates. The revelation that she wasn't high on pot didn't trouble her stoner fans, who simply didn't believe her. Feiss's ad on Apple's Web site is returned as the top hit on Google in response to the search item "stoned chick." Google's search algorithm ranks hits according to the number of other pages linking to it containing the search terms, among other things. Apple's page makes no mention of drugs, naturally.

According to the Rev. Samuel, who runs an online T-shirt business in upstate New York that sells a line of popular Smoke Different shirts, Apple is courting "tokers" with the ad. Feiss's ad is the only "Switch" ad from the original group still prominently displayed on Apple's site.

The Rev. Samuel said he recently attended a "hippie festival" and discovered a lot of young people are familiar with Feiss. "Apple is very cognizant of what Ellen represents: the stoner computer market," he said. "Obviously they are courting my people: the stoners, the pot enthusiasts, munchie mavens, which is fine with me. When more advertisers do, we will be seen as respectable."

STONER STAR: ELLEN FEISS BECAME AN INTERNET CELEBRITY AFTER STARRING IN A 30-SECOND SWITCH AD FOR APPLE, IN WHICH SHE TESTIFIED TO SWITCHING TO THE MAC BECAUSE A WINDOWS PC ATE HER HOMEWORK.
CREDIT: APPLE COMPUTER

MOCKERY: FEISS BECAME THE
SUBJECT OF NUMEROUS PARODIES
POKING FUN AT EVERYTHING FROM
APPLE TO DRUGS.
CREDIT: JEROME MAUREY-DELAUNAY

THE JOY OF TECH ON ELLEN FEISS.
CREDIT: GEEK CULTURE

Feiss Look-Alikes

If imitation is the sincerest form of flattery, let's hope Ellen Feiss was flattered by a look-alike contest held in Holland, which featured mostly men, none of whom looked like her. At an October 2002 gathering of members of the MacFreak online community, a Dutch Mac-oriented Web site and forum, attendees amused themselves by holding a look-alike competition to find the best Ellen Feiss, the teenage star of one of Apple's Switch commercials.

"We wanted to make spoof commercials, but people are too shy in front of a video camera," explained Peter Villevoye, who helps run MacFreak. "So we thought it would be fun to have an Ellen Feiss look-alike competition instead. A lot of people really got into the spirit of it."

The resemblances, as you can see, are not very striking.

APPLE AND THE CHURCH OF SATAN

Apple has always marketed itself as countercultural, but some people are too countercultural for Apple, it appears. In December 2000, lawyers representing Apple sent repeat notices to the Church of Satan's Web master, demanding that he remove from the site a "Made with Macintosh" badge and a "Think Different" parody featuring Anton Szandor LaVey, the Church's founder.

The site's Web master, Peter Gilmore, eventually complied after receiving a series of threatening legal letters, which he posted on the site. Gilmore, an avid Mac fan, said he merely wanted to demonstrate his loyalty to the company with a "Made with a Mac" banner. And the parody poster featuring LaVey, a consummate iconoclast, was entirely in keeping with the theme of Apple's Think Different campaign. Or so he thought. "It was a tribute and a parody at the same time," he said from his home in New York.

Apple disagreed. The firm's outside counsel, Arent Fox, insisted the images infringed Apple's trademarks and demanded they be removed immediately. Apple clearly disliked its brand being associated with the Church. A statement faxed to Gilmore said: "Apple believes that your use of the Made With Macintosh and Think Different badges in this manner is likely to tarnish the goodwill associated with the Apple [trademark]."

Apple has generally turned a blind eye to ad parodies and "Made with Macintosh" banners. Parodies of the Think Different campaign, featuring everything from Hitler to the Planet of the Apes, can be found all over the Net. The Church of Satan is one of the few to which Apple took exception.

Gilmore charged Apple with religious discrimination and threatened to take his case to the American Civil Liberties Union. He noted the Church of Satan is a legally recognized minority religion. "It's clearly religious discrimination," he said. "There are plenty of Christian sites that have the 'Made on a Mac' badge, and even some Wicca ones. They haven't asked them to take it down." Gilmore noted that LaVey was a big fan of Apple and owned several Macs before he died in 1997.

Ironically, Apple's demands garnered the Church considerable publicity; more in fact, than the Church had received in years. The story ran in numerous newspapers and on CNN. Gilmore said he received several thousand supportive emails from rank-and-file Mac fans.

Adweek awarded the LaVey poster its best advertising parody of 2001. The banner and parody poster had been on the site for almost two years before anyone noticed. "To Apple's chagrin, *Adweek* printed it," said Gilmore. "If they hadn't said anything, no one would have noticed. Only people who went to the Church of Satan Web site would have seen it. Now it's on the desks of advertising executives worldwide."

SATANIC WEB MASTER: PETER GILMORE, WEB MASTER OF THE CHURCH OF SATAN WEB SITE, CLAIMS APPLE'S LEGAL THREATS CONCERNING THE LAVEY POSTER WAS RELIGIOUS DISCRIMINATION.
CREDIT: PETER GILMORE

PARODIES OF THE THINK DIFFEREN
CAMPAIGN, FEATURING EVERYTHING
FROM HITLER TO THE PLANET OF
THE APES, CAN BE FOUND ALL
OVER THE NET.

TOO DIFFERENT: THE AMENDED LAVEY THINK DIFFERENT
POSTER. APPLE OBJECTED TO THE ASSOCIATION OF ITS
BRAND WITH DEVIL WORSHIP.
CREDIT: CHURCH OF SATAN

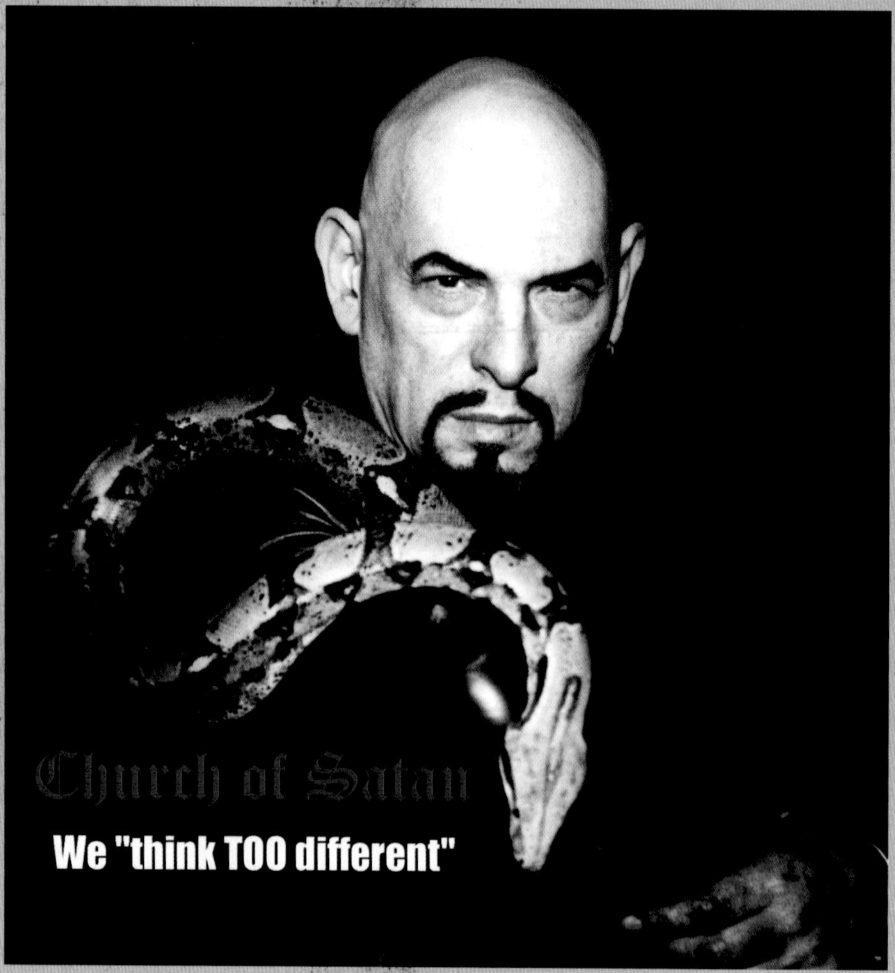

Church of Satan

We "think TOO different"

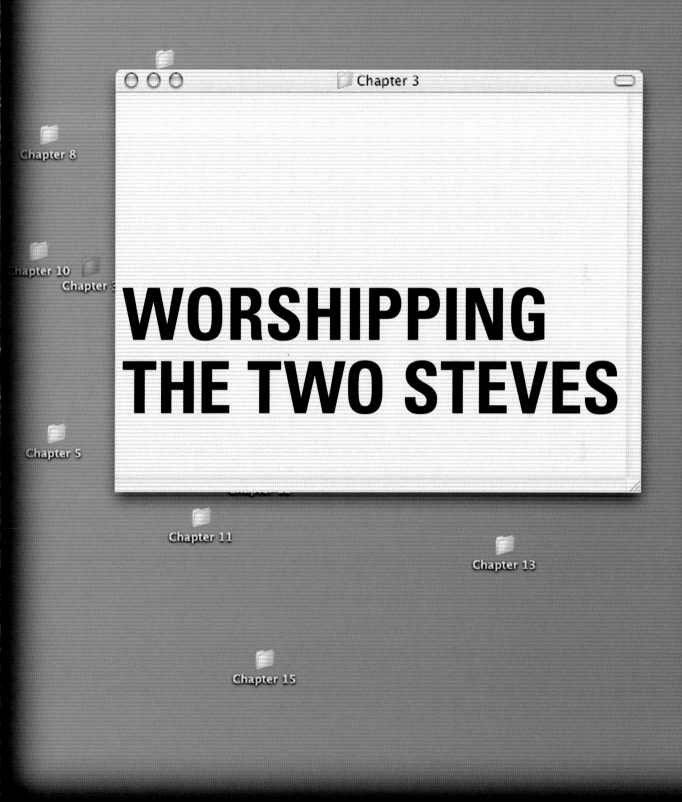

WORSHIPPING
THE TWO STEVES

THERE'S NO ONE IN AMERICAN BUSINESS WHO CAN ENTHRALL A CROWD LIKE JOBS ... YET ... HE IS WIDELY VIEWED AS AN ASSHOLE.

THE COFOUNDERS: JOBS AND WOZNIAK

A big part of the fascination with Apple stems from a fascination with the company's two founders: Steve Jobs and Steve Wozniak. They couldn't be more different. Jobs is worshipped like a rock star. Wozniak, the brains behind Apple's original machines, is revered as the ultimate hacker hero.

What is the attraction of these two very different icons? Jobs is the one who gets all the attention. He's the star, a regular fixture in newspapers and coverboy of magazines. Woz appears only occasionally in the public eye, yet in many ways his reputation is more secure and his fan base stronger.

Jobs is the charismatic face of Apple. He has undeniable sex appeal and is a master showman. There's no one in American business who can enthrall a crowd like Jobs. He is so charming, he has his own "reality distortion field," bending perception any way he chooses. The long-running joke at Apple is his ability to convince minions to drink poisoned Kool-Aid, a reference to the mass suicide at Jonestown.

Jobs is an aesthete, a style-seeking computer auteur. His stamp is on everything Apple makes, for good and bad. He has undeniably brought back a sense of innovation and excitement to the company.

Jobs is rightly called a visionary. He can see what people want or don't need—even if they don't know it yet. There was a huge flap about the original iMac lacking a floppy drive, then standard equipment on PCs. Jobs rightly saw that floppy drives were an anachronism, but he was ahead of the curve. On the other hand, the iMac had an unusable, single-button hockey-puck mouse, an unworkable concession to aesthetics.

Jobs gets an inordinate amount of press attention given the size of the Mac market. Although Microsoft has much more clout, Bill Gates just can't get the press's or public's interest like Jobs can. Alan Deutschman's 2000 unauthorized biography of Jobs was called *The Second Coming of Steve Jobs,* in reference to "the extraordinary reverence with which the media has treated him," said the author.

There may be a cult of the Mac, but there's definitely a cult of Steve Jobs. Huge lines form to see him talk at Macworld, and there's a near stampede to get seats. Bill Gates once remarked on Jobs' ability to elicit wild cheers for candy-colored computers. He was truly baffled.

I recall talking to some fans after one of Jobs' Macworld keynotes. One woman said, "Steve looks tired. He's been working hard for us lately." She had a dreamy look in her eyes. "Crikey," I thought. "She's a whacked-out Moonie."

Yet Jobs' reputation is tarnished. Although he is respected for being Apple's "savior" after returning to the troubled company in 1998, he is widely viewed as an asshole. "Jobs is not a role model," said John Manzione, who runs the Mac-oriented MacNet2.com Web site. "He's not someone to be admired. I would be saddened to hear someone desire to be like Steve Jobs."

Jobs portrays himself as a bohemian, yet stories abound about his greed. A disturbing story emerged a few years ago about how he'd stiffed Wozniak on an early deal. Jobs also makes a big deal about receiving only one dollar a year in salary at Apple, but he is one of the highest-paid executives in the industry. Bonuses, stock options, and other perks, like a private jet, put him in the top tier, according to a 2002 survey by the Economic Research Institute.

And then there's Jobs' reputation for being difficult to work with. His tantrums, outbursts, and verbal abuse have been well documented. Guy Kawasaki, a former Apple marketing executive, said working for Jobs was the greatest experience he'd never repeat. "He is a bundle of paradoxes," wrote Scott Rosenberg on Salon.com. "A manipulative cult-of-personality leader, he also brings egalitarian principles to his workplaces;

Would you buy a car from this man?

CONSUMMATE SALESMAN:
STEVE JOBS IS THE ULTIMATE SALESMAN—
CHARMING, CHARISMATIC, AND SEXY.
CREDIT: STEFAN TYNELL

STEVE WOZNIAK, ON THE OTHER HAND, IS ALMOST UNANIMOUSLY LOVED.

he longs to unleash the chaos of new technologies—as long as he can dictate the shape of their boxes and the color of their power cords. He is, it seems, a revolutionary control freak."

Deutschman, Jobs' unauthorized biographer, said many of Jobs' fans refused to believe the stories of bad behavior documented in his book. "The media has worshipped him as a modern hero," Deutschman said. "Many of his fans yearn so much for a inspiring hero figure that they simply don't want to believe a more balanced and realistic account."

Jobs' ego rubs a lot of people the wrong way. Here's a joke found in a newsgroup: "How does Steve Jobs change a lightbulb? He holds up the bulb and lets the universe revolve around him."

Steve Wozniak, on the other hand, is almost unanimously loved. Take his nickname, Woz, by which he is universally referred to. What could be more endearing?

Woz, a college dropout, is widely credited as the genius who launched the personal computer revolution with a series of elegantly designed, commercial machines. Both Jobs and Woz received a National Technology Medal from President Reagan in 1985, but Jobs is reportedly neurotic about his reputation as just a "marketing guy." Woz's accomplishments have received rock-solid recognition: He has a place in the National Inventors Hall of Fame, along with Marconi and Bell.

Woz is the blue-collar hacker, interested only in electronics, not empire building. He gave away the bulk of his $100 million fortune to early Apple engineers who weren't granted stock options, and he eventually dropped out of the industry altogether to teach high school. He spent more than a decade as a volunteer teacher at a local school.

Woz's heroes are his old high school teachers and his dad, an engineer. He often makes generous donations of equipment to local schools. Woz wanted to give the first Apple I, hand-built

in Jobs' parents' garage, to an itinerant computer teacher with the unusual name of Liza Lo*op. Jobs made Woz buy it, and then he gave it to her. Woz also has a great sense of fun; he once called the Pope pretending to be Henry Kissinger using a homemade phone hacking device.

Whereas Jobs is inaccessible—public appearances are carefully stage-managed by his handlers—Woz is anything but. He can be watched all day on his office Webcam (http://wozcam.woz.org/), which attracts about 250 visitors a day. The Webcam has regular viewers, who try to divine what Woz is up to by reading scribblings on the office whiteboard. However, true to character, all the messages are red herrings. "Anything you read on the whiteboard is misinformation," said Dan Sokol, Woz's Web master. "To put it another way, if you can see it on camera, it isn't true."

Woz personally answers most of the email he receives, which can be hundreds of messages a day. After the release of *Pirates of Silicon Valley*, a TV movie about the early days of Apple, Woz's major complaint wasn't about how he'd been portrayed, but about the volume of email he had to answer. He started spending 20 hours a day, rather than 5, answering email. "We see a lot of the adoration and respect he has from your average everyday geek through our work here," said Snaggy, who helps run the popular Geekculture.com Web site. "He just about always wins any poll he's mentioned in."

While Woz was out of the business pages for many years, he was a regular fixture on Slashdot.org, a news site for nerds. The site ran 11 features on him, all generously sprinkled with the word "hero." "I had never heard a negative word about the guy," wrote one poster. "Seems unique in this industry, especially because of his pairing with Steve Jobs. . . . We have here the nicest man in Silicon Valley. . . . If you have a story about him punching a busboy, stiffing a contractor, or making a child cry—I don't want to hear. I wouldn't believe it. You're only as rich as you are rich at heart."

GOOD OLD BOY:
THIS IS HOW A LOT OF FANS SEE STEVE WOZNIAK:
A NO-NONSENSE, BLUE-COLLAR ENGINEER.
SALT OF THE EARTH.
CREDIT: JOE PHILLIPS

STEVE
SUMMER 1997

HOMEBREW CLUB
ROCKS!

SUPERWOZ:
THANKS TO HIS DOWN-TO-EARTH
SENSIBILITY, WOZ IS A HERO TO MANY.
CREDIT: GEEK CULTURE

PRESIDENT JOBS:
SOME PEOPLE WOULD LIKE TO SEE JOBS RUN FOR
PRESIDENT. THE CEO OF APPLE IS A LONGTIME DEMOCRAT
AND A BIG DONATOR TO THE PARTY. HE ONCE
HAD PRESIDENT CLINTON OVER FOR DINNER.

CREDIT: UNKNOWN

JOBS FOR PRESIDENT

A grassroots campaign to persuade Apple's CEO Steve Jobs to run for President of the United States was launched on the Web in early 2003, but it was over almost as soon as it began. If successful, the campaign would have drafted Jobs as a Democratic Party candidate in 2004. The Steve Jobs for U.S. President campaign didn't fail because of a lack of interest. In fact, so many people rushed to the campaign Web site, it melted down minutes after it was put up. "We had 10,000 hits in 10 minutes," said William Foster, who dreamed up the idea. "It brought the server down. It was only up for 10 minutes." However, in that time Foster said he received numerous emails of support and encouragement and a couple of dozen donations of cash—he wouldn't reveal how much, but they were all under $10.

The other big problem was that Jobs wasn't interested. Thanks to the response, Foster considered relaunching the site. He decided against it after phoning Jobs' office. Jobs' personal assistant told him Jobs had seen the site but was too committed to his family to run a grueling political campaign. "He was flattered," Foster said, "but it was a job he wasn't interested in having. He wanted to concentrate on his family and his two companies."

Jobs, who heads up Apple and Pixar, an animation studio, is a longtime supporter of the Democratic Party. Jobs had Bill Clinton over for dinner in 1996 at his house in Palo Alto, California, and Clinton returned the favor. Jobs stayed a night in the White House's Lincoln bedroom, a privilege granted to big party donors. Jobs and his wife, Laurene, have contributed at least $250,000 to the Democrats since 1996, according to records available through the Center of Responsive Politics, a nonpartisan watchdog organization based in Washington, D.C. The couple hasn't made any donations whatsoever to the Republicans, according to the center. "They're heavily Democratic," said researcher Douglas Weber. "They've made quite a high number of contributions. It's a fair amount, but it doesn't put them up there in the top 100 contributors."

The idea for the campaign came to Foster, an information systems professor at Arizona State University, after watching President Bush's performance during his first two years in office. "He's an idiot," Foster said. By contrast, Foster said Jobs would make an excellent president. "He has shown over and over an ability to lead," Foster said. "He's brilliant."

As well as being a natural leader, Jobs has a great command of global issues and domestic politics, Foster said. He said he met Jobs in the late 1980s and was impressed with his knowledge of Congress. Foster has been a big fan since.

Jobs certainly has his fans, but not everyone agrees he's up to the job. Alan Deutschman's unauthorized biography said the Apple CEO is too abrasive. "He has the charisma and the will to power but not the diplomatic skills needed to govern effectively in a democracy," Deutschman said in an email. "He'd probably tell a number of important senators that they were bozos. I think Steve's better off as a corporate CEO, a position more akin to benevolent dictator than to president."

Foster also said Jobs may have too many skeletons in his closet to survive a cutthroat campaign. As a young man, Jobs fathered an illegitimate daughter and reportedly dabbled in psychedelics. "No president has ever admitted to taking psychedelics," Foster said. As opposed, of course, to cocaine, marijuana, booze, and a host of other substances.

Foster said that because his short-lived "Jobs for U.S. President" campaign fizzled, he planned to switch his support to Senator John Edwards, D-N.C.

Most of the traffic that brought down the Jobs for President Web site came from Slashdot, a popular technology Web site, which Foster used to publicize his freshly posted site. Slashdot readers made some good jokes about a Steve Jobs presidency. One suggested he invade Iraq and rename it iRaq. Another suggested Jobs would be barred from executive office because of the separation of church and state. As a deity, Jobs wouldn't be allowed to hold the nation's highest public office.

SLASH FICTION:
BILL/STEVE'S SEXCELLENT ADVENTURE

In real life, Bill Gates screwed Steve Jobs and everyone else in the computer industry. But in slash fiction, it's Steve Jobs who gets to screw Bill Gates—literally. In six short fictional stories written under the pen name Jezebel Slade, the long and ornery business relationship between Jobs and Gates is contrasted with their secret love affair, which is spelled out in pornographic detail.

Slash is homoerotic fan fiction that is usually written by women, for women. The stories detail erotic encounters between pop culture figures. Usually the works feature lead characters from popular movies or TV series: Spock and Kirk from *Star Trek;* Luke and Han from *Star Wars;* Mulder and Krycek from *The X-Files;* and Bert and Ernie from *Sesame Street.*

The term "slash" comes from the punctuation mark denoting paired lovers, as in Starsky/Hutch. Slash fiction arose in the '70s among straight female *Star Trek* fans who wanted to render the gay subtext between Kirk and Spock explicit through their own writings. Since then, it has flourished as a lively literary subgenre on the Net. There are dozens of sites, archiving thousands of stories.

According to her Web site, Slade's stories were inspired by the 1999 TNT movie *Pirates of Silicon Valley,* which chronicled the early history of Apple and Microsoft, personified by Jobs and Gates. Slade is at pains to point out that her fiction plays off the characters in the movie, not the real Gates and Jobs.

Slade's first story in the series, *I Have What You Need,* details a "missing scene" from the movie. Although it's not entirely clear from the text, the story appears to take place after Jobs shows Gates the Macintosh for the first time. Written in first-person narrative from Gates' point of view, Gates tells Jobs he "has what he needs." Jobs thinks it's software for the Mac, but quickly finds out Gates is referring to something else entirely.

"(JOBS) NUZZLES MY NECK, BITES MY EARLOBE," Slade writes. "I WATCH HIM GO TO HIS DESK AND RUMMAGE IN ONE OF THE TOP DRAWERS. WHEN HE COMES BACK, HE'S HOLDING A BOTTLE OF HAND LOTION.... HE HOOKS HIS HAND ON THE WAISTBAND OF MY CHINOS AND BRIEFS, SLIDING THEM BOTH DOWN AT ONCE.... HE RUNS HIS HAND UP MY BACK AND LEANS DOWN TO WHISPER, 'BILL, ARE YOU A VIRGIN?'"

"YES." Sort of.

"I'LL BE GENTLE."

The sex cements the relationship between Gates and Jobs, Apple and Microsoft. "WE'RE COMPATIBLE," the fictional Gates tells the fictional Jobs. But the sex simply lures Jobs into a false sense of security, which, of course, is exploited by Gates.

The remaining stories focus on the deteriorating business relationship between the two (Jobs accuses Gates of ripping off the Macintosh graphical operating system for Windows) and the enduring affair. Slade depicts business rows punctuated by bouts of hot, gay sex. And while Gates dominates the professional relationship, Jobs is the "top" in the bedroom.

"There's such an intense dynamic and history between [Jobs and Gates]," said Slade. "They changed the world together. And I just can't help wondering how it would have been different if they'd really been 'together.' It's just a matter of taking the tension that already exists and making it sexual."

Compared to most of the dull material published about Jobs and Gates, these stories are a rip-roaring read. But while the stories are clearly parody, Slade's choice of using real people is controversial. Slash purists insist only fictional characters should populate the canon. "The extension of slash from fictional characters to real people would be troubling to the original fans who conceived of the genre," said Henry Jenkins, a professor at MIT and author of *Textual Poachers,* a book about fan literature. "They maintained very rigorous ethical norms within the community against basing the stories upon real people and their actual sexual lives."

Jenkins said as slash moved onto the Internet, the genre's conventions began to be flouted, and there was a dramatic increase in stories featuring rock stars, politicians, and business leaders. Examples include pro wrestlers, boy bands like *NSYNC, and even the members of Metallica. Catherine Salmon, a psychology professor at Simon Fraser University and coauthor of *Warrior Lovers,* a book examining slash from an evolutionary psychology perspective, said the stories were anomalous. They weren't true RPS (real-person slash), but stories based on real people as portrayed in a movie.

As for the choice of characters: "There's often an appeal to powerful men—most slash focuses on the male leads of action-type TV shows—and certainly the relationship between these two men has had its ups and downs, which tends to lend itself to slash, the angsty factor," she said. "But I see these stories as an odd aberration in slash—part of the recent, you-can-slash-any-one-if-you-want-to mentality that has come with the Web. They may have been done more as a lark than as a serious attempt to explore the sexual-romantic nature of two characters."

MATING MOGULS:
BILL GATES AND STEVE JOBS ABOUT TO GET IT
ON IN THIS DOCTORED IMAGE FROM TNT'S
"PIRATES OF SILICON VALLEY."
CREDIT: TNT/JEZEBEL SLADE

Chapter 4

MAC TATTOOS AND HAIRCUTS

Chapter 12

Chapter 11

Chapter 13

Chapter 15

Chapter 6

TAT'S MY BUTT: ANNA M. ZISA, A GRAPHIC DESIGNER FROM MILAN, DOESN'T REALLY LIKE TATTOOS. BUT THE APPLE LOGO FELT SO RIGHT. "IT JUST FELT LIKE THE MOST 'ME' THING TO HAVE," SHE EXPLAINED. "I LIKE COMPUTERS. THE APPLE LOOKS GOOD AND SEXY. ALL THE COMMENTS I HAVE HEARD HAVE BEEN POSITIVE, EVEN FROM LINUX AND WINDOWS USERS." CREDIT: ANNA M. ZISA

TAT'S THE WAY MACHEADS LIKE IT

There's a clever hoax on the Web purporting to be the site of an advertising firm looking for people to become human billboards by getting corporate tattoos. The site is called Tadoos, and it has fooled dozens of Web surfers and at least one newspaper. But like all good hoaxes, it contains a nugget of truth. There are, for example, dozens of people sporting tattoos of Apple Computer's corporate logo. But none of them was paid to do it.

There are all kinds of people with Apple tattoos, from graphic designers to leading academicians. Most have Apple's famous logo tattooed on an arm, a leg, or their backside.

But it's not really about advertising for Apple. It's about homage. "I'm a Mac freak," said Mark Tappert, a graphic designer from Denmark who has a black Apple logo tattooed on his left biceps. "I identify strongly with Apple and Mac computers," he said. "I work on Macs every day, and a lot of nights. I got it done to convince myself I would always be true to Apple, not for religious or political reasons, but to convince myself that Macs are the way ahead."

There are, of course, other corporate brands that inspire tattoos: Coca-Cola, Nike, and Lacoste are some examples. However, Apple is one of the few companies that inspire tattoos through pure love of the product. There are perhaps only two other companies that enjoy similar devotion: Harley Davidson and Campagnolo, an Italian bicycle parts company.

The closest analogy is to fans of sports teams, members of fraternities, and other social groups, such as the Marines, Manchester United soccer fans, and gang members. And just as sports fans will often get team haircuts, Apple haircuts are another form of adornment peculiar to Mac fans.

"So many tattoos are about love, loyalty, and bravado," said Amy Krakow, author of *The Total Tattoo Book*. "Don't Mac users fall into all those categories?" Krakow, a Mac fan, said no other brand inspires as much loyalty, love, and devotion as Apple. And in the face of Apple's single-digit market share, Mac fans have to have "an awful lot of bravado. We are loud, vocal, vociferous. And we want the world to know where our loyalties are."

Although no one with an Apple tattoo has been reimbursed by the company for getting permanently inked, Doug Hardman came close. Hardman, owner of Silver Creek, a Web design firm in Akron, Ohio, almost got a free PowerBook laptop for his Apple logo tattoo. Hardman had a large rainbow-colored Apple logo tattooed on his left arm in March 1996 while visiting a buddy at a Marine Corps base. The tattoo was taken from a rainbow-hued Apple sticker, which Hardman still has on the windshield of his car. (He's transferred it to three different vehicles.)

(LEFT) MILESTONES: BRIAN OLSON'S THREE APPLE TATTOOS REPRESENT THREE MAJOR MILESTONES IN APPLE'S CORPORATE DEVELOPMENT: THE ORIGINAL RAINBOW APPLE LOGO, A BONDI BLUE LOGO FOR THE FIRST IMAC, AND A BLACK APPLE TO REPRESENT THE NEW G4 ERA. "THE TATTOO IS MEANT TO REPRESENT THE PROGRESS OF APPLE OVER MY LIFE SO FAR," OLSON SAID. "I HAVE ALWAYS DONE WORK WITH SPIRITUAL AND HISTORICAL SIGNIFICANCE TO MY LIFE, AND APPLE HAS BEEN A SHAPING FACTOR IN MY YOUNG LIFE. APPLE HELPED NURTURE MY CURIOSITY AND LOVE OF TECHNOLOGY THROUGH ITS EASY-TO-USE INTERFACE." OLSON IS THE HEAD OF MAC TECHNICAL SUPPORT AT THE UNIVERSITY OF WISCONSIN MEDICAL SCHOOL. HE'S ALSO BEEN A BARTENDER, BOUNCER, MOTORCYCLE MECHANIC, AND TATTOO ARTIST.
CREDIT: BRIAN OLSON

(BELOW) DESIGNER TAT: DANISH DESIGNER MARK TAPPERT WORKS ON HIS MAC NIGHT AND DAY, SO IT'S NATURAL THAT PART OF HIS IDENTITY SHOULD BE DEFINED BY APPLE'S LOGO. THE TATTOO WAS DONE BY THE SAME ARTIST WHO INKED PAMELA ANDERSON. GOOD THING HE DIDN'T GO TO HER PLASTIC SURGEON.
CREDIT: MARK TAPPERT

Hardman posted a picture of his tattoo on the Web and eventually received a phone call from the secretary of Gil Amelio, who was then Apple's CEO. "I was told that I'd be getting a new PowerBook in exchange for the lifetime of advertising," Hardman said. "About three days later, Steve Jobs came home [to Apple as acting CEO], and that was the last I heard from them."

Still, he doesn't regret it, although few in his social circle like it. His wife, for example, "just rubs at it, hoping it'll come off," Hardman said.

Tattoos often mark a rite of passage. People get tattoos after an engagement, wedding, or divorce; teenagers are tattooed to assert their transition into adulthood; and Cory Doctorow got a tattoo after spending an entire week salvaging a toasted Mac.

Doctorow, the Electronic Frontier Foundation's outreach coordinator and an editor of the Boing Boing Weblog, has a Sad Mac tattooed on his right bicep. It was inked after a marathon data recovery session when he was 18. "I felt the need to commemorate the event with an appropriately nerd-tough memento," Doctorow wrote in an email.

Doctorow's 27-pixel-square tattoo is based on the Sad Mac screen icon that is displayed when old all-in-one Macs have catastrophic hardware problems. The Sad Mac is a perversion of the happy, smiling Mac shown when a Mac boots up. Instead of a smiley face, the Sad Mac has a pout and crosses for eyes. It's the same icon Doctorow confronted one day, in the early nineties, when he tried to boot up his Mac SE with an 030 accelerator card.

The dead Mac stored all his email from several years, all the fiction and nonfiction he'd ever written, a lot of painstakingly collected software, a bunch of BBS numbers, and all the HyperCard stacks he'd authored. In other words, "a lot of important stuff was on that box . . . and not backed up, natch."

(LEFT) CLOSE, BUT NO
POWERBOOK: WEB DESIGNER
DOUG HARDMAN ALMOST GOT
A FREE POWERBOOK LAPTOP
FOR HIS APPLE LOGO TATTOO,
BUT A CORPORATE RESHUFFLE
NIXED IT.
CREDIT: DOUG HARDMAN

(RIGHT) CHEEKY: THIS BUTT TAT
WAS DISCREETLY REVEALED AT
A MACWORLD SHOW IN BOSTON.
ITS OWNER WISELY ASKED TO
REMAIN ANONYMOUS.
CREDIT: *MACWEEK*

Doctorow embarked on a painful, painstaking endeavor to recover the data. "This was about seven days' worth of miserable, round-the-clock trog-labor, locked up in my room with parts scattered all around me and notes with hex offsets scrawled on hundreds of scraps of paper piled . . . in the Sisyphean stable," Doctorow wrote. "I hardly bathed or ate, and smoked hundreds, if not thousands, of cigarettes. When I emerged, triumphant and exhausted, I felt reborn. . . . I was a new man and needed to commemorate the event."

Doctorow proceeded to collect a printout of the Sad Mac, which he took to his local tattoo parlor. "Took about 3 minutes, stung only a little, and has been with me ever since," he wrote.

In the late 1990s, *MacWeek's* now-moribund Mac the Knife Forums were a hotbed for Mac fans with Apple tats; a number of pictures were posted to the gossip column's online chat group. One of the first was taken by a *MacWeek* photographer at Macworld Boston in August 1997.

"[The photographer] came running in from taking photos of show-floor color to announce that he'd connected with this guy who claimed to have a Mac tattoo on his ass," recalled Matthew Rothenberg, an ex-*MacWeek* editor. "I believe it took a bit of cajoling, but he finally got him to nip around behind a curtain at one of the booths and pull out his buttock," Rothenberg added. "It was all very fast and anonymous, kind of like the Knife's love life."

Rothenberg said the man's identity is a mystery but remembered he was "a kind of furry, rumpled, middle-aged Mac enthusiast." The shot obviously couldn't be used for *MacWeek*, Rothenberg said, but made for a "cheeky" intro to the new Mac the Knife site.

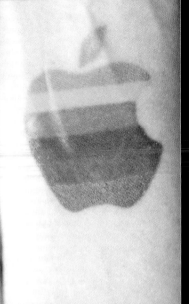 

LIFELONG DEDICATION: PAUL LOPICCOLO, A GRAPHIC DESIGNER FROM CHICAGO, HAS BEEN USING MACS SINCE CHILDHOOD. HE WAS INKED WHEN HE WAS 23. "I WANTED TO SHOW MY LOYALTY TO APPLE," HE SAID. "I USE MACS ALL DAY LONG AND I COULDN'T BE HAPPIER. PEOPLE REALLY THINK IT IS IMPRESSIVE TO CARE ABOUT SOMETHING SO MUCH."
CREDIT: PAUL LOPICCOLO

I WAS TOLD THAT I'D BE
POWERBO

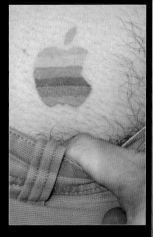

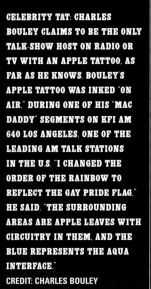

CELEBRITY TAT: CHARLES BOULEY CLAIMS TO BE THE ONLY TALK-SHOW HOST ON RADIO OR TV WITH AN APPLE TATTOO, AS FAR AS HE KNOWS. BOULEY'S APPLE TATTOO WAS INKED "ON AIR," DURING ONE OF HIS "MAC DADDY" SEGMENTS ON KFI AM 640 LOS ANGELES, ONE OF THE LEADING AM TALK STATIONS IN THE U.S. "I CHANGED THE ORDER OF THE RAINBOW TO REFLECT THE GAY PRIDE FLAG," HE SAID. "THE SURROUNDING AREAS ARE APPLE LEAVES WITH CIRCUITRY IN THEM, AND THE BLUE REPRESENTS THE AQUA INTERFACE."
CREDIT: CHARLES BOULEY

DEVOTED DAN: DAN BUCHAN IS THE DESKTOP COMPUTING SPECIALIST AT DICKINSON COLLEGE IN CARLISLE, PENNSYLVANIA—THE CAMPUS'S "MAC GUY." HE HAS TWO APPLE TATTOOS: A RAINBOW LOGO ON HIS HINDQUARTERS AND A "HAPPY MAC" ON HIS ARM. "I GOT THEM TO SHOW MY DEVOTION TO THE GREATEST COMPUTING PLATFORM THAT HAS EVER EXISTED," HE SAID. "TELL ME, HOW MANY PEOPLE DO YOU SEE WITH MICROSOFT, DELL, OR GATEWAY TATTOOS? HELL, I RARELY EVEN SEE ANYONE WEARING THEIR T-SHIRTS, LET ALONE MODIFYING THEIR BODY . . . I KNOW OF NO OTHER PRODUCT THAT INSPIRES THAT KIND OF DEVOTION."
CREDIT: DAN BUCHAN

INKED ALL OVER: ALESSANDRO CORTINI (PICTURED TO THE RIGHT OF GUITARIST PELLE HILLSTROM IN THE MODWHEELMOOD BAND PICTURE), A MUSICIAN WITH THE ALTERNATIVE POP/ROCK BAND MODWHEELMOOD, HAS THREE MAC-RELATED TATTOOS, NO LESS: AN APPLE LOGO ON HIS WRIST, A SAD MAC ON HIS FOREARM AND A MAC ON/OFF BUTTON ON THE BACK OF HIS NECK.
CREDIT: ALESSANDRO CORTINI

TRUE LOVE: ERIC GASTON, A DESIGNER FROM THE NETHERLANDS,
GOT HIS APPLE TATTOO BECAUSE HE FELL IN LOVE WITH MACS. "IT'S
KINDA LIKE WHEN YOU'RE A KID," HE SAID. "REMEMBER WHEN YOU
FELL IN LOVE WHEN YOU WERE A KID AND YOU WROTE THE NAME
OF THE ONE YOU LOVED ON YOUR ARM? IT'S THE SAME. ONLY THIS
FEELING WILL STAY."
CREDIT: ERIC GASTON

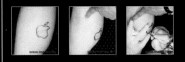

THE PROGRESSION OF PAIN:
GERMAN DESIGNER MARTIN
SCHOENBECK IS ONE OF MANY
WITH AN APPLE TATTOO.
CREDIT: MARTIN SCHOENBECK

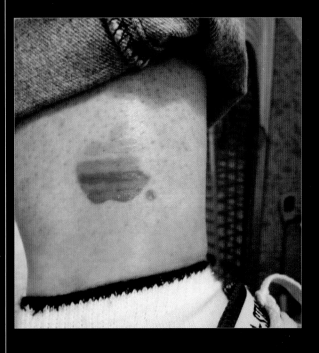

APPLE TAT ON CAMPUS: IN THE MID-1990S, JERRY MAJORS QUIT HER
JOB ON THE EAST COAST AND DROVE CROSS COUNTRY TO FIND WORK
IN SILICON VALLEY. THE APPLE TATTOO ON HER ANKLE DIDN'T HELP.
"THE TATTOO SCARED OFF EVERY INTERVIEWER I SHOWED IT TO," SHE
SAID. "I HAD TO GET A JOB AND PROVE MY SKILLS INCOGNITO. HIRING
MANAGERS...ARE A LITTLE SCARED OF PEOPLE WHOSE ONLY APPARENT
SKILL IS THAT THEY ARE A FAN. TODAY, I WORK IN HARDWARE
ENGINEERING AT APPLE AND THINGS HAVE NEVER BEEN BETTER."
CREDIT: JERRY MAJORS

...GE FOR A LIFETIME ...VERTISING.

INKED ACADEMICIAN: DR. CHRISTOF KOCH, ONE OF THE WORLD'S LEADING BRAIN SCIENTISTS, IS AN APPLE FAN.
CREDIT: NANA NAISBITT

THE PROFESSOR AND HIS MAC TATTOO

Some unlikely people get Apple tattoos. Christof Koch, a professor of computation and neural systems at the renowned California Institute of Technology and head of the Koch Laboratory, has a small rainbow-colored Apple logo tattooed on his right arm. "I always wanted a tattoo and I really love the Mac," Koch said. "There are very few artifacts that are so perfectly suited to their environment, that blend form and function. The Mac is like a perfectly designed organism."

Koch is one of the world's leading neuroscientists. He and Nobel Prize winner Francis Crick have teamed up to search for the neurological seat of consciousness, a philosophically contentious endeavor that has yielded some surprising results. A couple of years ago, Koch claimed to have found brain cells dedicated to recognizing Bill Clinton. The finding suggests the existence of the hitherto-elusive "grandmother cell": a neuron tuned to recognizing your grandmother. Before Koch's discovery, most cognitive scientists believed that higher-order functions like recognizing faces were conducted by large, complex networks of neurons, not individual cells. "There are grandmother neurons," Koch said, "even if people don't like the idea."

Koch got his Apple tattoo in 2000 while on a summer archeological dig in Israel with his 18-year-old son, Alexander, who pestered Koch to take him to a tattoo parlor. Koch eventually relented, but when they got there, his son couldn't decide what to get. On impulse, Koch decided to get an Apple tattoo, but the tattoo artist didn't know what it looked like. "If you just want an American corporate logo, we can give you the [McDonald's] Golden Arches," Koch was told.

Koch found a computer magazine at a nearby newsstand, and it contained the Apple logo. The tattoo artist "did a perfect job, it really looks good," Koch said. His wife didn't think so, though. "She does not like tattoos," Koch said. "That's why I had to get it done in Israel."

His son didn't like it either. "He thought it looked too whimsical," Koch said. "He wanted something more serious. If you're 18 years old, it's important to look serious and tough. But once you're 44, you don't need that image anymore."

Koch was surprised to learn he is not the only person with an Apple tattoo and that there are dozens of others. "It's pretty crazy," he said. "There's a whole community of us. "I bet you there's no person with a Microsoft logo," he added.

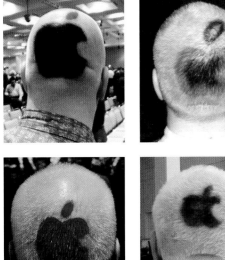

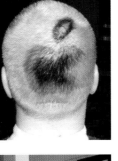

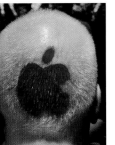

MAC HAIR TODAY, GONE TOMORROW

A few years ago, Peter Cohen was laid off from his systems administrator job. With time on his hands, he volunteered to cover the E3 gaming convention in Los Angeles for MacCentral, a Macintosh news site. A Mac aficionado and gaming fan, Cohen was so psyched to be at the show, he wanted a way to commemorate it.

And so began a tradition. Three times a year for the last four years, Cohen has had his hair styled into an Apple logo for E3 and the biannual Macworld shows in New York and San Francisco. "It's what I'm known for," Cohen said from his home in Cape Cod, Massachusetts. "I just show my loyalty to Apple in a different way than most people do. It's fun being a celebrity for a little while, as freakish as it may be."

Cohen usually shaves his head, but for the conferences he grows his hair and has it styled into a large, eye-catching ad for Apple. "I start growing my hair out four to six weeks before the show to give the artist a palette to work with," he said. As well as the Apple logo, he's also had large, colorful, "X" haircuts, celebrating Apple's Mac OS X operating system.

His unique hairstyles always attract a lot of attention. A couple of years ago, a German with limited English asked him, "May I take a picture of your backside?" Cohen was momentarily puzzled. "May I take a picture of your rear parts?" the German elaborated. The following year they ran into each other again. The German simply said, "Backside?"

Cohen, now a senior editor at MacCentral, is used to a variety of reactions. "Sometimes a PC user will pick a fight," said Cohen, who is a big, somewhat fierce-looking guy. "People have tried to make it heated, but it's not something I get into an argument about."

However, he failed to get Apple CEO Steve Jobs' attention at the opening of the Apple store in Manhattan. "I was practically doing back flips," Cohen said. But Phil Schiller, head of Apple's marketing, noticed. "That's pretty hard-core," he told Cohen. "I would never do anything like that."

Now that he's comfortable with the haircuts, Cohen is planning the next step: a pair of tattoos. "The first will be my wife's name," Cohen said. "The second will be Apple. These are my two loves."

...MEG RYAN'S CUDDLY, DOWN-TO-EARTH

MACSPOTTING: THE NEW OBSESSION

Did you know Bill Gates uses a Macintosh? So do Bill Clinton, Boris Yeltsin, Sylvester Stallone, and Martha Stewart. The late Princess Diana and King Hussein of Jordan were Mac users, too. And did you notice the distinctive Macintosh system beep in *True Lies*? Or that Jean-Claude Van Damme used a PowerBook 1400 as an offensive weapon in *Knock Off*? Well, legions of Macspotters remark such things. They're compiling long lists of all the celebrities, world leaders, captains of industry, athletes, and musicians who use Macs.

Like an ornithologist spending hours in a bog to spot a rare bird, some Mac fans will sit glued to the TV for a glimpse of some Apple hardware. Mac fans note every appearance of a Mac in a movie or TV show, as well as every mention of a Mac in magazines and newspapers, on the radio, and on pop albums—even in cartoon strips. The phenomenon feeds a regular column on MacCentral, a Macintosh news site. Based on a steady stream of reader tips, the Famous People column features celebrity Mac users and Mac appearances in movies, TV shows, and myriad other media.

Having become popular on MacCentral, Macspotting has now spread to numerous Mac sites. Perhaps the most comprehensive database of Macs in movies and on TV is the French MacStudios site (http://www.cruniac.com/index.php).

It's taking on shades of an obsession; the following comes from a recent Famous People column: "During an episode of *The X-Files*," the column noted, "if you look close . . . you can briefly see the left corner of a laptop . . . the curve of the display case looked like a G3 Series PowerBook to me."

The column, which began on an irregular basis, has become a daily fixture and is one of the site's biggest draws, said MacCentral publisher Stan Flack. "It's become one of the most popular things we do," Flack said, "which is quite strange." Flack attributed the column's popularity to a combination of fanaticism, an underdog mentality, and the fact that people like to read about celebrities, no matter what the topic. "Underdogs like it when a superstar or a celebrity uses the same system they do. Nine out of 10 people don't use a Mac. They need some comfort," he said. "If we did a column about stars that ate peanuts, people would read that, too."

Dennis Sellers, the column's author, said he gets at least 100 emails a week on the topic. He gets the most when Macs show up on TV, especially during *The X-Files* or *Felicity*. "I get inundated with emails saying a PowerBook popped up for two seconds on Sunday night," he said.

Sellers' column pointed to Bill Gates as a Mac user: A reader "happily noted" an aging Mac in the background of a photograph of Microsoft's Steve Ballmer and Bill Gates while studying Stephen Segaller's book, *Nerds 2.0.1: A Brief History of the Internet*. "No wonder Bill is so rich," the reader wrote. "He uses a Mac."

Lists of celebrity Mac users can also be found at the Apple Museum (http://www.theapplemuseum.com) and the Celebrity Macintosh Page (http://www.owt.com/users/sdechter/celeb.html), where the number of stars, authors, producers, musicians, theater types, athletes, politicians, and corporate bigwigs who use, or have used, a Mac runs into the hundreds.

Probably the most obscure is Sir Roger Banister, the first man to run a four-minute mile, but the lists also include actors

CORNER-BOOKSTORE CHARACTER USES A MAC...

Sly Stallone, Gary Oldman, Dolly Parton, and Goldie Hawn; President Clinton and Vice President Al Gore; cyberpunk writers William Gibson, Bruce Sterling, and Neal Stephenson; and G. Gordon Liddy, jailbird-cum-columnist. Gates is mentioned, as is Bill Lowe, the former head of IBM's PC Development Team. So, too, is Seymour Cray, supercomputer designer; Martha Stewart; Malcolm Forbes, Jr.; and Disney's CEO, Michael Eisner.

The Apple Museum also houses a long list of Apple sightings in movies dating back to 1983. Even the briefest glimpse warrants a mention. Macs seem to be getting more and more popular. Only two 1983 movies featured an Apple machine: *WarGames* and *Trading Places*. But in 1998, Macs were spotted in 17 movies, including *The Faculty*, *Godzilla*, and *You've Got Mail*.

Sometimes a Mac is not seen, just heard. The list notes the distinctive booting blips and beeps of Macs on movie soundtracks, such as *True Lies*.

The Mac also seems to be a TV staple, appearing regularly on *Spin City*, *Melrose Place*, *Veronica's Closet*, and many other shows, according to the lists. Who, for example, failed to notice on *Seinfeld* the 20th Anniversary Mac, the PowerMac 6100, the Mac SE, the DuoDock, the Apple keyboard, and the Multiple Scan monitor? And surely you spotted the MacWarehouse mail-order catalog? Someone did.

APPLE PRODUCT PLACEMENT

The number of Macs shown in movies and TV is way out of proportion to the number used in real life. By Hollywood standards, everyone uses an iMac or an iBook, instead of occasionally, which is the unfortunate reality. There are a number of reasons why. Chief among them are Apple's vigorous product-placement efforts.

In 1982, a fleeting glimpse of some Reese's Pieces in Spielberg's *E.T.* sent sales of the candy through the roof. Since then, getting products into movies has become a major focus for companies like Apple. According to Apple's Web site, Macs have been featured in more than 1,500 movies and TV shows since the early 1980s. Most of the machines are simply loaned to the producers. For the cost of shipping a computer to Hollywood, the hardware can be seen in movie theaters all over the world. Occasionally, movie makers will buy the machine after the film has wrapped, so Apple gets a sale out of it, too.

In the movies, 1996 was the high point of Apple's product-placement efforts. Under the guidance of marketing whiz Satjiv Chahil, Macs had starring roles in *Independence Day*, *Mission Impossible*, and *Ransom*, the first, third, and fifth highest-grossing movies of that year. "By putting one PowerBook in a movie like *Mission Impossible*, you get your product shown in every country in the world," Apple's product-placement manager, Suzanne Forlenza, told Apple's Web site. "You look at that and say, wow, our product has been seen by this many people for the cost of loaning the product."

Apple also scored a big hit with *Forrest Gump*. The film's producers used Apple's corporate logo for a scene in which Gump discovers he's a millionaire after investing in what he thought was a fruit company. Apple estimated that nearly 80 million people worldwide saw the free endorsement.

Macs are especially popular on television. Shows like *Sex and the City*, *Dharma and Greg*, *Felicity*, *The X-Files*, *The Drew Carey Show*, *Spin City*, *Beverly Hills 90210*, *Northern Exposure*,

WHILE TOM HANKS' PREDATORY, CORPORATE

NYPD Blue, *Home Improvement*, *Melrose Place*, and *Seinfeld* have all prominently featured Macs. "The Apple brand makes a statement about the character in the movie," Forlenza said.

But another big reason Macs are featured so prominently in the entertainment industry is because they are used so widely in that industry. Plus, of course, many directors, prop managers, and set designers appreciate Apple's unique aesthetic. "We're lucky that Apple is so entrenched in the entertainment industry," Forlenza said. "It's sometimes as easy as the director saying, 'It has to be a Mac, and we can't use anything else.' That happens a lot."

HOLLYWOOD: GOOD GUYS USE MACS

Hollywood uses a handful of clichés to denote villainy. The bad guys are Nazis, Soviets, or Arabs. They wear black clothing or have stubbly chins. Now there's a new one: The baddies use Windows PCs.

In Fox's hit TV show, *24*, starring Kiefer Sutherland, the villains used PCs running Microsoft Windows. The good guys, of course, used Macs. The show was a blockbuster hit for Fox and earned star Kiefer Sutherland a Golden Globe award.

The show, which debuted in November 2001, traced 24 hours in the hectic life of counter-terrorism agent Jack Bauer (Sutherland), who struggled to rescue his kidnapped wife and daughter while simultaneously foiling an assassination plot. Each hour-long episode unfolded in real time.

The action was full of plot twists. Central to the drama was figuring out the identity of the moles in Bauer's group; there were traitors in their midst, but no one knew who they were. No one, that is, except Dean Browell, a Web designer for a small college in Virginia.

Browell is an avid Macspotter. He keeps his eyes peeled for glimpses of Macs on TV and in the movies and sometimes sends notes about sightings to Web publications MacCentral and Mac Observer. Watching *24* with his wife, Browell quickly noticed that all the good guys use Macs, while the antagonists use PCs. "I made an off-the-cuff remark to my wife," Browell said. "It was obvious from the first episode that the assassins use PCs, but Kiefer Sutherland and his gang all use Macs."

Bauer uses an Apple Cube and a titanium PowerBook. Most of his fellow agents use PowerBooks, iBooks, or Power Macs with flat screens. The baddies, a group of renegade Serbs, use Dell machines. However, after a few episodes, Browell noticed that one of the CIA agents, the trustworthy Jamey Farrell (Karina Arroyave), uses a Dell PC.

"I thought my theory had been blown," he said. "My wife was quite entertained when my theory was shot down." But Farrell was subsequently exposed as a traitor and committed suicide, bolstering Browell's theory. "She was supposed to be the one everyone trusted," he said.

A character widely suspected of being a traitor—Tony Almeida (Carlos Bernard)—used a Mac, which convinced Browell that his characterization was a red herring. And one of Bauer's most trusted colleagues, Nina Myers (Sarah Clarke), used a Dell laptop. She was ultimately exposed as the main traitor. "It is really odd," Browell said. "It almost seems like a visual clue that was there from the beginning. It would be a really big coincidence if they didn't put that in there intentionally."

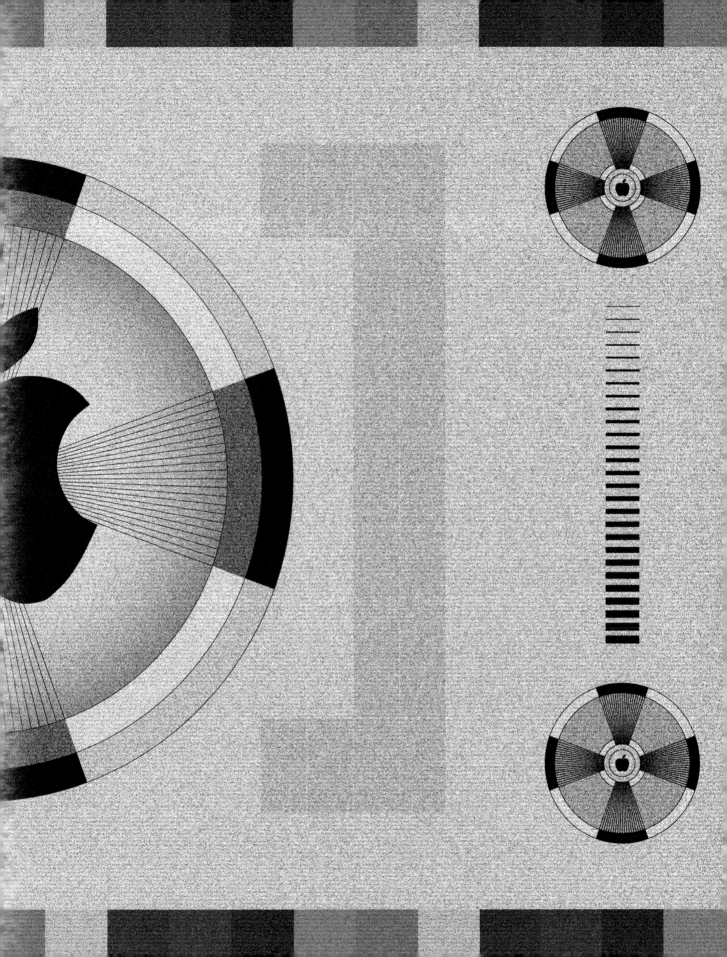

MEGA-BOOKSTORE-CHAIN OWNER USES AN IBM...

Garrett Beauvais, a marketing executive at Advanced Micro Devices, which makes chips for PCs, suggested that Apple's famously vigorous product-placement efforts are the source of the plot device. "Apple Computer outspends all other PC companies in product placement and is perhaps more active in the area than any other technology company outside of Microsoft," Beauvais wrote.

Naturally, the producers of *24* pooh-poohed the idea of any connection between computing platform and moral fiber. "Very clever of you to figure this out," said writer Michael Loceff in an email. "But your powers of observation could have carried you a little further. For instance, the bad guys use Nokia and the good guys Ericsson. The good guys play chess and the bad guys play Go. The good guys eat popcorn and reconstituted soy protein and the bad guys eat red meat. The good guys are on the quarter system and the bad guys on semesters. However—both the good guys and the bad guys read Wired [News]."

Despite Loceff's sarcastic denial, observant pop culturists have noticed the good-guys/bad-guys platform dichotomy in a number of other movies. In the film *Mission: Impossible*, Tom Cruise plays a government agent frantically trying to foil a fiendish plot. The bad guys use Windows notebooks, while Cruise and friends use Apple PowerBooks.

Charles Colombo noted that in *You've Got Mail*, Meg Ryan's cuddly, down-to-earth corner-bookstore character uses a Mac, while Tom Hanks' predatory, corporate mega-bookstore-chain owner uses an IBM ThinkPad. The two companies bid to have their machines used in the movie. Apple came out best, it seems.

Sara Tripp noticed the same thing in *Legally Blonde*—the free-spirit heroine Reese Witherspoon uses an Apple laptop, while everyone else at Harvard Law, who are portrayed as a bunch of stiffs, own PC notebooks. "There is a great scene where [Witherspoon] is pictured sitting in a lecture hall with her orange-colored iBook among a sea of black laptops," wrote Tripp in an email. "Once again, the good person is seen owning a Mac."

In HBO's *Sex and the City*, Sarah Jessica Parker plays a sympathetic writer who uses an iBook. Her manipulative boyfriend, Mr. Big, uses a PC.

There are, of course, exceptions. In the 1997 movie *Most Wanted*, Jon Voight leads a team of assassins who use PowerBook Duos to plot their evil schemes. In *Jurassic Park*, the money-grubbing bad guy uses a Mac to sabotage the park and unleash the dinosaurs. And at the end of *Unbreakable*, Samuel L. Jackson's character is revealed to be not only bad, but a Mac user to boot.

Chapter 7

Chapter 6

Chapter 2

Chapter 6

Chapter 13

MAC EVANGELISM

Chapter 15

THE EVANGELIST

In the mid- to late 1990s, Apple might have gone out of business if it hadn't been for a crusading army of evangelists led by a charismatic marketing executive. The executive—Guy Kawasaki—was an early proponent of what has come to be known as "evangelist marketing"—turning your customers into messianic proponents. Kawasaki's primary tool was a popular Internet mailing list called the Mac EvangeList. It not only had a profound influence on Mac culture, it arguably saved Apple.

In the mid-1990s, Apple was the biggest computer maker in the U.S., but increasing competition from Microsoft, as well as a series of botched products and business blunders, led to a long string of heavy losses. Apple appeared to be in a "death spiral," from which it couldn't pull out. It's hard to kill a company as big as Apple, but in 1996 and 1997, it looked doomed.

A big part of the problem was negative press. Bad news about Apple became a self-fulfilling prophecy: stories about Apple's decline made customers nervous. They bought fewer computers, and the trouble deepened. Realizing this, Kawasaki launched the EvangeList in July 1996 to provide a daily stream of "good news" about Apple. "The whole reason that EvangeList was started was because the press was so negative," said Kawasaki recently. "I decided that instead of trying to convince the press, we would become the press."

The EvangeList, sent out daily, was a breezy mix of news, tips, queries, and job postings. Thanks to Kawasaki's sharp wit, and often hilarious diatribes against Microsoft, the EvangeList quickly became popular. At its peak, the EvangeList boasted 44,000 daily subscribers, although Kawasaki has suggested the list actually reached about 300,000 Macintosh fans, because it was so widely passed around in email, newsgroups, bulletin boards, and Web sites. Kawasaki eventually archived the list on an affiliated "Macway" Web site, which is now gone.

As well as news, the EvangeList had a big activist component. Kawasaki urged subscribers—known as EvangeListas—to proselytize the Mac by engaging Windows PC users in debate. EvangeListas were urged to wear Apple-logoed T-shirts and baseball caps "to show the world we're not crawling into holes and dying." He recommended leaving Macintosh magazines in doctors' waiting rooms and seat pockets on airplanes. And he suggested asking store clerks why they weren't stocking more Macs, fixing up neglected machines, and talking to potential customers about buying a Mac. Many subscribers spent their weekends as unpaid salespeople at CompUSA, steering customers to the Mac section.

But the list was most famous for marshalling a formidable force of Mac fanatics when it appeared that the platform needed defending in the press. Kawasaki urged subscribers to "educate" wrongheaded journalists who wrote negative stories about Apple; and he often provided the appropriate email address. "Write a letter to the publications that publish stupid, insipid, inaccurate, and unfair stories," he wrote. "Most journalists are insecure and perceptive: after the 300th flaming message, they'll get the picture." Kawasaki's 300 flames was conservative: some journalists got hundreds—sometimes thousands—of angry, abusive emails. This was in the early days of the Net, before spam, when most reporters got a handful of messages a week and dutifully responded to each one.

James Coates, a technology columnist with the *Chicago Tribune*, received more than 500 emails after writing a story about Apple that was posted to the EvangeList. He likened the two-week flood of abusive email to a "cyberlynching," an "online necktie party" at the hands of "virtual vigilantes." "The [emails] included unkind words about the moral character of my poor late mother, suggestions that I perform mechanically impossible actions with my new IBM ThinkPad laptop computer, and sadly, a few death threats," he wrote. "'Come to Texas,' wrote one. 'We haven't shot a tourist in a car since 1963.'"

Henry Norr, a former editor at *MacWeek*, said he would get scores of "nasty, hostile" email if he wrote anything critical about the Mac. Some were polite and thoughtful, he said, but in general the experience was like being "besieged by zombies," some of whom were "really unbalanced."

In his defense, Kawasaki frequently urged subscribers to be on their best behavior. He forbade sabotaging Windows machines and told EvangeListas to be nice and polite. As well as pointing out negative press, Kawasaki suggested readers send love notes to journalists who wrote nice things about Apple.

Kawasaki left Apple in 1998 to start Garage.com (now Garage Technology Ventures), a "boot camp" for entrepreneurs. He folded the list in April 1999. The final posting, signed by Kawasaki ("who is and shall remain pure Macintosh"), cited Apple's "stunning turnaround" as the main reason for discontinuing the list. "The original purpose of EvangeList was to counteract the

"This COMPUTER stands for a DREAM... Let me show you the DREAM."

negative news about Apple and Macintosh, and I believe that EvangeList has served its purpose—fantastically," Kawasaki wrote. "So, after discussing what we should do with EvangeList with the folks at Apple, we've decided to retire the list."

Oddly, it was mourned by some of its "victims." Dan Gillmor, a columnist with the *San Jose Mercury News,* who had been a faithful reader for many years, was sad to see EvangeList pass. "Hearing from people who want to change your mind is really useful in the business of journalism," Gillmor said. "I learn more from people who disagree with me than I do from those who agree. But after hearing from several hundred, you do get weary."

James Coates, the *Chicago Tribune* columnist, had mixed feelings about the list's passing. "I did suffer the brunt of an awful lot of abuse from Guy Kawasaki and the EvangeLists, and I am even bitter about it in some ways," he said. "But I learned a tremendous amount of things Macintosh there. I also made a lot of friends and things like that, so I mourn its passing."

The "education" of journalists had a mixed effect. The negative stories didn't stop altogether, but a lot of journalists were more careful when reporting news about Apple. "This writer will never again write about an Apple-related story without a keen gun-shy appreciation that critical hordes are judging every word," Coates wrote after getting flamed.

On the other hand, some journalists complained that the fanaticism was harming Apple. "Overreliance on fanatic faithfulness led to years of complacency at Apple, the business," wrote Charles Pillar in the *Los Angeles Times* in 1997, when Apple was in deep trouble. "And it's not working now—just look at Mac sales figures."

Whatever the effect on the media, there's the widely held perception that the EvangeListas saved Apple's bottom line—it has been argued that millions of little acts of Mac evangelism stopped the company from sliding into bankruptcy. During the EvangeList years, there was a lot of committed and energetic lobbying for the Mac in schools, universities, and businesses threatening to dump them. Who knows how many would have abandoned the platform if a committed friend, relative, or workmate hadn't convinced them not to? "Thanks to the Macintosh loyalists, [and] people like Guy Kawasaki who are out championing the cause for the underdog, Apple, you know, still is a contender," Jim Carlton, author of *Apple: The Inside Story of Intrigue, Egomania, and Business Blunders*, told National Public Radio.

However, there were a number of high-profile institutional switches to Windows PCs at big Macintosh sites, Dartmouth College being the best known, that mobilized scores of EvangeListas to no effect. "I don't think it helped a lot," Cheryl England, a former editor of MacAddict, said of the EvangeList. "It's obvious to say Apple's loyal customers saved the company; of course they did, it wasn't saved by its disloyal customers. But it's hard to judge how much of an effect the EvangeList had, rather than Mac users generally. The return of Steve Jobs to the company in 1998 and popular products like the iMac probably had more to do with it."

While the EvangeListas tried to help Apple in retail stores, Apple eventually dumped a lot of the chain stores in favor of a "store within a store" at CompUSA. The company also started concentrating on specialist Apple retailers and its own Web site.

The most profound effect of the EvangeList was to energize the Mac community in its darkest days. The EvangeList unified Mac users and gave them an identity. Its championing spirit of evangelism survives today, and, in fact, has never been stronger. People are as passionate as ever about Macs and are just as committed to cheerleading them.

"The one good thing it did is provide an early platform for people who love the Mac," said England. "It was a club. It was their friend. It was a place they could go and not get picked on by [Microsoft] PC suits."

SOME OF THE GUYS IN AISLE SIX

A lot of men get dragged to the mall on weekends to go shopping with their wives. But for Eddie Clipper, the opposite was true. He'd drag his wife to the mall, but not to go shopping—to voluntarily help sell Macs. Many weekends Clipper would go to the mall or a local computer superstore to fix up the Macs on display and persuade customers to buy them. "My wife knows that if we stop in the computer department, I will be talking to people for a while," he said. "She usually goes elsewhere in the store and drags me away later."

K. Jerry Smith was the same. Every month or so, he'd take his son to a local Sears or Circuit City, and they'd spend the day fixing up the Macs. "My son and I, like so many other Macheads, have always cleaned up the Macs on display at stores that could care less whether they were properly displayed—usually major retailers," he said. "To this day, one can almost always find Macs with frozen systems after the kids of busy shoppers have banged on the keyboards. We restart and repair whatever damage has been done. We want them to look and operate at their best."

Jeff Sepeta is another who acted as a voluntary salesperson. "Although you're not supposed to solicit business inside CompUSA, I have often caught sales reps saying bad things about the Mac to people who are clearly interested in buying one," he said. "I generally step in, explain why the Mac is better than the sales rep would admit, and generally make the sales guy look like cow pie."

Clipper, Smith, and Sepeta, and dozens of others like them, perhaps hundreds, were doing their bit to help Apple in its darkest days. In the late 1990s, Apple's showing at retail stores was below par: indifferent staff at computer stores often relegated Macs to the quietest aisle. Machines were left turned off or were badly neglected, and stocks of Mac software were often out.

Without the resources to tackle every store, Apple's chief evangelist, Guy Kawasaki, urged Mac fans to rectify the miasma through his popular Mac EvangeList mailing list. Kawasaki suggested subscribers tidy up displays, buttonhole salespeople, and counter pro-Windows sales patter. It worked pretty well. For a while, many of the thousands of stores selling Macs were visited by well-intentioned Mac enthusiasts. Collectively, the volunteers came to be known as "the guy in aisle six."

"I started doing this because none of the sales associates could ever answer any questions about Apple products and I could," said WilliamLH (http://www.mymac2u.com/), one of the guys in aisle six. "Why did I do this, with no pay, no outright reward? Because that is the type of people Mac users are. It is a passion, an obsession, a religion if you will." WilliamLH started visiting stores when he was out anyway, he said, but eventually he went every weekend when he had free time.

Occasionally, extra-zealous Mac fans would sabotage Windows PCs at stores, though it was more common to rearrange a magazine stand so that Mac magazines obscured the Windows ones.

The army of volunteer salespeople worked so well, Apple eventually co-opted the idea, first with "Demo Days"—one-off sales events coinciding with big shopping days or product launches—and then with a longer-term program overseen by MarketSource, a marketing firm.

Dan Oblak (http://macbigot.com/) became a Demo Day "volunteer"—paid $75 a day—and then an Apple Power Rep, which was more of a part-time job. As a Power Rep, Oblak spent about 10 hours a week, on top of his day job, supporting the staff at five local Circuit City stores. "These are usually not people who spend every waking hour reading about and discussing the Mac," he said. "But I do; and the exposure I've had to the questions and concerns of the potential Mac customer is a tool that these stores can take advantage of."

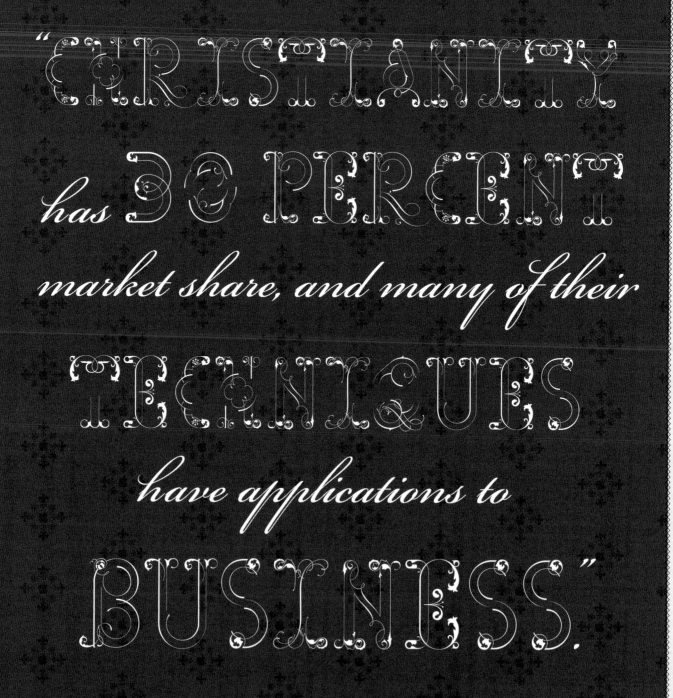

"CHRISTIANITY has 30 PERCENT market share, and many of their TECHNIQUES have applications to BUSINESS."

Oblak was responsible for making sure all the Macs were running, the display area was neat and tidy, and all the signage was present and correct. On top of this, he put together a weekly Mac newsletter (http://homepage.mac.com/jdoblak/) for the sales staff and often made himself available throughout the week for advice. He didn't do any selling directly, although he often talked to potential customers.

"My wife is a Mac widow," he said. "It's a challenge. Many of these salespeople are a bit green, and there is high turnover in any retail environment, but little victories here and there make it all worthwhile."

CASE STUDY—LEWIS PERELMAN

In 1996, writer Lewis Perelman went through some of the darkest days of his career as a reporter, thanks to a story he wrote for *Wired* magazine that was critical of Apple. The article, "Opportunity Cost," published in the November 1996 issue, argued that Apple's "obsession" with selling computers to schools and universities cost it dearly in the quest for bigger markets (http://www.wired.com/wired/archive/4.11/es_apple.html).

Shortly after it was published, a scathing criticism of the article—or more accurately, a rant—was sent to the Mac EvangeList by one of its subscribers. Kawasaki duly posted it, and it was soon in the in-boxes of thousands of subscribers. "*Wired* magazine has succumbed like so many others to the let's-kill-Apple syndrome," the message said. "Lewis J. Perelman's 'Opportunity Cost' article in their recent issue is just sickening. . . . There is so much to be angry at, I better not start." The post included Perelman's email address.

For the next six weeks, Perelman received a steady stream of uncouth email about the piece. Perelman estimated he received thousands of messages. Most were rude, and some included violent threats against himself and his wife. When Perelman showed his wife some of the messages, she burst into tears. "It was really nasty," Perelman recalled recently. "It was very unpleasant. My in-box was being flooded with hate mail. It was incredibly vicious."

Perelman likened the EvangeListas to the "digital Taliban" and the flood of invective to "cyberterrorism," and a "digital riot." It was his first experience of Internet-mediated criticism, he said,

and it appalled him. The most galling thing was that most of his critics didn't appear to have read the article. The same phrases were repeated over and over, suggesting people were copying phrases from the same source. "The overwhelming majority of them never read the article," he said. "I called them on that. That's the mentality of the mob. There's no accountability and no intelligence. It's the digital equivalent of a riot."

Perelman was so shocked by this, he decided to track down the author of the original EvangeList post. "I did it because I wanted to know how it started," Perelman said. "Who did this to me? I eventually found him [and] asked him, who put you up to this?"

According to Perelman, even the original poster had never read the article; he'd merely been told about it. "That's what I found most outrageous," Perelman said. "Everyone's entitled to their opinion and to respond to your work. That's the chance you take when you express a strong opinion. But 90 percent of them had never read the article. That's frightening, not just personally, but socially."

GUY KAWASAKI

Steve Jobs and Steve Wozniak get all the praise, but Apple's one-time chief evangelist, Guy Kawasaki, has possibly done as much as anyone to shape Mac culture. It was Kawasaki, for example, who united Mac users during Apple's darkest days and helped to mold a community identity that persists strongly today. The fervent, pro-Mac stance among Mac fans is a clear legacy of Kawasaki's evangelist approach to marketing, as is the community's united front against Microsoft.

Kawasaki, a native Hawaiian, was first hired by Apple in the mid-1980s to evangelize the nascent Mac platform to software developers. He had an uphill battle. The Mac had just been launched. It faced tough competition from dozens of different computer platforms, led by the IBM PC and the Apple II. In this environment, software developers were wary of committing resources to a new, unproven platform like the Mac. But software was critical to the Mac's success. Without a library of applications, no one would buy Mac hardware.

Kawasaki hit the pavement, visiting hundreds of developers with nothing more to offer than a dream: the dream of the power and ease of use of the Macintosh. "Full of fervor and zeal, I would meet with developers, show them a Macintosh prototype, and convince them to develop Macintosh software," Kawasaki said in an article for *Forbes Magazine*.

He was phenomenally successful. By July 1985, little more than a year after the Mac's launch, its software base had grown from a handful of titles to more than 600 programs, according to *InfoWorld*. "Kawasaki was a central character in Apple's ascension from garage startup to multibillion-dollar powerhouse," said the *San Jose Business Journal*.

Kawasaki's success was due to the near-religious enthusiasm he induced in others for the Mac. As he wrote in his best-selling book, *The Macintosh Way*, he sold the dream first, the product second.

"[The Mac is] like any other personal computer," he wrote. "It's glass, silicon, rubber, metal. A typical salesperson would say, 'I'll give you this box; you give me $3,000.' But an evangelist would say, 'This computer stands for a dream. The dream is productivity and creativity for people. Let me show you the dream. If you buy into it, let us go off together and sell it.'"

Kawasaki left Apple in 1987, only to return to the company in 1995 as chief evangelist. He was also made an Apple Fellow, an honorary title awarded to "those rare individuals who have made extraordinary technical or leadership contributions to personal computing," according to Apple.

At first, Kawasaki understood the title of chief evangelist to mean he was a marketer-cum-preacher: he got out there, met lots of people, and extolled the virtues of the machine, rather than its speeds and feeds. But soon after launching the EvangeList, his most powerful vehicle for spreading the "good news," Kawasaki realized his preaching had a secondary effect: the more people he convinced to believe, the more people they convinced to believe.

"We didn't plan it that way; it just happened," Kawasaki said in an interview with Wabash & Lake, a marketing company. "Apple has thousands of user groups. Those are truly the evangelists. They're not paid. They're not employees. They tell people to use Macintosh solely for the other person's benefit. That is the difference between evangelism and sales. Sales is rooted in what's good for me. Evangelism is rooted in what's good for you."

In effect, Kawasaki was using the EvangeList to recruit and train tens of thousands of salespeople for Apple. "Apple has 600 salespeople in the field," Kawasaki said in one interview, "but there are really about 100,000 out there spreading the word. If you own a Mac, you were probably evangelized by another Mac owner, not by a sales representative."

Kawasaki was one of the first people in the technology industry to link evangelism and business. A Christian, Kawasaki was heavily influenced by religious evangelism. He attended Billy Graham's School of Evangelism to learn more about it and intentionally used a lot of religious terminology in the EvangeList and in interviews. Here's a typical quote, mixing piety and humor: "Saying Windows 95 is equal to Macintosh is like finding a potato that looks like Jesus and believing you've witnessed the second coming."

Kawasaki often characterized Windows PC users as "heathens" or "unenlightened" and claimed Mac users were being "persecuted" for their beliefs. "Christianity has 30 percent market share, and many of their techniques have applications to business," he said in one interview. "I ripped it off from the Bible," he said in another.

One of Kawasaki's central strategies was to identify and demonize a common enemy. In the early days, when he was dealing with software developers, it was IBM. Later, it was Microsoft, even though the company was, and still is, one of the biggest publishers of Mac software. During the EvangeList days, Kawasaki's rallying cry was "Stop the Microsoft hegemony!"

In addition to founding Garage Technology Ventures, Kawasaki has also written half a dozen best-selling books on business evangelism, including *The Macintosh Way, Rules for Revolutionaries,* and *How to Drive Your Competition Crazy.* Kawasaki has been anointed "the father of evangelism marketing" by the fast-growing guerilla marketing industry, which has adopted many of the practices he pioneered.

"We were learning evangelism as we were doing it," he told *IndustryWeek.* "There were no courses, books, or training sessions. Looking back, maybe one of the reasons we succeeded is that we were too naive and ignorant to know how difficult our task was. The key to evangelism is a great cause. If you love the cause enough, you'll find a way to make it succeed...I just know how to take a cause, fall in love with it, evangelize others to share it, and change the world. Isn't that enough for a third-generation Japanese-American from Hawaii?"

ARUN GUPTA AND THE SPA

Can one man make a difference? Arun Gupta certainly did. Gupta, an AT&T systems analyst from Middletown, NJ, almost single-handedly shut down a bogus research program by the Software Publishers Association (SPA), which incorrectly reported Mac software sales were in chronic decay.

Throughout 1996 and the latter half of 1995, the Washington, D.C. trade association released a series of quarterly reports, which appeared to show the Mac software market in chronic decline. The reports always garnered a lot of attention, particularly from the Mac trade press, and were taken as signs of

Apple's imminent demise. Not only that, the negative reports persuaded software developers that writing software for the Mac was a bad business move. Why bother, if it wouldn't sell?

But subsequent numbers from the SPA told an entirely different story. While the SPA's quarterly reports were based on estimates of projected sales from the Association's members, later reports—based on actual sales—often showed growth instead of decline. The difference between the SPA's initial estimates and final numbers were sometimes as much as 50 percent, which equated to hundreds of millions of dollars in sales. For example, the SPA reported 1995 Mac software sales were $1.05 billion, down 14 percent from 1994 sales of $1.22 billion. However, the SPA's revised numbers, published in 1996, said 1995 Mac software sales actually grew to $1.52 billion, a 45 percent increase over 1994 sales.

The SPA always buried the revised figures in its reports, and no one noticed the discrepancies except for Gupta. Poring over the SPA's numbers, Gupta noticed that revisions often turned declining sales into growth sales. Gupta contacted *MacWeek,* which had been reporting the SPA's numbers without noticing anything awry. Prompted by Gupta's concerns, *MacWeek* published a couple of stories critical of the SPA's methodology.

The SPA tried to put a brave face on its research program, but in July 1997, the association's Web site announced the program had been "suspended." "The SPA Data Programs are currently suspended," the site read. "Details will be posted about a new software sales tracking program as they become available." Needless to say, no new program has been launched.

THE MAC
WEB

INDIVIDUAL RUMOR SITES MAY COME AND GO, BUT TRADING IN RUMORS ABOUT APPLE HAS BECOME ONE OF THE MOST SUCCESSFUL NICHES ON THE MAC WEB.

APPLE'S UNOFFICIAL PR CORP

The locus of the Mac community is the Web. It's where Mac users congregate, get their news, solve problems, and show off their creative efforts. There are hundreds, perhaps thousands, of active, regularly updated Mac Web sites, collectively known as the Mac Web.

The breadth is remarkable: there are sites devoted to news, rumors, opinions, how-tos, problem solving, Apple's history, specific products like the Newton or the iMac, music or movie making, and finding bargains. There are community forums and sites for trading desktop pictures, icons, and shareware. There are guides to games, upgrades, and benchmarks. You name it, there's probably a site devoted to it. There's even a site given to academic analysis: Applelust.com. "We talk of life, death, nihilism, God and the Mac," wrote editor David Schultz.

According to the interactive database at MacPiCkS (http://macpicks.com/), there are nearly 900 active Mac sites with registered domain names as of spring 2003. "It's taken me over four years, and I've assembled all of them by hand," said Greg Piper, who built the database. "I made it my mission to find every Mac site." Piper said the MacPiCkS database is one of the most comprehensive on the Web, listing 80 to 90 percent of all the Mac sites with registered domain names. If someone has gone to the trouble to register a domain, pay the annual fee and bandwidth costs, and maintain the site, it means it is likely to stick around.

MacPiCkS points to about 40 percent of the more ephemeral sites, hosted on free servers like Apple's Mac.com domain, GeoCities, and the like, Piper said. MacPiCkS includes a built-in link checker, which weeds out sites that are down, and a click-through link popularity system, indicating the most popular sites and those that have been around for a while.

What's perhaps most interesting about the Mac Web is that all but a handful of sites are published by small, independent publishers, often an individual or a small team of part-time volunteers. A good number of the more popular sites clearly make enough money to keep going. Overhead is low, but there's money to be made in publishing Mac-oriented material.

Because the Web makes it so easy for anyone to set up a site and publish their thoughts, excellence is far from guaranteed.

"Like just about every other topic on the Web, quality and attention to detail vary widely," wrote Charles Piller, a columnist with the *Los Angeles Times,* about the Mac Web. "Many of the sites clearly come from rank amateurs with a Mac chip on their shoulder or a desire to make a buck online. Still, there's a lot of great stuff if you show a little discrimination. You could spend weeks perusing just U.S. sites."

At one time, the center of the Mac universe was *MacWeek,* the much-missed trade paper that chronicled the Mac world for almost a decade and a half. Thanks to the declining advertising market in the late 1990s, *MacWeek* transformed into the cross-platform *eMediaWeekly*, an attempt to reflect changes in the creative computing space and attract more advertisers. Unfortunately, it was short lived, and *eMediaWeekly* ceased publishing. *MacWeek* continued to live online, but news sites like MacCentral were eating its lunch.

APPLE'S OBSESSION

MacCentral was started by Stan Flack and run by a handful of staffers working from home across the U.S. and Canada. MacCentral was eventually acquired by *MacWeek's* publisher, Mac Publishing, LLC, for a couple of million dollars, according to a source.

Meanwhile, the explosion of the Web heralded an explosion of Mac-oriented Web sites. The Web is the natural medium for trade news, providing a timely and diverse source of information, knowledge, and opinion. In general, the Mac Web is mostly about cheerleading. The vast majority of sites passionately advocate the Mac. Even the most trivial items are prominently featured if they contain good news about Apple. When there's bad news, it is often accompanied by mental acrobatics to put the best spin on it. The Mac Web is Apple's unofficial PR corp.

On the other hand, Mac users have a sense of humor and can be stunningly creative. The Mac Web feeds on a regular diet of parodies and jokes at Apple's, and the community's, expense.

Everyone has their favorite Web sites. But every year, Low End Mac (LEM), a popular site about older Macs (http://lowendmac. com), runs a "Best of the Mac Web" survey. According to LEM's readers, these are the top 10 most highly rated Mac sites:

1. **TIDBITS.** Adam Engst's long-running email newsletter of Mac news and tips (http://tidbits.com).

2. **MACSURFER'S HEADLINE NEWS.** A near-comprehensive, daily update of links to Mac news around the Web (http://www.macsurfer.com).

3. **VERSIONTRACKER.** A popular database of mostly Mac software (http://versiontracker.com). (Windows, Linux, and Palm are also included on separate pages.)

4. **MAC OS X HINTS.** Hints and tips for running Mac OS X (http://www.macosxhints.com).

5. **AS THE APPLE TURNS.** Humorous daily commentary on events in the Mac universe (http://www.appleturns.com).

6. **OS X FAQ.** Another OS X–dedicated site (http://www. osxfaq.com).

7. **JOY OF TECH.** Publishes three Mac-oriented editorial cartoons a week (http://www.joyoftech.com).

8. **MAC MINUTE.** Headline links, updated several times a day (http://www.macminute.com).

9. **CRAZY APPLE RUMORS.** Satirical rumor site (http://www. crazyapplerumors.com).

10. **MACINTOUCH.** Ric Ford's long-running Mac news and information site (http://www.macintouch.com).

RUMOR SITES—PICKING UP WHERE MAC THE KNIFE LEFT OFF

Once upon a time, *MacWeek's* weekly Mac the Knife column was the place to go for the best gossip and rumors about Apple and its upcoming products. But after the column was discontinued, its fiefdom was fought over by a handful of upstart Web sites.

WITH SECRECY MAKES GOOD BUSINESS SENSE. IN THE TECH INDUSTRY, SOMETHING BETTER, FASTER, AND CHEAPER IS ALWAYS AROUND THE CORNER.

Mac the Knife was superceded by Ryan Meader's Mac OS Rumors (http://www.macosrumors.com/), which ruled the roost for a while, until it too was pushed to the side by AppleInsider (http://www.appleinsider.com/). As AppleInsider's popularity waned, Spymac (http://www.spymac.com/) and Nick dePlume's Think Secret (http://www.thinksecret.com/) became the places to go. Others include MacRumors (http://www.macrumors.com/); macosXrumors (http://www.macosxrumors.com/); and RumorTracker (http://www.rumortracker.com/), an über-rumor site that tracks scuttlebutt at the other sites.

Individual rumor sites may come and go, but trading in rumors about Apple has become one of the most successful niches on the Mac Web. There's a huge, insatiable appetite for rumors and gossip about Apple's upcoming products. The rumor sites are a mixed bunch, taking a scattershot approach to news. Sometimes they hit the bull's-eye; often they are wide of the mark.

The rumor sites are most active in the run up to Macworld Conference & Expo, when Apple's CEO Steve Jobs typically introduces new products during the opening keynote speech. The secrecy-obsessed CEO likes to keep a tight lid on information to preserve the element of surprise, which induces a frenzy of speculation on the rumor sites. So great is the hunger for news, some rumor sites see the same people coming back hour after hour, day after day, in search of the latest tidbit.

Armando Santana, a 37-year-old San Francisco Web developer who runs RumorTracker, said about 1,300 regulars visit the site seven or eight times a day—every hour, on the hour, every day of the week. "They're Mac fanatics," he said. "They're itching to get news about Macworld. They're itching to know what Apple will come up with." Santana created the site because he and a friend spent hours every day reading the rumor sites, and they wanted a convenient one-stop shop. He still spends an hour a day discussing rumors with his friend.

Apple has always taken a dim view of speculative press. New York Macworld in the summer of 2001 was widely deemed a failure because rumor sites whipped up unrealistic expectations of flat-screen iMacs and video-capable handhelds, which the company failed to introduce. (The flat-screen iMac was subsequently launched at the San Francisco show in January 2002.) To dampen speculation, Apple took the unusual step of deflating expectations for Macworld Tokyo in March 2002 by announcing there would be no new computers at the show.

Apple was also widely believed to be behind a crackdown on press passes to the July 2002 Macworld in New York. Despite being granted press credentials to previous shows, various Web sites that printed "rumor and speculation" were denied access. Apple has also been very active in sending threatening cease-and-desist legal notices to sites that publish pictures of forthcoming hardware. There aren't many rumor sites that haven't received a nastygram from Apple at one point or another. And the last time an Apple employee leaked product details to the Net, he was summarily dismissed and slapped with a multimillion-dollar lawsuit. How's that for a deterrent? (Apple eventually dropped the suit against Juan Gutierrez, known as "Worker Bee.")

Apple's obsession with secrecy makes good business sense. In the tech industry, something better, faster, and cheaper is always around the corner. Early information about future products gives people pause about buying products in the current lineup. The case of Osborne Computer in the early 1980s is the industry's cautionary tale. Osborne sold a popular portable, but made the mistake of publicizing its successor before it was ready. Sales ground to a halt, and the company went out of business before the new machine came out.

LAIN WORKED PART TIME AT LOCAL COMPUTER SUPERSTORES FOR THE PURE PLEASURE OF PREACHING AND SELLING

RODNEY O. LAIN: THE iBROTHA

The suicide of controversial Mac columnist Rodney O. Lain prompted a mass online mourning. Lain, the iBrotha, had more friends than anyone suspected.

Lain was an online columnist known as the "Angry Mac Man" and the iBrotha. He shot himself at his home in Eagan, Minnesota, in June 2002. He'd been treated for depression. Friends say he stopped taking his medication a few days before his death. Lain, 34, was found by his widow, Irma. The couple had no children.

The iBrotha: Rodney O. Lain visiting the local Apple Store in his home town in Minnesota. Although he always had a full-time job, Lain worked part time in computer superstores for many years just to help sell Macs.
CREDIT: RODNEY O. LAIN

Lain's death was widely mourned in the online Mac community. Hundreds of people posted messages of condolence on forums at the Mac Observer, MacAddict, and MacNN, and eulogies have been published by former editors at Applelinks, Low End Mac, the Mac Observer and MyMac. "I'm amazed at how many people knew him," said friend Bill Ferguson. "I'm getting emails from editors and readers everywhere who loved his writing."

Lain, an African American, was an indefatigable Mac evangelist who styled himself as the "black Guy Kawasaki" after Apple's former pitch man. He gained a wide audience as a prolific and provocative Mac pundit. In the last few years, he had been published by most of the major Mac-related Web sites, including Applelinks, Applelust, Low End Mac, MacAddict, and the Mac Observer. Much of Lain's writing is archived at his iBrotha Web site.

Lain held various full-time day jobs, but for six years, he also worked part time at local computer superstores for the pure pleasure of preaching and selling Macs face-to-face. "That was one of his outlets for evangelizing the Mac," said friend Juan Cabanela, an astrophysics professor at Haverford College in Pennsylvania. "It wasn't about money. He did it to meet people.

He was an incredibly gregarious person. He liked to talk about Macs more than anything."

As a columnist, Lain was a passionate Mac advocate. But he also liked to court controversy. He was often critical of Apple and the Mac, a heretical attitude in the largely conformist Mac world. And like all good columnists, he wrote to provoke. One piece entitled "The Macintosh Is the Nigger of the Computer Industry" caused a storm of protest. In it, Lain compared Mac users to America's black underclass.

His writing earned him a large and dedicated audience on the Net. A small group of detractors even created an entire site devoted to ridiculing him and his articles. "His passion seemed disturbing but also fascinating to watch from a hack-sociological perspective," said programmer Montgomery Gabrys, who helped create the T.E.M.P. site. "Vaulting computer users to civil rights martyrs was perverse enough to grab our attention."

Lain often used the Mac platform as a way of writing about issues like poverty, racism, and politics. His columns were often prefaced with a quote from literature or popular culture. Friends say Lain had a masters degree in English literature and had taught at universities in Macon, Georgia, where he grew up, and St. Paul, Minnesota. For the last couple of years, Lain worked full time as a technical supervisor at UPS. But evenings and weekends, he had a second career in the Mac section of various computer superstores, earning a reputation as a star salesperson. There are reports of customers leaving with basket-loads of merchandise. "If I had 10 Rodney Lains, I wouldn't have to worry about anything," one of his CompUSA managers told the *Twin Cities Pioneer Press*.

Lain was hired full time at Power On Software, a Mac software publisher, after one of the company's executives saw the way he worked a crowd of shoppers at CompUSA. "I saw Rodney, and he was speaking with a whole group of customers," said Corey Johnson, Power On's operations manager. "He had gathered a crowd. His speaking skills were something to behold. He could really keep people's attention. He was selling Macs to several people there at the same time.

"It was like preaching. He was preaching the Mac gospel. He was showing them the light, which is something people don't get when they go into CompUSA. It was really quite something. When I saw that, I said we really have to hire this guy."

After working in tech support at Power On for about two years, Lain joined UPS. At the same time, he sold Macs at Best Buy, CompUSA, and Micro Center. Two weeks before his death, he started a new job at Apple's store in Minneapolis's Mall of America, a position he had coveted. "He will be sorely missed on this earth," said Johnson. "He was an incredible talent."

Before his association with the Mac community, Lain was active in various Christian churches. "I've been a fanatic," he told Minnesota Public Radio. "I've been a mainstream church fanatic; I've been a fringe church fanatic. I've been all over that stuff. It helps me understand this Macintosh thing, too. I know not to take it too seriously like some of the other people do. If Apple were to die today, I'd find something else to write about.

"Maybe (the Mac) is my religion," he added. "In a way, this is the serving and stuff I used to do when I was in the church. I was always one of the most active people; always the first to step up and do something. It's no different now. And I believe I can worship God by just helping people, and that's what I'm doing."

Lain's friend Bill Ferguson said, "The Mac community gave him an outlet for his preaching tendencies. He was very involved in the Mac world. He told me he was too honest to be a preacher and that he loved Macs. It gave him something larger than himself to help him deal with his depression."

Ferguson said Lain had been on a manic-depressive cycle for a number of years. When he was up, he was friendly, sociable, and productive. But every few months he would withdraw and spend a week or so in bed. "He had problems with depression going back to his youth," said Ferguson. "His father abandoned the family when he was young. He was raised in poverty and always told he would never amount to anything. Despite what was said, he did amount to something."

INSIDE THE MIND OF A MACCOMMUNIST

Technology columnists aren't, as a rule, a controversial bunch. But New York writer Lukas Hauser, who writes Mired's occasional MacCommunist column, has upset more than his fair share of readers. Hauser, 26, writes about Apple and the Mac with a unique Marxist spin, a wicked, inflammatory sense of humor, and plenty of profanity.

Mired is the creation of five Brown University graduates who live in New York City. They met at Brown's independent newspaper, the Indy, in the mid-1990s. Mired bills itself as a lowbrow digital magazine, obsessed with hip-hop, celebrities, sleazy politics, fast food, and, of course, Macs.

Hauser came up with the MacCommunist idea after pondering Apple's Think Different advertising campaign, which starred counterculture figures like Joan Baez, Mahatma Gandhi, Ted Turner, and Cesar Chavez. "It was mostly comprised of such terribly bourgeois iconography, it got me thinking about the real revolutionaries out there," said Hauser. Like a lot of people at the time, Hauser made his own Think Different posters. He chose Marx and Freud because they are "still the two most unpopular intellectuals of all time."

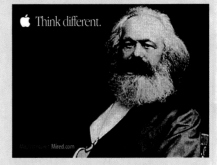

"The more I thought about the similarities between left-wing politics and the left-coast computer platform, the more a tasty synergy emerged," he said. Inspired, he drafted the MacCommunist manifesto, in which he compared Mac users to victims of the 1950s Red Scare. "Mac users resist The Man," he wrote. "There's a revolutionary tendency in deciding to use the protest platform. After all, what Apple fan hasn't envisioned a utopian state with Macs for everyone?"

Marx and Macs: Is the Mac the opium of the people? Controversial columnist Lukas Hauser mixed Macs and Marxism in his online MacCommunist columns.
CREDIT: LUKAS HAUSER

In the three years since, Hauser has taken a controversial stand on issues closest to Mac users' hearts. He's compared Mac users to homosexuals and opined that Apple's Flower Power iMacs are "gay." He criticized the widely lauded new iMacs and Apple Stores and produced a unique show-floor photo gallery from the 2001 Macworld in San Francisco. By comparison, most other publications focus on booths and products.

On the plus side—at least as far as Mac users are concerned—Hauser regularly refers to Dell's CEO Michael Dell as a "Texas hick" and his firm as a "ku klux komputer company." He wrote an unerringly accurate deconstruction of the cookie-cutter stories about Apple common in the trade press.

THE WEAPONS OF CHOICE

"Macs appeal to socialists because Apple is the model of a planned economy," one irate reader wrote him. "Totally anti-free market (no clones). No free choice of Mac supplier.... No free choice of hardware configuration. You get what the central planners (aka Steve) say you need and don't ask for nothing different. . . . Yep, Apple is for socialists."

Hauser does have his fans. Mired was the subject of an admiring review in glossy hip-hop magazine *The Fader*. Hauser's annual guide to New York for Macworld attendees prompted a protest from a local record store for being left out.

Oddly, MacCommunist earned Hauser a lot of money. During the Internet bubble, a lot of companies were desperate for content for their Web sites, and many syndicated Hauser's column. For a couple of years, syndication earned him more money than his job as principal of Phatinum, a digital production collective. "MacCommunist was syndicated by dim-witted content purchasers at OmniSky and Hewlett-Packard, among hundreds of smaller Web startups," said Hauser. "They were paying thousands of dollars a month for my descriptions of how terrible these companies were and how to destroy them. What a bizarre era."

APPLE HATERS

In 1998, Apple ran a television commercial aimed squarely at its competitors. The Toasted Bunny ad, as it came to be known, portrayed one of Intel's bunny-suited workers being hosed down by a firefighter. "Apple Computer would like to apologize for toasting the Pentium II processor in public," the voice-over intoned. "But the fact remains, the chip inside every new Macintosh G3 is up to twice as fast."

The advertisement so enraged Todd Arneson, at the time a 13-year-old fan of Windows PCs, that he launched Ihateapple. com, a Web site devoted to countering what he called Apple's "propaganda." Thanks to mentions on Web sites like CNET and a plethora of outraged Mac-advocacy sites, Ihateapple.com quickly became one of the major battlegrounds in the "platform wars" waged on the Net during the late 1990s and early 2000s.

The platform wars were an escalation of the never-ending argument between Mac users and Windows users about which platform was better. The weapons of choice were benchmarks, statistics, price comparisons, insults, flames, and threats. This so-called infowar was conducted in magazines, Usenet newsgroups (such as comp.sys.mac.advocacy and alt.flame.macintosh), innumerable chat forums, Web site message boards, and IRC channels. Oddly, the arguments were often as inflammatory as debates about abortion, gun control, or religion.

Apple did its part to fan the flames with calls to fight the Windows "hegemony" on the popular Mac EvangeList mailing list. Feeding on the controversy, Epinions.com created a television ad showing a Windows PC fan blasting an iMac to pieces at a firing range.

But while Apple continues to press the issue with its Switch campaign, which features disgruntled Windows users who switched to the Mac, a détente seems to have been reached among ordinary Mac and Windows users: Apple-hating sites have all but disappeared, Mac OS X is getting widespread respect, Mac fans are more confident, and Windows users apparently couldn't care less what computers other people use. Even Microsoft is trying to be friendly, running print ads for its new Mac Office software portraying Macs and Windows PCs as best buddies. Apple's one-sided battle makes it look like the

WERE BENCH MARKS, STATISTICS, PRICE COMPARISONS, INSULTS, FLAMES, AND THREATS.

lone soldier marooned on a forgotten island, fighting a private war long after a ceasefire has been called.

Among users, "Mac or Windows?" will probably remain one of the Net's never-ending debates, but instead of insults and diatribes, it has mostly transformed into a sober, rational discussion. Ihateapple.com, for example, is now a forum known for its balanced deliberation on the pros and cons of each platform. About a third of the site's regular visitors are Mac users, and one of the forum adminis-trators reportedly even uses a Mac. Talk touches on interface differences, software issues, and getting the machines to work together. "It really doesn't live up to its name anymore," said Jesse Stengel, the site's current Web master. "I think people just got tired of it, fighting over what was silliness, really."

The same is true of the Platform Wars mailing list, once a hotbed of com-puter-choice skirmishes. These days, the most heated arguments are between advocates of different versions of the Mac operating system. "For a while, some of the most animated discussions were not about Mac versus Windows, but Mac OS 9 versus Mac OS X," said listmom Bruce Giles.

Even Slashdot, the popular Linux-advocacy site, which often adopted a cool attitude toward Mac users, is becoming a major Mac hangout. Rob Malda, one of the site's cofounders, uses a Titanium PowerBook (though the company continues to use "all the major operating systems"), and Slashdot's Apple section is updated frequently and gets heavy traffic. "We have a lot of Unix users on Slashdot, and OS X is one of the biggest things to happen to Unix since Linux," explained Malda in an email.

Longtime Mac advocates, like Adam Engst, publisher of the online Mac magazine TidBITS, agreed that the ferocity of the fight against Windows has faded signifi-cantly. "On the one hand, I agree that we've seen a bit less invective than before, but on the other hand, the entire Switchers campaign is keeping the whole thing on the front burner," Engst said. Mac users are more confident, Engst said, and they don't feel the need to defend Apple quite so vigorously now that the com-pany isn't in imminent danger of going out of business.

The MacCommunist: Lukas Hauser looking not very communist.
CREDIT: TIMOTHY GREENFIELD-SANDERS

ARNESON SAID ZEALOUS MAC USERS WERE EASY TARGETS

Dheeraj Vasishta, who runs fuckMicrosoft.com, another platform-wars battleground, said he'd seen a sharp decline in anti-Mac email and a significant decline in email from Microsoft's "apologists." "More and more Windows users are starting to seriously question Microsoft's motives, as well as the quality of its products," he said in an email. "And Apple took a lot of the wind out of its critics' sails with the introduction of Mac OS X."

And then there are the anti-Apple Web sites, which at one time included Smackintosh, Macs Suck, and the Why Apple Macintosh Computers Are Worthless Homepage, which are now mostly gone. Arneson's Ihateapple.com site is one of the few that remain, but it's a shadow of its former Mac-baiting self. At its height, it attracted hundreds of people to aggressively debate the pros and cons of Macs and Windows machines.

Needless to say, the debate frequently descended into invective and abuse, partly because Arneson and the group of friends who helped run the site took great pleasure in taunting Mac fans with insults and jokes about the Mac platform. "It was a propaganda war," Arneson said recently from his home in Gilbert, Arizona, a suburb of Phoenix. "We were just sitting around thinking up things to piss Mac users off. We were baiting them. We were trolls."

A common theme was the kid appeal of the new colorful iMac and iBook. "Apple has a new notebook," ran a joke from the time. "It's an Etch A Sketch."

One of the most controversial parodies on the site was a poster mocking Apple's Think Different ad campaign, which highlighted famous iconoclasts. The parody featured Adolf Hitler.

Arneson initially thought it was funny but eventually took it down because it was just a bit too edgy.

Arneson said he derived great pleasure from posting a note denigrating the Mac platform and watching as hundreds of angry emails poured in. Arneson estimated he received 10,000 or more nasty messages in the five or six years he was at the helm.

The site wasn't a Windows advocacy vehicle per se, like the hundreds of pro-Mac sites on the Web. Arneson said he doesn't know if such a thing even exists. "When you're the big guys, no one needs to defend you," he said. Arneson said zealous Mac users were easy targets; it didn't take much to get their blood up. Apple, at the time, was in financial trouble, and the Mac community was feeling very, very threatened, he said.

The downside was a number of death threats, which he never took seriously, and a series of sinister letters mailed to a post office box he used to register the site. The letters would occasionally arrive from California. They contained newspaper clippings of an advertisement for a Windows conference or training seminar. The clips were accompanied by a sarcastic, handwritten note signed with an anonymous smiley face. The notes were never overtly threatening, but their cryptic nature really unnerved him. "They sent a shiver up my spine," he said. "I had no clue what they meant.

"We were never too serious about what we were doing. We liked the attention. We mostly didn't care if people used a Mac or not."

If you build a computer
that idiots can use...

...only idiots will want
to use it

Apple

More Pain.
Less brain.

The new PyroBook G3.

PART 2: GATHERINGS OF THE CLAN

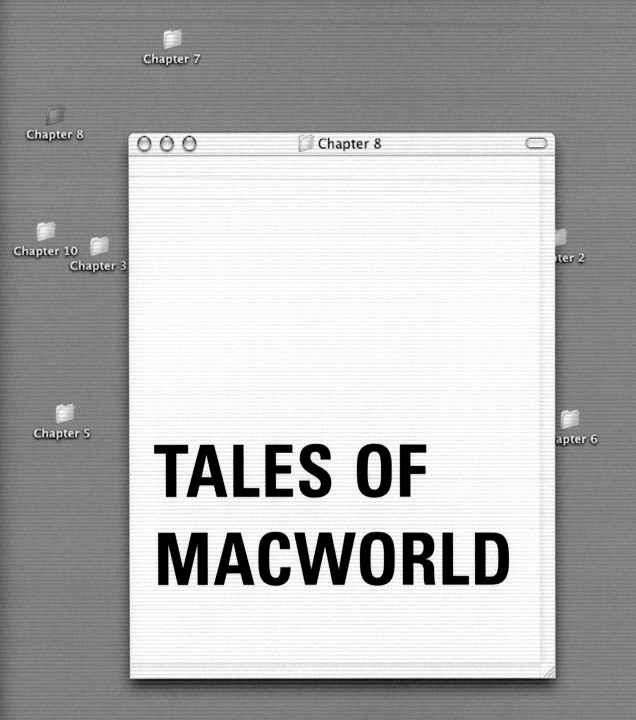

CREDIT: JEREMY BARNA

CREDIT: JEREMY BARNA

"I'm a borderline MAC nut," said GEORGE MASTERS, a graphic designer from Long Beach, California, who was visiting MACWORLD with his daughter EVELYN. "I read the rumor sites and like the stuff, but you see some guys and you think, 'I'm not quite there yet.' I didn't name my daughter iBABY."

KEVIN WILLIAMS, SHARIF MUSTAFA, and JENEE DAVIS (pictured left to right) all just graduated.

Williams is thinking about YALE, Mustafa and Davis, HARVARD. Before they go, they're working on a PC repair program for the Treasure Island Job Corp. "I'm probably going to get an iBOOK, but a POWER BOOK would be nice," said Mustafa. "Macs are easy, but they're so expensive," said Davis. "I'm a Linux guy," said Williams.

WHEREVER MACWORLD GATHERING

THE GATHERING OF THE MAC CLAN

Conferences are an American institution. Ostensibly for business, people get drunk, have a good time, and fool around on their spouses.

Macworld Conference & Expo is no exception. Since 1985, the show has been held twice a year in the U.S.—in San Francisco in January and New York in July. Overseas, Macworld shows have also been held in Tokyo in the spring and France in the fall.

The first Macworld shows were held in 1985, at San Francisco's Brooks Hall in January, and in Boston in the fall. For many years, Boston and San Francisco were the show's traditional venues. Over the years, however, there was some shuffling of the conference from city to city.

In the late 1980s, a one-off Macworld was held in Dallas, and there were a few shows in Toronto. In 1989, the East Coast show attempted to move to Washington, D.C. to go after the government market, and again in May 1994, after the Power Mac came out. But Boston, a hotbed of academics and developers, held sway over alternative venues until 1998, when the East Coast show was moved to New York to focus on the Big Apple's cre-

ative types. In 2002, the show's organizer, IDG, announced a plan to move the show back to Boston in 2004. Apple balked, pledging not to participate if the show left New York. Apple said it would continue exhibiting at the San Francisco Expo.

In 2002, the Tokyo show folded after Apple dropped out. The three-day show had run for 12 years, and year after year attracted audiences in excess of 180,000 people.

Wherever it is held, Macworld is the great gathering of the Mac clan.

The show floor is like a Las Vegas casino, without the cigarette smoke: lights, deafening noise, and rude crowds of people who constantly bump each other or congregate in the most inconvenient places, usually the aisles.

The exhibition hall is full of companies clamoring for attention, shouting over each other to attract people to their booths. They give out truckloads of inexpensive gifts: buttons, T-shirts, pens, CDs. Attendees fill their bags with all the giveaways and literature they can lay their hands on. Out-of-towners can be overheard discussing where to buy jumbo-sized luggage for all the stuff they've collected.

IT IS HELD, IS THE GREAT OF THE MAC CLAN.

(LEFT) WORLD OF MACS: MACWORLD CONFERENCE & EXPO IS LIKE A CACOPHONOUS LAS VEGAS CASINO, WITHOUT THE CIGARETTE SMOKE.
CREDIT: JEREMY BARNA

(BELOW) MAIN ATTRACTION: APPLE'S BOOTH IN THE MIDDLE OF THE SHOW DOMINATES THE MACWORLD PROCEEDINGS. THE PRODUCT DISPLAY STANDS, SHOWN HERE, ARE OFTEN CROWDED WITH GAWKERS FOUR OR FIVE DEEP.
CREDIT: JEREMY BARNA

Macworld is a good time. People attend the show to see new products, network, and meet old friends. User groups host big dinners at local restaurants. There's a lot of joking and horsing around and a palatable sense of solidarity.

Andrew Orlowski, a reporter with the Register (http://www.theregister.co.uk/) and a Mac user, likened Macworld to a naturist's semiannual holiday to a nudist camp. "All year you're poked and teased for your weird habit," he wrote. "You suffer: the shelves of CompUSA are filled with nothing but Windows stuff, except for that bit under the stairs marked "Freaks." But for two weeks a year, you're surrounded by people just like you! Except they're nothing like you! But it doesn't matter!"

A lot of business is conducted behind the scenes. In hotel suites and in booths off the show floor, companies demonstrate new products to big customers and the press. The press is particularly courted. Everyone wants some ink. Reporters are invited to all the parties and get to meet the top executives, who hand out their business cards to everyone in reach. (Call them after the show, and they defer to a stonewalling PR team).

Most attendees don't get invited to the parties. For the rank and file, the highlight of the show is the keynote speech, delivered in recent years by Steve Jobs. A Steve Jobs keynote has to be seen to be believed. They are pure show business. A Jobs keynote at Macworld is by far the most entertaining event in the technology industry; no one can excite a crowd quite like he can. The common comparisons to a rock concert are appropriate: the crowd cheers and applauds wildly with each demonstration of shiny, new Apple technology.

(LEFT TOP) STANDING OUT: A GEEKY TEENAGER SPENDS AN AFTERNOON AT MACWORLD. THE SHOW ATTRACTS A DIVERSE CROWD. SOME PEOPLE PLAN THEIR VACATIONS AROUND THEM. CREDIT: LUKAS HAUSER

(LEFT BOTTOM) ARTISTIC URGES: MACWORLD OFFERS MANY DISTRACTIONS, ASIDE FROM EATING AND DRINKING ON THE COMPANY EXPENSE TAB. HERE, SHOW-GOERS DABBLE WITH ELECTRONIC EASELS. CREDIT: JASON O'GRADY

(RIGHT) WAIT, THERE'S MORE: MACWORLD ATTENDEES LINE UP FOR HOURS TO SEE STEVE JOBS' KEYNOTE SPEECH. CREDIT: LEANDER KAHNEY

"The enthusiasm for software and hardware at Macworld is almost touching," wrote Katharine Mieszkowski on Salon.com. "To make light of it feels like sucking a sourball at a chocolate convention; it's just beside the point."

People line up for hours to get in to the keynote. The most dedicated camp out all night. There's a near stampede when the doors are thrown open, and the cavernous hall, which seats several thousand, fills like a flood. In past years, hundreds have been turned away, disappointed, from the overfilled hall.

When he stalks onstage, Jobs is greeted with wild applause, which sometimes goes on for several minutes before he cuts it short. One of his best entrances made use of the actor Noah Wyle, who played Jobs in TNT's *Pirates of Silicon Valley*. When Wyle emerged on stage to introduce Jobs, most people thought it was Jobs; he'd nailed his mannerisms so well.

The keynote is usually wrapped up with Jobs' trademark "one more thing" shtick, when, as an apparent afterthought, he introduces a major new product. This, of course, is what everyone's been waiting for. Jobs is parodying infomercials and their breathless, "wait, there's more" commercialism.

In January 2001, Jobs' "one more thing" was the sleek Titanium PowerBook G4. Within minutes of Jobs announcing its availability, people in the audience were ordering it wirelessly from Apple's online store using their current laptops, according to reports.

WAITING, WAITING: TO KILL TIME IN THE LINE FOR THE KEYNOTE, PEOPLE MAKE MUSIC, PLAY MULTIPLAYER GAMES WIRELESSLY, OR CATCH A NAP.
CREDIT: LEANDER KAHNEY

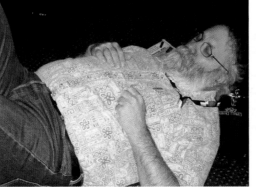

LETA JUSSILA, a 30-year-old acupuncture student from Santa Cruz, California, was airlifted out of SAIGON as a child and raised by an American foster family on CAPE COD. A few years ago, she began to search for her mother, who was left in VIETNAM. But to find her, Jussila needed money and technology: she started her search on the Internet. Working as a waitress, she managed to save $30,000. "I sweated for that," she said. "I sweated."

She dropped $11,000 on a high-end POWERMAC tricked out for digital video. She's making a documentary about her search. Last year she went to Saigon and shot 17 hours of video. She hasn't found her mother but got a tip that she's living in Australia. "Sometimes I regret spending the $11,000 because I need it now for food," she said. "But [the documentary] is how I can get closer to her."

It's Jussila's first trip to MACWORLD—she's looking for sound-engineering software. She started editing her film with APPLE's consumer oriented iMOVIE but now uses FINAL CUT PRO. "The MAC is so easy to use," she said. "Anyone can buy a camera, edit, and produce a DVD. It's that easy."

DON PETERSON is a general building contractor from Los Altos Hills, Ca, who became so good at fixing broken-down Macs, his reputation spread by word of mouth and he was able to launch a fix-it business, the MAC MECHANIC, on the referrals. "I've been doing Macs about 15 years now, I guess," he said. "I'm a Mac addict."

Six months later, at Macworld New York in July, Jobs' keynote was a letdown. For weeks, rumor sites had been predicting he would unveil amazing new hardware, such as flat-screen iMacs, wireless Web pads, or Newton-like handhelds. When these technological marvels failed to appear, some people left the keynote in tears, according to reports. Another group attempted to storm the stage and buttonhole the departing Jobs. The reaction online was vociferous. People felt cheated.

Before the Internet, Macworld was the best opportunity for companies to show their public face and demonstrate new products. Companies were especially keen to court volume buyers—corporations, education, and government—and spared no expense on custom booths and lavish parties. One company built a working waterfall into its booth; another had a theme park–like ride towering above the show floor. The size of a company's booth was key: the bigger the booth, the more successful the company appeared. Companies would spend hundreds of thousands of dollars on booths, expensive custom favors like swimsuits or underwear, and sumptuous parties.

"The parties also reflected how a company was doing, and vendors made sure they had plenty of food and drinks for analysts, partners, customers, and the press," said David Morgenstern, former editor of *MacWeek*. "Around 1988 or so, Jasmine, a leading hard drive vendor, held a huge party during Expo. Three floors in a galleria, each with its own food section. A band or two. The company was having cash flow problems and would go under in a few months, but management couldn't afford to give the world the wrong impression."

BLANKET COVERAGE: DURING THE WEEK OF MACWORLD, NEW YORK SEEMS TO BE COVERED IN APPLE ADS. IT APPEARS THAT EVERY BUS STOP IN TOWN SPORTS AN APPLE POSTER.
CREDIT: LUKAS HAUSER

CREDIT: AP/WORLD WIDE PHOTO

CREDIT: MACCENTRAL

MESMERIZING: THERE'S NOTHING AS ENCHANTING IN THE BUSINESS WORLD AS A TOUR THROUGH THE WORLD OF APPLE, COURTESY OF STEVE JOBS. FOR A COUPLE OF HOURS, WORLD-WEARY MACWORLD ATTENDEES FIND THEMSELVES AT THE CENTER OF STEVE JOBS' LEGENDARY REALITY-DISTORTION FIELD.

THE LINE FOR MACWORLD KEYNOTES

At 2:30 a.m. on a crisp January morning in 2002, Christian Huffman, an engineer from San Jose, stood alone outside the Moscone Center near downtown San Francisco. Steve Jobs' keynote speech would start in six-and-a-half hours, and Huffman wanted to get a good seat.

He chatted for a while with a security guard on a cigarette break. An hour later, he was joined by Melody and Glenn Batuyong, who'd flown up that morning from San Diego bearing a hand-lettered "We love Steve Jobs" sign. A bike rider pedaled by. "You're macadamia nuts," he yelled. He wore a helmet covered in flashing lights.

More Mac fans started to turn up. The line steadily grew. Huffman and the Batuyongs shook a lot of hands as people congratulated them for being first in line. At about 5 a.m., someone turned up with two big boxes of doughnuts. He handed one box to Huffman. "Pass them down," he said. The other box went farther down the line. "It's a Mac community thing," said Glenn Batuyong. "He did it just to be cool."

People got out their laptops. Chris Catherton and Alexander Profeit, a pair of 12-year-olds, started playing Starcraft wirelessly with a couple of others in the line. Where their opponents were exactly, Catherton and Profeit didn't know. Andrew Koss, who owns a Boston recording studio, unpacked a portable keyboard, plugged it into his Mac, donned headphones, and started composing. "It's better than reading a magazine," he said.

By 9 a.m., thousands of people stood patiently behind Huffman and the Batuyongs. The line snaked out of the cavernous Moscone complex, around the corner, and down the block. Huffman and the Batuyongs were flagging just a little, but anticipation was building. "This is my fifth Macworld keynote," said Huffman. "I'm excited about it. I'm glad the rumors are all over the place. There's nothing really concrete this time, no secret diagrams or anything like that. It's more exciting when you don't know what's going to happen."

The line for a Macworld keynote is unlike anything else in the business world, comparable only to rock concerts or sports matches in the competition to get in. Since 1996, when Steve Jobs returned to Apple, even those who begin queuing in the early hours aren't guaranteed a seat. Five thousands seats at a Macworld keynote speech go very, very quickly. The cavernous hall at San Francisco's Moscone Center, venue of Steve Jobs' Macworld keynote speech, usually fills within minutes.

"It was like the famous Who concert in Cincinnati in 1979 when people got trampled," said Hoke Greiner, a restaurant owner from Gaffney, South Carolina, who was caught in the mad crush to get in for Jobs' keynote in 2001.

(BELOW) SPREAD THE LOVE: MELODY AND GLENN BATUYONG, WITH CHRISTIAN HUFFMAN, AT THE FRONT OF THE LINE TO SEE STEVE JOBS. THEY CAMPED OUT ALL NIGHT TO BE AT THE FRONT OF THE LINE. **CREDIT: LEANDER KAHNEY**

105

PEOPLE ATTEND THE SHOW TO SEE NEW PRODUCTS, NETWORK, AND MEET OLD FRIENDS.

MACWORLD: VACATION DESTINATION

What does Macworld have in common with Hawaii, Disneyland, Las Vegas, or Europe? People go to the Macworld trade show on vacation. A surprising number of people take their two weeks' annual vacation at Macworld: one week in San Francisco in the winter and a week in New York in the summer. "This is our annual vacation," said Nina Benami, who had come from Canada with her husband, Lior, to attend Macworld in San Francisco. "A little bit of Macworld, a little bit of San Francisco."

While Nina was more interested in the city, her husband was more interested in Macworld. "This is his thing," she said. "For him, it's a dream come true. I was a bit dubious about this, but it's quite exciting. My husband's not alone with his obsession with the Mac. There's lots of them, and they seem like nice people."

At Macworld in New York, Nancy Boover, an elementary school teacher from New Jersey, told Wired News she was also killing two birds with one stone. "This really is a lovely way to chill out," she said of the show. "I get a nice little holiday in a happy place, I learn a lot, and it's a valid deduction on my taxes. Otherwise, I'd never be able to afford to visit New York City." Boover said she attends Macworld religiously for reasons ranging from "the total creative inspiration" to "it's the only techie show that you can meet girls at."

Mick McGee, a graphic artist from Milwaukee, said: "I met my wife at Macworld five years ago, I proposed at Macworld two years later, we eventually conceived a kid while attending a Macworld, and I've gotten a lot of jobs at Macworld. I wouldn't dream of missing a show."

Likewise, Mark Matten's life revolves around Macs. "I work on my Mac, I make art and music with my Mac, and in my spare time I play games on my Mac," said Matten, a writer and artist from Florida. "And obviously, I also center my vacations on my Mac...I'm having an excellent time on my summer vacation at Macworld."

MAC THE KNIFE PARTY

For many years, the hottest ticket at Macworld was an invite to the Mac the Knife party, an uninhibited bacchanal thrown by the editors of *MacWeek*. The party was considered the most important gathering of the Macintosh development community.

The idea was to get everyone drunk enough to talk about the secret product plans, bitch about their employers, or dish dirt on their competitors. Naturally, the tips would then be reported exclusively in *MacWeek*. "It wasn't a soirée," said former *MacWeek* editor Matthew Rothenberg. "It was a blowout. A lot of straight-laced people letting their hair down."

The party was named in honor of *MacWeek's* Mac the Knife rumor column. Over the years, the column was penned by a number of anonymous writers, whose identities were closely guarded and frequently speculated on.

Like the names of the writers, the location of the party was always a secret. Tickets were very hard to come by. Attendance was strictly limited. The only rule was no marketing flaks or PR people. "We wanted the Mac geeks coming to this," Rothenberg said. "We wanted the people who had the 411 on the latest and greatest in Mac technology. Just add alcohol and loud live music." Most invites were given out by *MacWeek* reporters who often demanded a tip for a ticket.

Some years, resourceful partiers would try to pass off forged tickets at the door. There were often altercations with bigwigs who demanded entry. "It was a bit like getting into CBGB," recalled Rothenberg. "Doing the door was always a lovely spot to hold down. It was strictly one ticket per person. You'd always get a group of drunks saying 'this is the vice president of sales; he's got to come in with us.'"

PARTY HEARTY: THE MAC THE KNIFE PARTY WAS THE MOST UNINHIBITED PARTY AT MACWORLD. THROWN BY THE EDITORS OF *MACWEEK*, THE IDEA WAS TO INVITE INSIDERS, WHO WOULD GET DRUNK ENOUGH TO TALK ABOUT ALL THE THINGS THEY WEREN'T SUPPOSED TO TALK ABOUT. CRAIG ISAACS, A MAC THE KNIFE REGULAR, ALWAYS KEPT HIS MOUTH SHUT. **CREDIT: ELENE HOFFMAN**

Unfortunately, the party died with a fizzle, not a bang. When *MacWeek* killed the Mac the Knife column in 2000, it also killed the party. Not to be denied the biannual bacchanal, Ilene Hoffman, a consultant and editor at MacFixIt (http://www.macfixit.com), took on the task of organizing the "Not the Mac the Knife Party," but it slowly fizzled out.

CREDIT: JEREMY BARNA

CREDIT: JEREMY BARNA

"MAC is just feeling good," said Akihiro Okashita, from the Mac Treasure Trailing Club, a Mac user group from Tokyo. "To make to work in. And it's just MAC have fun. It create something. MAC is very different from Windows or Linux. Mac share in JAPAN is 5 to 7 percent. The new iMAC is very surprised Japanese people. It is in the newspapers not just for computers — very famous newspapers in Japan. This design, it is nothing like in the past. The iMAC is not like PCs and computers. It is like furniture."

PAM PETTIT, PHYLIS ALMANZA, TRENA TERRELL, and CORRINE KISTLER (pictured left to right) took the bus from Sacramento to attend MACWORLD for the day and would rather be at the trade show than shopping in nearby Union Square, San Francisco's famous shopping district. They all work for POWERSCHOOL, a software publisher and a division of Apple. "We love MACs," said Terrell. "And we're not just saying that since our checks come from them." Two of the women said they were going to order new Macs online the minute they got home. "They have some really great stuff," said Terrell. "The iMAC is sooooo cool."

108

CREDIT: JEREMY BARNA

"If I had a choice, I would kill PCs," said CHRISTINA BERGSCHNEIDER (right), a 3D animation student from San Francisco. "PCs must die. They crash all the time, and they're NOT fun to play with. I hate them." Her companion, Andre Williams, owner of Avarija Sound Design, chuckled. "There's a growing synergy between the Mac and Unix, especially in the design and entertainment industry. A lot of people are saying, 'Hey, it was worth waiting for MAC OS X."

CREDIT: JEREMY BARNA

CHARLES PHILIPS is five years old and the youngest accredited journalist at MACWORLD. He reviews education and game software for FAMILY MAC. when we caught up with him, he'd just finished a radio interview and had been stopped by someone for an autograph. He has three rules: Rule 1: You can never have enough RAM. Rule 2: Get a good disk utility. Rule 3: If you don't buy a MAC, you're an idiot. Pictured are his dad, Robert Philips (right), mum Cyndi Tester (center), and "auntie" Sharon Hosler. "PCs suck," he said. "Macs are easy to use."

MAC DEADHEAD CAMPS IN STYLE

Who is the biggest Mac eccentric at Macworld? There are a few contenders, but perhaps Taylor Barcroft takes the title: Barcroft has spent the last decade videotaping almost every keynote speech, press conference, and booth presentation given at the Macworld trade show.

For 11 years, Barcroft has crisscrossed the country in his custom-fitted RV, attending Macworld conferences on both coasts and perhaps hundreds of other Mac- and multimedia-related trade shows in between. "I've attended scores of shows, a different one every week," he said. "It's amazing what I've gone through, considering I haven't been paid for it."

Supported by an inheritance, Barcroft has devoted his life to obsessively taping speeches, conference sessions, booth presentations, and convention parties. Always managing to secure media credentials for the shows he attends, Barcroft describes himself as a "multimedia historical videographer." One day he hopes to produce a series of videos about the history of multimedia. He claims to have more than 3,000 hours of video stored in boxes at his home in Altadena ("Altadena is close to Glendale, where the first Apple store opened," he explained). Barcroft also rents a giant storage locker filled with all the press releases, marketing materials, and free software samples he has acquired over the years.

However, he has yet to produce anything. "I haven't edited any footage," he said. "I haven't even gone back and looked at it. My dream is that somebody will like it and organize an army of interns to produce a detailed log of everything, and then develop some really interesting DVDs."

Barcroft is a curious mix between a Mac deadhead, an eccentric, and, perhaps, a visionary. Tall and slim, he is 55 years old, though he looks ten years younger, thanks, no doubt, to his vegan diet. He has two business cards: one for his Web site, FutureMedia.org, which is empty, and another inscribed with his Buddhist name, Kunga.

Barcroft talks in a booming voice, oblivious to the attention he attracts. He's friendly and has a self-depreciating sense of humor. His outfit is cliché filmmaker—a black beret and photographer's vest with bulging pockets. The look is undermined, however, by the battered laundry cart he pushes, containing his expensive digital camera and tripod, along with all the stuff he collects.

For Macworld, Barcroft parks his RV among some homeless encampments under a freeway flyover, near San Francisco's Moscone Center where the event runs. He chose the space because it was free, but the white Tiger RV looked incongruous among shopping carts and cardboard shacks.

The van is outfitted with an expensive audiovisual system—a flat-screen TV is mounted above the sink, and another unfurls from the dashboard. Cost: about

MAC TRAVELER: TAYLOR BARCROFT SPENT A DECADE TRAVELING TO TECH CONFERENCES, MOSTLY MAC SHOWS, TO SHOOT VIDEO OF KEYNOTE SPEECHES AND PRESENTATIONS. HE HAS BOXES FULL OF UNEDITED TAPES HE HOPES ONE DAY TO TURN INTO A HISTORY. **CREDIT: JEREMY BARNA**

109

(ABOVE TOP) AUTEUR: BARCROFT
AND HIS PRICEY VIDEO SETUP.
HE HAS ALL THE LATEST GEAR,
THANKS TO AN INHERITANCE THAT
FINANCED HIS TRAVELS.
CREDIT: JEREMY BARNA

(ABOVE BOTTOM) ROAR: BARCROFT'S
TIGER RV HAS A PERSONALIZED
"MAC" PLATE. SO DO HIS FORD
AEROSTAR MINIVAN (MAC STAR)
AND HONDA DEL SOL SPORTS CAR
(MAC SOUL).
CREDIT: JEREMY BARNA

$50,000. It sports a vanity plate, MAC TIGR, that echoes those on his two other vehicles: a Ford Aerostar minivan (MAC STAR) and a Honda del Sol sports car (MAC SOUL).

Apart from occasional writing for Web sites and magazines, Barcroft doesn't work. For years he was supported by a rich aunt, who left him an inheritance when she died. "I've been lucky," he said. "I've been totaled by the crash though. I wasn't paying attention. But we don't want to get into that."

Every year, he roams the country attending technology conferences: four or five conventions in Las Vegas; Macworld in San Francisco in January; and in July he drives across country to Macworld in New York. Add to that several conferences in the Los Angeles area, a couple in Chicago, and the occasional New Orleans National Cable convention. "I've been back and forth," he said. "I've put several hundred thousand miles on that Aerostar."

Of all the shows, Macworld is his favorite. "I love the Mac," he said. "The Mac is so much better for multimedia than Windows." Barcroft said he still has all 17 Macs he's ever owned, from early models to the Cube, which he bought in 2001. "I'm too emotionally attached to my Macs to sell them," Barcroft said. "So they're being donated to a private museum in a friend's barn in Boulder Creek (in rural northern California)."

Barcroft got his first Mac in 1985, shortly after the computer was introduced, and started publishing Mac Briefs, a monthly newsletter detailing every Mac-related article published in dozens of magazines, newspapers, and newsletters. It was during this time that he rented a booth at the early Macworld shows and developed his love of technical conferences. Mac Briefs folded in 1987, so Barcroft got a video camera and started filming instead.

"I have some incredible footage," he said excitedly. "I was in a jammed room full of print-shop operators when [publishing guru] Jonathan Seybold told them the Internet is going to change everything, and they have to scrap their businesses. I was the only one in the room shooting. I've got some incredible footage."

Among Barcroft's other accomplishments, he was president (self-proclaimed) of the "Adam Users of America," a user group devoted to an early home computer made by the maker of the Cabbage Patch Dolls. "I was featured in *USA Today*," he said. "I was the guy who told *USA Today* everything that was wrong with the Adam computer, and there was a lot wrong with it."

He helped produce the first copy of *Mondo 2000*, the influential techno culture magazine that preceded *Wired* magazine, and was one of the first people to try transmitting text over TV, a technology overtaken by the Internet.

Although he was married briefly and had a son, Barcroft has only recently started to settle down. "I've been doing this so long I'm sick of it," he said with a laugh. "When I started, I was very anal. I was shooting every-thing, but now I'm like 'whatever.'" Besides, his girlfriend, a Hollywood costume designer, won't come to trade shows. "She's not into technology," Barcroft said. "There's only so much she can take."

"At a certain point you get burned out," he added. "It's not as easy to shoot as intensely as I was. You realize no one may ever see this stuff."

ICELAND'S HOT FOR MACWORLD

While thousands of Mac fans gather in hot, sweaty New York to hear Steve Jobs' keynote speech at Macworld Expo, in a remote, frosty part of the world, oppressive humidity isn't a problem. In Reykjavik, Iceland's capital city, hundreds of Mac fans rent out a local movie theater to watch the speech broadcast by satellite. The gathering attracts 500 to 600 Mac fans from the city and surrounding towns to Reykjavik's larg-est cinema, Haskolabio (University Cinema). Some even drive hundreds of miles across the island to attend.

"The atmosphere is like a cult gathering," said Andrés Magnússon, a 37-year-old journalist, PR consultant, and Web designer who lives in Reykjavik. "There is a buzz in the room. Usually the crowd is almost giddy, flush with expectations and the confidence of the righteous."

Although Mac fans all over the world get together to watch the speech by satellite or Webcast, this may be the only place fans rent out a large movie theater. An Apple spokeswoman said she hadn't heard of anything like it. Last year, more than 250,000 people watched the keynote webcast, according to Apple.

The crowd sips free Tuborg beer and munches on compli-mentary Subway sandwiches. The event is sponsored by a local Apple dealership, which sets up a stand in the foyer to demonstrate its wares. The gathering attracts the usual crowd of Mac users: graphic artists, designers, videographers, and photographers. "When Jobs appears on the stage, there is much clapping and whistles, and his presentation is interrupted by applauses and cheers, with the odd boo if Bill Gates is men-tioned," Magnússon said. "When the new iMac was uncovered, there was one shout of 'Hallelujah!'"

Jobs' speech has become an annual pilgrimage for Icelandic Mac fans, who also get together to watch the keynote from Macworld San Francisco, which is held in January. A few years ago, small groups of Icelandic Mac users started gathering at each other's homes to watch Steve Jobs' keynote speeches. They were so popular that the Apple dealer started renting out a small confer-ence room and a large-screen TV. Every year, the events kept growing, from about 40 to 300 people, Magnússon estimated. "This year it has grown to a mini-conference," he said.

The driving force behind the event is Steingrimur Arnason, a senior programmer with Apple-Umbodid, who supports Icelandic Mac software. "Arnason is a Mac zealot, but he is also extremely concerned with the Icelandic language," Magnússon said. "Icelandic is a hot issue here, as it should be on the endangered languages list."

Arnason has created software to localize popular programs from Adobe, Macromedia, Microsoft, and others, Magnússon said. Icelandic has six special characters unique to the lan-guage and a few special requirements that preclude using International English versions of some software. Many soft-ware companies ignore the language because of Iceland's tiny population (280,000 people; about 100,000 live in Reykjavik). The Mac OS has been localized for Iceland for many years. Mac OS X is still being translated, Magnússon said.

PCS DON'T GO GENTLY INTO MACWORLD

In *Some Like It Hot*, Jack Lemmon and Tony Curtis evaded the Mob by dressing as chorus girls. At Macworld in January 2002, a Web site editor tried to evade the Mac mob by disguising his Windows notebook as an Apple laptop.

Ben Stanfield, an executive editor at MacSlash, the Macintosh version of Slashdot, is an avid Mac user, but his Apple lap-top—a Titanium PowerBook G4—was in the shop during January 2002's Macworld Expo in San Francisco. Forced to borrow a friend's Toshiba Satellite laptop to cover the show, he tried to disguise it by sticking a large, white Apple decal on the lid. "Knowing I'd get endless grief about it, I stuck a white Apple decal on the front of it to lessen the snide comments," he explained.

But Mac users aren't so easily fooled. Stanfield was heckled by the crowd when he pulled out the laptop to cover Steve

(TOP) SOME LIKE IT HOT: AN ATTEMPT TO SMUGGLE A HATED PC INTO MACWORLD BY DISGUISING IT WITH AN APPLE STICKER GARNERED THE OWNER MORE ATTENTION THAN HE BARGAINED FOR.
CREDIT: DAVID ENGSTROM

(BOTTOM) NO PEEKING: SECURITY GUARDS WATCH OVER A MYSTE-RIOUSLY SHROUDED BOOTH IN APPLE'S DISPLAY AREA ON THE EVE OF MACWORLD TOKYO.
CREDIT: LEANDER KAHNEY

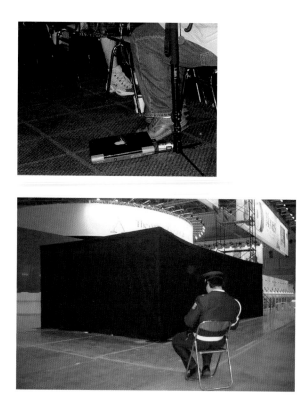

Jobs' keynote speech on the first day of the show. "Some good-natured ribbing and catcalling went on, and the guy with the laptop looked kind of embarrassed," said David Engstrom, a senior editor at MacSpeedZone and MacReviewZone, who witnessed the deception.

Engstrom said he feared the Mac mob would chase Stanfield down and stone him, like a scene from *Zorba the Greek*. Luckily, Engstrom said, Stanfield was surrounded by guys the size of defensive linebackers. "Like a Roman cohort, they formed a protective ring around their beleaguered member and moved him out of harm's way," Engstrom wrote about the incident on his site. "Entering Macworld with the wrong technology is like wandering the Casbah with money hanging out of your pocket...just ain't prudent."

Needless to say, Stanfield wasn't stoned. But his attempts to disguise the machine only made people more curious. Some thought the silver and blue computer was a new Apple laptop, yet to be released to the public. "One person actually begged to hold it and look at it, believing that it was a new portable Steve would be announcing during the keynote," Stanfield said. "I played along and told him it had a 1.8 GHz G4 in it, and ran Windows XP as well as Mac OS X." Stanfield said the gullible fellow actually believed him.

"I didn't feel the need to give him the real story," Stanfield said. "I was hoping he'd figure it out when Jobs didn't announce it."

WHAT'S BEHIND APPLE'S CURTAIN?

Apple usually reveals major new products at Macworld. To maintain secrecy, security at the Apple booth is always very tight. In the past, Apple has draped its entire booth in a giant, 150-foot curtain that is 30 feet high. Only a small number of vetted Apple employees are allowed anywhere near it.

"Macworld is one of the most secure events in the industry," said Rob Scheschareg, vice president of events for IDG World Expo, which puts on the show.

At Macworld Tokyo in 2001, Apple wasn't expected to reveal anything new. But before the show opened, the company had a pair of large and mysteriously shrouded booths in its display area on the exhibit floor. The draped booths resembled something from a Stanley Kubrick movie. Even the tops of the booths were draped in thick, black material, preventing workmen on ladders or lighting gantries from peeking inside. Adding to the air of mystery, a fluorescent glow from inside the booths could be seen where the curtains met the floor.

"I'm a MAC nut," said GRAZIELLA DANIELI, a community liaison with SAN FRANCISCO State University. "I think the MAC empowers you to feel imaginative. It makes you feel like an artist, even though you're not. You feel it's not corporate. It makes you do things that are original. The mac has that quality. It's so friendly and endearing all the time. It's really a good companion. It has personality. It's a tool for expression, for personality. Sometimes people have a boring job, but the MAC encourages them to add things to their memos, their messages little pictures or videos. It's a good tool to express your personality and not just be another person at that desk."

ROSENDA SALDANA (left), a musician from Reno, Nevada, was dragged to MACWORLD by his friend JOSHUA SMITH, a graphic artist. "I said, 'I don't know man, a computer show? I'm a musician.' But I think it's way cool. I'm enjoying it, seeing all kinds of weird shit, seeing all kinds of weird people. Same as everywhere I go." Smith, who said people (like cops) never believe Joshua Smith is his real name, said he comes to Macworld every year and stays all week. "It's about art," he said. "I've been an artist my whole life. I started with Photoshop, and since you learn the tools, you learn the computer also. Macworld is where the hip stuff happens."

"I DON'T GIVE A DAMN WHO YOU ARE... NO ONE GETS IN WITHOUT A BADGE."

Each booth was under the watchful eye of a pair of uniformed guards, stationed at opposite corners to give them a commanding view of all four sides. No one was allowed to approach the booths, which were located on each side of the large stage. When approached, one of the guards said he had no idea what was inside. But he said firmly that no one without a special Apple badge was allowed anywhere near it. Another guard just sternly shook his head when approached.

In addition, there was a large, metal box on wheels at the corner of Apple's display area. The box, which appeared to be designed for air freight, was also watched over by a uniformed guard. It was adorned with a prominent red sticker that read, "Apple Booth: Secret."

Despite some Apple employees from America milling around, I was able to snap a picture by hiding behind a stack of iMac boxes. I got some suspicious glances from the Apple employees, but that was the only sign of security at Macworld Tokyo. Apart from the secret booths, the entire show floor was more or less freely accessible, and so was a lot of expensive equipment scattered about. I was able to freely wander the show floor on the eve of the conference by simply saying "Press."

The booths turned out to contain new iPods, which Steve Jobs introduced in the show's opening keynote speech.

JOBS' POTTY MOUTH

In public, Steve Jobs comes across as sophisticated and urbane. So it's something of a relief to know that, in private, he swears like a sailor.

At a big meeting of Apple's resellers at the Macworld Expo in 2001, Apple's CEO Steve Jobs unexpectedly dropped in. According to those in attendance, the "great man" gave a short talk and then took questions from the floor for more than an hour. The resellers—a bunch of no-nonsense business types—were impressed by his candor.

Jobs gave frank and honest answers to tough questions in this time of trouble for the company and its partners, they said. They were also impressed by his incredible potty mouth. Every sentence he uttered—every single one—contained an expletive.

"I was surprised," said one reseller, who asked not to be named. "He wasn't like he was during his keynotes."

No One Gets In Without a Badge

Everyone needs a badge to get into Macworld, even Steve Jobs. At one show in New York, right after delivering the opening keynote speech, Steve Jobs was collared by a security guard for trying to get onto the main show floor without a badge. Naturally, Jobs tried to explain who he was.

"I don't give a damn who you are," replied the sassy New Yorker. "No one gets in without a badge."

After some discussion with his group, which included the singer and dancer Gregory Hines, and an unsuccessful attempt to sneak by the guard, Jobs was forced to retreat and borrow a lackey's badge. He stayed only a minute or two before leaving for his flight back to California. Meanwhile, the guard got a rocket from unhappy superiors, or so the story goes.

GOING THE DISTANCE TO GET TO MACWORLD

For three years in a row, Randy Nauert attended Macworld with his dog, but had trouble finding a hotel that will allow the animal to stay in his room. So Nauert, who's had a colorful and varied career in the music and film industries, slept in his car with the dog.

Nauert, 57, drives up to San Francisco from his ranch in Malibu, pays for an expensive hotel room, and parks in the hotel lot. He uses the room to take a shower and go to the bathroom, but he spends the night in the car. "I can't leave her anywhere," he explained about the dog, a 3-year-old Weimaraner called Valentina. "I've tried all kinds of different things. I've tried leaving her with the neighbors, but she just howls." During the day, while he tools around at Macworld, Valentina stays in the car. She's quite happy, Nauert said.

Nauert is a part-time Macintosh consultant, offering computer advice to his friends in the music and film industries, some of whom are pretty famous (Mark Hamill, Daryl Hannah), but he's never sent them a bill, he said. He's also active in the Camarillo/Ventura Macintosh User Group and friendly with some Apple executives.

ONE MAN AND HIS DOG: MUSICIAN RANDY NAUERT BRINGS HIS DOG, VALENTINA, TO MACWORLD EVERY YEAR AND SLEEPS WITH HER IN HIS CAR. MOST HOTELS DON'T ALLOW DOGS.
CREDIT: LEANDER KAHNEY

116

MATT CARLSON, NATHAN KLINE, and TIFFANY THOMPSON (pictured left to right) took the train up from BAKERSFIELD to attend MACWORLD for a few days. Kline helps run Bungie.org, a fan site devoted to Bungie, the veteran MAC game company. Kline is working on a project based on an open source version of Marathon, a creaky old first-person shooter that's getting very long in the tooth. "It's still hopping," insisted Kline about the Marathon community. "There's a lot of cool stuff going on."

On Wednesday, PABLO PAVIA walked onto the MACWORLD show floor without a pass. "I was just passing by yesterday and I wandered in no problem," said the freelance artist. But on Thursday, the floor guards stopped him and turned him away. "I guess you need a pass to get in," he said, shrugging his shoulders. "I just bought a computer, a MAC. That's why I was drawn to this. Oh well."

Nauert got his start in the music business as a member of The Challengers, the surf group that helped popularize such hits as "Wipe Out." The band went through various incarnations, eventually recording 28 albums under different names and recording contracts. Nauert said he met Ravi Shankar, the famous sitar player, and was invited to India, where he spent time with George Harrison.

Returning to the United States, Nauert reentered the music business as a manager and music publisher, becoming involved, he claimed, in the careers of some of the era's most famous artists, including Bob Dylan, Jimi Hendrix, Janis Joplin, The Band, Peter, Paul & Mary, the Beach Boys, and the Rolling Stones, among many others.

He also worked in film, he said, acting as associate producer of the 1985 Oscar-winning documentary, *Broken Rainbow*, and as music supervisor for an Antonioni film, *Zabriskie Point*. Meanwhile, he built a handful of houses in Malibu, including the one where he now lives. "The damn house is nothing but gold records on the walls," said John Bass, an editor at CNN's Los Angeles bureau who has known Nauert for 20 years. "His picture is on the freakin' cover of Sergeant Pepper's Lonely Hearts Club Band."

These days, in addition to serving as a free consultant to the stars, Nauert is the unofficial U.S. manager of the German rock band The Scorpions, but he spends most of his time hanging out at his Malibu ranch. "So what exactly do you do for a living?" his Web site asks. "Nothing, exactly. But I do follow 'the inspiration' and have been able to survive and enjoy life."

In 2003 he devised a new plan for bringing his dog to the show. He's put Valentina in a harness that identifies her as a service dog. Under the law, Valentina is supposed to be allowed anywhere her owner goes, including hotel rooms.

Nauert booked into a fancy hotel, and was told the dog would be no problem as long as he had some paperwork (which he didn't have). Luckily, the hotel accepted the sheaf of Internet printouts Nauert made explaining the law.

Nauert and Valentina volunteer for arson watch in Malibu's fire-prone canyons, which is how Nauert got the harness. He refuses to wear dark glasses to make him look blind, or pull any other kind of deception. "I shouldn't need to make an excuse," he said. "She's a service dog. She needs to be with her trainer."

Perhaps the farthest-flung Macworld attendee is Raena Armitage, a self-confessed "Mac geek" who flew halfway around the globe from Tasmania to attend the show.

Armitage, a 22-year-old computer technician for an Australian government–sponsored scientific research center, is also visiting

her cyberboyfriend, Dan Miller, a 31-year-old photojournalist who lives in Ohio. But instead of spending her two-week visit in Miller's hometown of Sandusky, Ohio, the couple decided to cover Macworld for the Mac Observer, a Mac-oriented news site. The couple met and have been "dating" for about 18 months through the site's forums. Miller flew out to visit Armitage in Tasmania last June.

"I'm really, really happy to be here and see so many Mac geeks together," Armitage said of Macworld. "We just don't have them [in Tasmania]. I can count them all on the fingers of one hand. All my geek friends are PC geeks."

"I'm glad [her friends use PCs]," chimed in Miller. "She wouldn't have spent so much time on the Mac Observer."

Macs are the couple's "common language," Armitage said. "We do different things; we live in different countries," she added. "This is the first thing we have to share."

According to IDG World Expo, which organizes Macworld, the show attracts visitors from 70 to 100 different countries. "The majority are from the U.S.," a spokesperson said, "but we have some really interesting visitors from far-flung places."

MACS IN JAPAN

「古い」と「新しい」

TOGETHER: USER GROUPS ARE VERY POPULAR IN JAPAN, A REFLECTION ON THE JAPANESE GROUP ETHIC. **CREDIT: UNKNOWN**

OLD AND NEW: HIROKAZU KUWATA'S BEAUTIFULLY CUSTOMIZED POWERBOOK G4 TITANIUM EPITO-MIZES MAC CULTURE IN JAPAN—THE SEAMLESS BLEND OF CUTTING-EDGE TECHNOLOGY WITH TRADITIONAL HANDICRAFT IN JAPAN—THE SEAMLESS BLEND OF CUTTING-EDGE TECHNOLOGY WITH TRADITIONAL HANDICRAFT. **CREDIT: HIROKAZU KUWATA**

MAC LOVE: JAPANESE STYLE

If you thought U.S. and European Mac users were nuts about their Macs, they're nothing compared to the Japanese. Japanese Mac users are absolutely bonkers about their machines. The most obsessed are known as "Mac otaku," a term taken from fans of Japan's sexually explicit, hyper-violent manga comics. An *otaku* is a fanatic who knows every detail of their adopted hobby. Roughly translated: a geek.

Take, for example, Mitsuaki Ohashi, a self-confessed Mac otaku who has created dozens of dinky replicas of most Apple's more recent machines out of paper. He has modeled all the flavors of the iMac, including the flat-screen iMac, and dozens of desktops and portables. (See Chapter 13, "Paper Macs.")

Making paper Macs is just one of the unique twists of Japanese Mac culture. Japanese Mac users are also generally more technical than U.S. Mac users, and there's a strong hacker ethic that seems to have largely disappeared from the U.S. and European Mac scenes.

User groups are also important in Japan. Japanese culture encourages many activities to be conducted in groups. It's considered weird, for example, to take a solo vacation. Hence, there are all kinds of clubs, including regional user groups and groups devoted to particular machines or technologies.

Japan is Apple's second-largest market outside the United States. Apple's market share in Japan is similar to in the U.S.: Apple had a 3.2 percent share of the total Japanese PC market in 2001, and it is the tenth largest computer manufacturer in Japan. Apple is particularly strong in consumer and graphic arts–related markets: DTP, design, and music. Apple has a 5.1 percent share of the home market, according to IDC Japan. In one strange quirk, Macs are particularly popular with doctors, who imported a lot of the machines in the late 1980s after seeing them at international medical conferences, according to Nobuyuki Hayashi, a freelance writer for Japanese Mac magazines.

As in the U.S., the Macworld trade show is the big gathering of Apple fans. In fact, the Tokyo Macworld trade show is the biggest gathering of Mac fans in the world. Held at the ultramodern "Big Sight" International Convention Center, the show attracts more than 180,000 Japanese Macintosh users. Attendance is almost double the U.S. Macworld Expos in San Francisco and New York.

Design is also important to Japanese Mac users, something that Apple excels at. There's a word in Japanese that describes something never done before, something totally new and totally amazing: kakkiteki. According to the dictionary definition, the word literally means "epoch making," but it's a common term often applied to new products or things like Hollywood's special effects. *Terminator 2* was described as kakkiteki. Apple's flat-screen iMac is also kakkiteki. With its flat screen and rounded base, the Japanese think it is truly epoch making; computers will never be the same again.

Thanks to the kakkiteki factor, the flat-panel iMac is attracting more Japanese women to the platform, according to reports. Manami Shimomura, a 30-something piano teacher from Kyoto, told MacDirectory that the iMac greatly appealed to style-conscious women computer buyers. "After the iMac arrived, so many girls started appearing in the computer shopping district," she told the magazine. "The iMac was so cute!"

Japanese Mac users know the specs of all the machines and love to take them apart. Trouble is, messing with the innards voids a machine's warranty. So average users leave their Macs alone and have the computer magazines do it for them. There are six or seven Japanese Macintosh magazines on the market, and every review of every product includes a detailed breakdown of the product's internal components. There is almost always a detailed set of photos documenting the innards of a piece of dismantled hardware.

A recent edition of the popular *Mac Power* features a review of the flat-panel iMac featuring six pages of glossy, full-color photographs of its internal components, including a detailed map of the machine's circular motherboard. "Every Mac that comes out, we take apart," said Nobuyuki Hayashi, a veteran freelance writer for many Japanese Mac magazines. "In Japan, a review of a Macintosh isn't complete until we break it apart." Even a review of the PowerMate—a simple volume knob—includes pictures of its internal components. It doesn't happen with PC magazines, Hayashi said. There are so many different components and configurations, the exercise is meaningless.

Mac Power employs three full-time writers just to analyze the internal components of products that cross the review department's desk, Hayashi said. "Japanese and German Mac users all want to know what's inside the machine," he said. "They all

want to open it up and touch the motherboard. But they don't want to open up their own machine because of the warranty."

MACWORLD TOKYO

Before it was canceled in 2002, Macworld Tokyo was the biggest Macintosh convention in the world, with almost double the attendees of the U.S. Macworld Expos in New York and San Francisco.

The show, which ran for 12 years, regularly drew in excess of 160,000 attendees. In 2001, Macworld Tokyo celebrated its biggest audience to date: 180,000 Macintosh fans turned out, largely because the show coincided with a national holiday.

Macworld Tokyo was held over three days in one of the cavernous halls at the ultramodern Big Sight International Convention Center, which is located on a reclaimed island in Tokyo Bay. The Big Sight center's architecture resembles one of the terraforming plants in the movie *Aliens*.

Although the number of visitors was double the U.S. shows, the number of exhibitors was about half. The conference drew the usual crowds of designers, artists, filmmakers, and musicians, and boy, did they look good. Contrary to Western cliché, dress-wise the Japanese are anything but conformist. There's a vast array of different street styles, and the crowd drawn to Macworld was young and hip.

Whereas Macworld San Francisco is geeky, and New York a little less so, Macworld Tokyo was full of well-dressed, well-groomed, style-conscious young people. Sometimes it looked more like a rave or a fashion show than a computer convention. There was a nerd factor, of course, but the dominant look was cool. Tokyo's ubiquitous salarymen and office ladies were sparsely represented.

たくさんの人たち

[TOP] PACKING 'EM IN: MACWORLD TOKYO SURE ATTRACTS A CROWD. MORE THAN 180,000 MAC FANS VISIT THE SHOW OVER THE THREE DAYS.

CREDIT: LEANDER KAHNEY

[BOTTOM] ENGINEERING INGENUITY: KEN NAKAO, A JAPANESE DESIGNER, MADE HIS "HALLI MAC" BY INSTALLING THE GUTS OF AN IBOOK INSIDE A HIGH-END ALUMINUM TRAVEL CASE FROM ZERO HALLIBURTON, A U.S. CASE MANUFACTURER. THE EXTERIOR LOOKS LIKE A PHOTOGRAPHER'S CASE, BUT FLIP THE LID, AND A FULLY FUNCTIONING IBOOK IS REVEALED. NAKAO'S HALLI MAC IS EXTREMELY WELL MADE. THE MELDING OF CASE AND COMPUTER IS SEAMLESS. THE CD TRAY POPS OUT OF THE SIDE, AND THE USB, ETHERNET, AND MODEM PORTS ARE CAREFULLY CUT OUT OF THE BACK. THE MACHINE SEEMS PERFECT FOR TRAVEL, RUGGED AND PORTABLE. IT EVEN INCLUDES A WIRELESS AIRPORT CARD.

CREDIT: KEN NAKAO

124

TRENDY TOKYO: MACWORLD TOKYO ATTRACTS A HIP, GOOD-LOOKING BUNCH OF MAC USERS. THE SHOW'S NOT AS NERDY AS MACWORLD IN SAN FRANCISCO.

CREDIT: LEANDER KAHNEY

流行を行く

For the past few years, Apple CEO Steve Jobs delivered the opening keynote address at Macworld Tokyo. Major new products were not usually announced at the show—that's reserved for the U.S. Macworlds—so Mac fans were mostly curious about whether or not Jobs would wear a suit. In 2000, Jobs dispensed with his trademark jeans and black turtleneck for business attire. It was a change of habit that made more of an impression than the Blue Dalmatian and Flower Power iMacs he introduced.

Jobs picked an auspicious time to come to Tokyo in 2001. The Expo coincided with one of the biggest and happiest festivals in the Japanese calendar: hanami, the festival of "looking at the flowers." The festival changes its date every year, occurring on different dates in different regions, depending on when the cherry blossoms bloom. For weeks before the festival, Japanese meteorologists include a blossom report on the evening weather forecast to help people plan for hanami.

Thanks to unseasonably warm weather, Tokyo's famous cherry blossoms bloomed early, just in time for the Expo. The vast, ultramodern megacity was awash with delicate pink flowers. Many shops and restaurants were decorated with sprigs of fake blossoms made from silk. During the festival, most of Tokyo takes to the city's parks with a blanket, a picnic basket, and lots of beer and sake. Sitting under the blossoms with a group of friends, people tend to get a little drunk and sing karaoke.

Because of hanami, the opening day of Macworld Tokyo was particularly well attended. However, the response to Steve Jobs' keynote speech was surprisingly frosty. Sitting as impassively as Easter Island statues, the audience—maybe 6,000 people—was stonily unmoved by demonstrations of magical technology like Bluetooth or amusing iMac TV advertisements. By contrast, U.S. audiences are riotous, clapping, cheering, and wolf-whistling at regular intervals.

However, most of the audience listened to a translation of Jobs' speech through wireless headphones, and there was a lag. Had they applauded, they would have interrupted Jobs, which would have been impolite. When Jobs shared the stage with a couple of Japanese CEOs talking about their products in Japanese, the audience sprang to life, laughing and applauding.

Jobs motored on, oblivious. Had he paused occasionally, the audience could have shown its appreciation. The same phenomenon is demonstrated every day on Tokyo's roadways. Even though everyone drives like a New Yorker, there's no honking of horns. It's considered bad manners.

Inside the exhibition hall, the show was much like its U.S. counterparts. The hall was divided into booths staffed by a large number of glamorous "campaign ladies": hired models and aspiring actresses who spend most of their time posing for photographs.

CAMPAIGN LADIES: TO ATTRACT WANDERING MALES TO THEIR BOOTHS, MOST MACWORLD EXHIBITORS HIRE A CONTINGENT OF GLAMOROUS "CAMPAIGN LADIES"—THE JAPANESE EQUIVALENT OF "BOOTH BABES," A DENIGRATING TERM APPLIED TO HIRED FEMALE GLAMOUR AT U.S. TRADE SHOWS. HOWEVER, CAMPAIGN LADIES ARE FAR MORE COMMON IN JAPAN—ALMOST EVERY BOOTH HAS ONE OR TWO. CAMPAIGN LADIES ARE RECRUITED BY TALENT SCOUTS WHO SCOUR THE STREETS AND SUBWAYS FOR TALENT. IT'S A MINI-INDUSTRY IN JAPAN. CAMPAIGN LADIES HAND OUT FLYERS, GIVE AWAY FREEBIES, AND ENCOURAGE PEOPLE TO SIGN UP FOR PRODUCT LITERATURE. BUT MOSTLY THEY POSE FOR THE CAMERAS—OFTEN THREE OR FOUR AT THE SAME TIME.

CREDIT: LEANDER KAHNEY

綺麗なモデル

127

人気のマック

MMUJ: THE MOBILE MAC
A POPULAR USER GROUP.
MACWORLD TO SHOW OFF THEIR MATCHING T-SHIRTS.
USERS OF JAPAN IS
MEMBERS GATHER AT
CREDIT:UNKNOWN

POPULAR/UNPOPULAR: AT MACWORLD TOKYO, THE USER GROUP
PAVILION WAS ONE OF THE MOST POPULAR ASPECTS OF THE SHOW.
WHEN THE EXPO'S DOORS WERE FIRST OPENED, MOST ATTENDEES
RUSHED TO THE USER GROUP PAVILION, TUCKED AWAY IN A
FAR-FLUNG CORNER OF THE EXHIBIT HALL, LEAVING CORPORATE
BOOTHS—LIKE MICROSOFT'S AT RIGHT—NEARLY EMPTY.
CREDIT: LEANDER KAHNEY

A small number of Macworld Tokyo attendees preferred to be squired around the show floor as a group rather than wander around on their own. Catering to this crowd, iTours offered a guided group tour of the Expo every hour or so. The tour leader held aloft a cardboard sign on a pole. Every time the group came to a booth with something to give away—a pen, a T-shirt, a baseball cap—the group played rock, paper, scissors to see who got it. Everyone gathered around to play the tour leader. Whoever beat him got to play the others until the winner was chosen. It was a small group, so the winner was usually selected within a couple of rounds.

At the back of the hall, Rochambeau was played all day. Fifty to 60 people gathered around while an announcer on stage yelled into a microphone. A couple of helpers added to the cacophony, while another took photographs. Everyone played the guy on stage. At his command, everyone held up their hand—fist clenched or flat, or fingers extended—and then fell about laughing. It didn't take long to whittle the crowd down to two, who played off on stage. The announcer carried on like a game-show host, whipping everyone into a frenzy. The winner, who chose rock over scissors, won a PlayStation 2 game system. Before leaving the stage, the winner bowed deeply and posed for a picture taken by the camera-toting helper.

The show finished at 6 p.m. every day. There were a couple of announcements over the PA system, but to make sure everyone got the message, "Auld Lang Syne" was piped over the sound system.

USER GROUPS AND UPGRADE CLUBS

Everyone has seen Japanese tourists herded around foreign landmarks in groups. So strong is the collective ethic, it is unusual—and considered weird—for people to shun organized group activities. So it should be no surprise that Mac user groups are very popular in Japan. There are 114 Mac user groups registered with Apple Japan, and probably another 30 unregistered groups. Many have hundreds of members; some have thousands.

Some user groups are organized by geography, such as MacTokyo, the Hokkaido Macintosh User Group, and the Kinki Macintosh User Group, which is based in Kobe and Osaka. Others are virtual: members meet on electronic bulletin boards or Web sites dedicated to Mac news and chat. A lot of user groups focus on a particular technology or product, like HyperCard Park, the QuickTime Users Group, and the iMac User Group. Some of the most dedicated groups are devoted to mobile technology, such as the PowerBook Army, the PowerBook Owners' Club, and the Newton Japan User Group.

The PowerBook Army is more of a Web publishing ring than a user group. Members run a popular mailing list, and the group's central Web site, http://www.powerbook.org, is a jumping-off point for specialist sites run by the PowerBook Army's "officers."

Of the 50 or so people who maintain Web sites devoted to PowerBooks, many are specialists in different, often narrow, niches. One is expert in maintenance issues, like mending hinges; another focuses on upgrading old machines with new chips; another is an expert in customizing keyboards.

MobileDog, a Web site run by Yuko Tanaka, a former Canon engineer, concentrates on upgrading PowerBooks. Tanaka's site is full of technical information, schematics, and instructions on taking the machines apart, all of which she figured out herself with a volt meter and soldering iron. Her site is reputedly the best place to find out how to upgrade the 2400's processor, a tricky operation. "It's very hard to do this. It requires special skill," she said.

The PowerBook Army reveals the strong hacker ethic of Japanese Mac users. Japanese Mac users tend to be very technical and hands on, unafraid to dismantle machines and break out the soldering iron, and capable of figuring out for themselves the problems Apple ignores or buries. They are also happy to help each other. Everyone chips in their expertise for the group's benefit, freely sharing knowledge and assistance.

Customizing machines is popular in Japan. It is partly driven by the desire to make mass-produced products more personal, and it is also a way to stand out from the crowd. Like Tokyo street fashion, computer customizations can be extremely varied. "Most people dye their hair, especially women," said Francis Boisvert, an expatriate American and founder of MacTokyo, an English-language Mac user group. "They want brown or blonde or orange—anything except black. The same is true of their computers. People are concerned with distinguishing their machines as much as their appearance."

As well as making them look good, Japanese Mac users like to hold on to their machines. Unlike their U.S. counterparts, they don't trade in their computers every couple of years. Rather, they upgrade them with newer components and faster chips.

Sonnet Technologies (http://www.sonnettech.com/default.html), an accelerator manufacturer, sells about two dozen different upgrades for scores of machines dating back more than a decade. In the U.S., the company's most popular product is an upgrade for the first generation iMac, which is only a few years old. But in Japan, the company's second biggest market outside the U.S., Sonnet still sells a lot of upgrades for the Mac Classics, the LC line, and other dinosaurs.

"It's funny. It's totally different here," said Vicki Burkhard, Sonnet's vice president of international sales. "Most of these products are sold in Japan. Hardly any are sold in the United States. We sell maybe 50 a month. Japanese people have to take their computers apart and play with the insides. It's part of the hobby." Sonnet will query mailing lists for particular machines to see if there's enough interest to justify making a particular accelerator. Even a modest response, such as a few hundred dedicated users, is usually enough for Sonnet to release a product.

There are dozens of clubs devoted to upgrading these older machines. For example, there is the Club for Creating the Strongest Color Classic (see Chapter 15, "Antique Macs"), the Strongest 6100 Owners' Club (http://the6100.pos.to/), and the PowerBook 150 Fan Club (http://www.powerbook.org/pb150/). A lot of these clubs are competitive; members playfully vie to see who can create the "strongest"—or most powerful—model of a certain machine through upgrades and hardware modifications. The Strongest 6100 Owners' Club is one of the most singular of these clubs. It boasts an incredible 2,200 members.

The Power Mac 6100 was one of the first Power Macs, an entry-level 66 MHz machine introduced in 1994. It did, however, have a slim "pizza box" case, which makes it attractive to Japanese users, who are obsessed with diminutive computers. Members of the Strongest 6100 Owners' Club have figured out how to improve the cooling system, install better video cards, and upgrade the processor with fast G3 and G4 chips. One fanatic upgraded his 6100 to a G3 and painted it silver (http://www.success1.co.jp/61seal/).

"The proportion of these maniacs is higher than those in the U.S.," said writer Hiroo Yamagata. "But there's a good amount of humor in all this. It's just to see how far they could push the thing. The 6100 club is, to an extent, a half-joke, half-serious project. It's fun, trying to figure out how to extract the maximum amount of life out of a machine."

IN JAPAN, UPGRADING BEATS BUYING

The Japanese love to consume as much as Americans, but they're not as keen on disposing of obsolete Macs. They love their Macs, and some people just keep upgrading old ones. Really old ones.

The Japanese have a deep and abiding love for well-made objects. If something is well made, it will be taken care of until it wears out. Taking this principle to the extreme, Nonki, a 29-year-old soldier, has gone to great lengths to keep his beloved PowerBook 550c contemporary, even though it's woefully obsolete.

Launched in 1995, the PowerBook 550c was sold only in Japan. It came with a 33 MHz processor, 8MB of RAM and a 750MB hard drive. By today's standards, the machine is painfully slow and too limited to do anything useful. However, thanks to countless hours of tinkering and about $1,000 in upgrade parts, Nonki's machine is almost as serviceable as a modern laptop.

Nonki has upgraded his machine with a 163 MHz chip, 40MB of RAM, and a whopping 48GB hard drive. He has a wireless modem in the PC Card slot that provides always-on, fast Internet access for $50 a month. "This is the first computer I owned, and it is still my main machine," he said through a translator. "I've been using it for seven years now."

Nonki belongs to the BlackBird Club, a group of about 700 fans of the PowerBook 550c and the PowerBook 540, the American equivalent. Polite and shy, Nonki declined to give his full name, just his nickname. He was, however, very keen to show off the innards of his machine. Fiddling furiously, he dropped some of the delicate components on the floor. He was urged not to go to the trouble, but the interpreter said it didn't matter to him; he liked taking it apart.

The hard drive—a modern IBM drive—had a special circuit board strapped to it to convert the IDE interface to Apple's old standard, SCSI. Nonki also showed how he had replaced the LCD and a bunch of other parts. He has another machine just for

進化するマック

TINKERER: NOTHING CAN STOP NONKI FROM TAKING HIS MACHINE APART TO SHOW PEOPLE HOW HE HAS UPGRADED IT. HIS HOMEMADE BATTERY PACK CAN BE SEEN AT RIGHT, HANG-ING OFF THE BACK OF THE MACHINE. HIS MUM SEWED A SPECIAL POUCH TO HOLD IT.
CREDIT: LEANDER KAHNEY

BEER SERVER: THE BEER SERVER WAS A BIG DRAW AT MACWORLD TOKYO, ATTRACTING CROWDS OF GRINNING SHOW ATTENDEES. MADE BY SOMEONE FROM A MAC USER GROUP, THE SERVER IS CONSTRUCTED OUT OF A BLUE AND WHITE G3 TOWER, A BEER TAP, A CANISTER OF CARBON DIOXIDE, AND A BIG CAN OF ASAHI BEER.
CREDIT: LEANDER KAHNEY

UPGRADER: NONKI, A 29-YEAR-OLD SOLDIER, HAS GONE TO GREAT LENGTHS TO KEEP HIS BELOVED POWERBOOK 550C CONTEMPORARY, EVEN THOUGH IT'S WOEFULLY OBSOLETE.
CREDIT: LEANDER KAHNEY

parts, he said. He has decorated the sides of the machine with strips of decorative red-and-white checkered paper.

The biggest problem Nonki faces is the machine's limited battery life. It's impossible to get good batteries for the 550c these days, so he has rigged up an external battery pack. The homemade pack has a dozen rechargeable AA batteries strung in two lines inside a transparent plastic tube. The pack hangs below the computer in a red cloth sleeve sewed by his mother. The cloth sling slides over and around the keyboard, and the battery attaches by a pair of wires to the AC power jack in the back. The wires are held in place by scotch tape. Even with this elaborate setup, battery life is still only about an hour—two if he's lucky.

Why doesn't he just get a new computer? "I like the beauty of it and the functionality," he said, smiling, knowing he sounded slightly crazy. "I like the slope of the keyboard—it's ergonomic—and the speakers on the top of the screen." Besides, he's waiting for a portable with a really big screen—at least 16 or 17 inches, a wish Steve Jobs granted in 2003, with the world's first widescreen notebook — a PowerBook with a 17-inch screen.

THE UNDYING DEVOTION TO THE POWERBOOK 2400

An old Apple laptop that didn't sell well when it was released in Japan a few years ago has subsequently achieved cult status, with fans paying up to $25,000 to upgrade and decorate their aging machines. Launched in 1997, the PowerBook 2400 was a small light subnotebook designed especially for the Japanese market, although it was later also sold in the U.S. At the time, the 2400 was praised for its power, size, and good looks. It was small—it weighed only 4.4 lb.—but performed like larger, fullsized laptops weighing twice as much. And it looked good; fans

liked its smooth, black curves. But the machine was expensive, $3,500, which put off a lot of Japanese buyers.

Since then, the 2400 has become a hot ticket. Used machines, if they can be found, go for more than $1,000. Even broken machines command more than $800. In the U.S., they sell for about $200 to $300. Fans go to great lengths to upgrade their machines with more memory and newer processors. They also spend a small fortune decorating their laptops with colored or transparent cases, or custom Yuzen designs (found at http://member.nifty.ne.jp/crystal/profile.html), a style used in traditional Japanese kimonos.

"The 2400 people are crazy," said Nobuyuki Hayashi, a freelance writer for Japanese Mac magazines. "Japanese people tend to extend the life of their machines because they love them so much. Instead of buying a new machine, they want to extend the life of their old machine. And people spend thousands of dollars to modify their machines."

Demonstrating the attachment to the machine, one of its most influential fans, Naritomo Mizutani, wrote a lot of articles about the PowerBook 2400. He is so enamored with the machine's design, he created an entire Web site about the "bottom of the machine." It was Mizutani's contention that the 2400 was more beautiful because its entire case had been carefully designed, not just the parts that most people see. To prove his point, he created a Web page with pictures of the underside of the 2400, which he compared to the undersides of about 100 other laptops, in particular Windows machines (http://www.powerbook.org/2400/ura/adult.html). "He was trying to prove the Apple was more beautiful because it used less screws and stickers and panels," Hayashi said.

There are dozens of other fan sites devoted to the machine, as well as user groups with hundreds of members. In 1999, about

250 PowerBook 2400 fans gathered at Macworld Tokyo for a group picture.

There have also been a number of books published in Japan about the 2400, detailing every aspect of maintaining, repairing, upgrading, and modifying the machines (http://www.powerbook.org/book/). According to Francis Boisvert, founder of MacTokyo (http://www.mactokyo.com/), an English-language Mac user group, people will spend up to $25,000 to customize their machines. Boisvert said transparent cases are a popular option. Each part has to be made individually, often by denture manufacturers, who have expertise in creating custom-molded, transparent plastics. "They'll spend $10,000 on see-through keyboards, battery covers, lids, or other parts," he said. "A lot of people do it one piece at a time. It can add up to $25,000 easy." To save money, groups of 40 or so PowerBook owners will band together to get volume discounts.

Hayashi said Japanese fans like the 2400 because it was designed for them. "It has a special place in their hearts," he said.

One of the reasons the 2400 has continued to be popular is the lack of a replacement. Until the small white, dual USB iBook came along, many 2400 owners couldn't find an Apple machine small enough for their tastes. Even the early "toilet seat" iBook was too big for Japanese users.

The 2400 was the idea of former Apple CEO Gil Amelio, who, realizing that Japan was the second-biggest market for Apple, dispatched a team of engineers to Japan to develop something special. After riding on Tokyo's crowded commuter trains every day, they came up with the small, lightweight machine. "It didn't sell well because it was expensive," Hayashi said, "but people who bought one are crazy for it."

"The PowerBook 2400 was the turning point for Japanese Mac culture," Hayashi continued. "Many users saw it as the first Mac made for Japanese people. They went crazy for it. They started the culture of tuning up their machines and decorating their machines."

KAIZO

A traditional kimono maker living in Japan's ancient city of Kyoto runs a sideline business painting PowerBooks with intricate kimono designs. Yuho Hayashi is a master craftsman, an expert of the Yuzen style of kimono design, a technique of dyeing and painting silk dating from the 17th century.

Hayashi, a favorite with Mac owners who want to customize their machines, will paint a traditional Yuzen design on the lid of a PowerBook for about $300. He uses real gold dust suspended in paint, gold leaf, and little strips of decorative paper lacquered onto the lid. To drum up business, Hayashi has exhibited at Macworld Tokyo, and he's done a roaring trade: dozens of examples of his work can be found on his Web site.

It's rare for the 50-year-old kimono maker to work on Windows PCs—there just isn't the interest. But he has decorated a lot of Palm and Sharp organizers, cell phones, and, occasionally, a PlayStation game console. He charges about $100 to paint the lid of a Palm.

Hayashi's customizations are just one of the many ways Japanese Mac users like to decorate their machines—customizations range from painting the lids of laptops to replacing the entire shell with custom-made transparent plastic. The Japanese word for it is *kaizo*, which means "modifying," "upgrading," or "remodeling." A thriving market exists in Japan for after-market kaizo mods. Many Mac computer stores sell items like thin metal skins for reupholstering a PowerBook's cover with funky zebra stripes or austere brushed aluminum.

CLASS PICTURE: IN 1999, HUNDREDS OF POWERBOOK
2400 OWNERS GATHERED AT MACWORLD TOKYO
TO HAVE COMPUTERS POSE IN A CLASS PHOTO.
CREDIT: MOBILE MAC USERS JAPAN

POWERBOOK LOVERS: DEVOTEES OF
THE POWERBOOK 2400, WHICH APPLE
MADE SPECIFICALLY FOR THE JAPANESE
MARKET, GATHER FOR A GROUP PICTURE
AT MACWORLD TOKYO.
CREDIT: MOBILE MAC USERS JAPAN

ANOTHER VIEW OF THE POWERBOOK
CLASS PHOTO, AS A 3D PANORAMA.
CREDIT: MOBILE MAC USERS JAPAN

綺麗

KIMONO TO GO: A HAYASHI DESIGN ON THE LID OF A PALM COSTS ABOUT $100. **CREDIT: LEANDER KAHNEY**

KIMONO COMPUTERS: SOME OF THE BEAUTIFUL TRADITIONAL KIMONO DESIGNS PAINTED ON THE LIDS OF POWERBOOKS BY MASTER CRAFTSMAN YUHO HAYASHI. **CREDIT: YUHO HAYASHI**

Keita Suyama is a prolific Macintosh "modder." The 32-year-old has customized a half-dozen machines, including his flat-panel iMac, which he painted black. The process required entirely disassembling the machine, stripping the white paint from the inside of its plastic shell, and painting it black. Trouble is, it didn't work. When he put the machine back together, it wouldn't start up. Having grossly violated his warranty, and unable to buy spare parts, Suyama had to buy another iMac to cannibalize.

In the hope of encouraging others to paint their own iMacs, Suyama documented the entire operation on his Web site with dozens of step-by-step photos. In fact, the Web site for his family business, a dental lab in Tokyo, is dominated by Macintosh news and instructions for taking apart computers.

So dedicated is Suyama, he has employed soundproof chambers, heat-sensitive cameras, and other scientific instruments in his search for the perfect mod. For example, he took a picture of a new iBook with a thermographic camera at a friend's dental lab. The photograph helped him design an external cooling fan that he added to the machine. To measure precisely the noise coming from the iMac's fan, he rented a soundproof chamber.

Suyama has at least nine Macs in his tiny bedroom in Tokyo, including a Color Classic, a couple of iMacs, and a 20th Anniversary Mac, all of which he has taken apart and tinkered with. The question is, why bother?

"Tough question to answer," he wrote in halting English. "I am interested in the structure of a computer. If a new product is released, I will decompose a model." He said he likes to take machines apart and look for new ways to customize them.

素晴らしい コンピューター

WHERE TO SLEEP? KEITA SUYAMA'S BEDROOM IS SO FULL OF APPLE HARDWARE, THERE'S BARELY ROOM FOR HIS BED. **CREDIT: KEITA SUYAMA**

MAD MAC MODDER: IN HIS QUEST FOR THE PERFECT MAC MOD, KEITA SUYAMA HAS EMPLOYED THERMOGRAPHIC CAMERAS, SOUNDPROOF CHAMBERS, AND SCIENTIFIC THERMOMETERS. **CREDIT: KEITA SUYAMA**

PAINT IT BLACK: DENTAL TECHNICIAN KEITA SUYAMA IS CONSUMED WITH A PASSION TO MODIFY MACS. HIS ATTEMPT TO PAINT HIS IMAC BLACK DIDN'T WORK THE FIRST TIME, SO HE WENT OUT AND BOUGHT ANOTHER, WHICH HE IMMEDIATELY PAINTED BLACK. **CREDIT: KEITA SUYAMA**

138

とても輝いている

POWERMATE: VOLUME CONTROL KNOB TURNS HEADS

Who but a jewelry designer could have created a computer peripheral that appears to be almost useless but became a hit based on its good looks? Takahiko Suzuki, a jewelry designer from the industrial city of Nagano, Japan, designed the PowerMate, a volume control for computers. The PowerMate is sold by Griffin Technology, a company based in Nashville, Tennessee, for about $40, which sounds like a lot for a simple volume control. But people are snapping it up. In the first three months, 10,000 PowerMates were sold. At first, Griffin couldn't make enough to keep up with demand, the company said.

Made of brushed aluminum, the PowerMate looks like a large volume knob from a regular stereo, but it sits on a desktop instead. The silver metal knob attaches to a USB port of any Mac or Windows PC. Turning it adjusts the computer's volume; tapping it pauses or plays the music. Around the knob's base is a ring of transparent plastic that glows blue. The light dims or brightens as the volume is adjusted. When the computer is idle, the light pulses.

It's the light at the base that attracts people, a stroke of genius suggested by Suzuki's wife, Naoko, a Web and graphics designer. In fact, it was his wife's constant requests for him to turn down the music on his computer that led Suzuki to design the PowerMate. "Touching the buttons on a computer does not agree with me very well," Suzuki said.

Thanks to clever software, the PowerMate is much more than just a volume control. It is actually a universal controller, capable of performing any command that has a keyboard equivalent, such as Control-S for Save. It can be used to close and open windows, forward or rewind audio, scroll up and down pages, or scan through movie files. It can be clicked to follow a hypertext link or double-clicked to launch an application. It can even be scripted to launch a chain of complex predefined actions. The software is fully configurable and automatically recognizes whatever application is being used, so that it can be set up to do different things in different programs.

For example, video editors use it as a jog wheel for editing video, and digital artists use it to change the size of brushes in applications such as Photoshop.

Paul Griffin, the company's founder, said initial sales were slow but grew exponentially on word of mouth. "People see it on someone's desk, glowing and pulsing, and they've got to know what it is," he said. "We get people saying, 'It's incredibly useless; I use it every day.'"

Griffin said he decided to market Suzuki's design after seeing a prototype in San Francisco. "I couldn't take my eyes off it," he said. "It was just compelling. We had to redesign it and we developed the software, but we kept all the metalwork. It's just beautiful."

Suzuki, who makes a line of techno jewelry and runs a three-person design company called Pro-tech Design, said the product is made in the tradition of his home city, Nagano. Famous for the 1998 Winter Olympics, Nagano became a center for precision engineering after World War II, specializing in watches, cameras, and computer components. Seiko and Epson are based there. "It's not like a plastic gadget," Suzuki said. "You can throw it against a wall. It's strong. You can use it for ten years. It will last."

Suzuki, who has long hair and fidgets a lot, said he is getting into mobile phones. He's designed a cell-phone clip that will attach phones to most surfaces, he said. He hopes to license it to a big manufacturer, like Sony-Ericsson. Suzuki said he is interested in universal design—products that are so simple they can be used by anyone without special training or even instructions. To illustrate, he pulled out a simple Casio calculator that he carries around. The calculator has ten buttons for the numbers and eight for the basic arithmetical functions. "Everyone can understand [how to use it]," he said, nodding his head vigorously with satisfaction. "Words are not necessary."

COMPUTER MAC KAN

Apart from Apple's headquarters in Cupertino, California, perhaps the only other Macintosh mecca on the planet is the giant Computer Mac Kan store in Tokyo's famed Akibahara "Electric Town" district. Visitors from around the world flock here to a 10-block neighborhood of electronics stores that is known as one of the biggest electronic shopping districts in the world.

Rising five stories, the Computer Mac Kan store is an Aladdin's cave of goodies that would make any Mac fanatic dizzy with excitement. The store stocks absolutely everything from the latest flat-screen iMacs and little iPod players to obscure flexible keyboard covers to keep the keys of a laptop clean. In between, there are entire floors devoted to books and magazines, software and games, monitors, and peripherals like printers and scanners. The store also stocks digital cameras, hardware upgrades, and a wide variety of doohickeys like corkboard place mats for the flat-screen iMac, or zebra-striped covers for customizing PowerBooks.

In the United States, there are also specialist Macintosh stores, and Apple is busy opening a string of boutiques in upscale malls. But for most Americans, shopping for Macintosh gear means venturing into a backwater corner of a giant computer mart like CompUSA. The display machines sometimes work and often don't, the staff is not always Mac-educated, and the stock on hand is often limited.

It's different at the Mac Kan store. There are more than 60 uniformed staff at any given time, and many speak English. Every few minutes somebody yells out "Irasshaimase" (pronounced era-shai-mah-say—meaning "welcome"), a Japanese retail custom that can have a disconcerting effect on people unaccustomed to it. A female staff member stands at the front door chirping "Irasshaimase" at everyone who comes through the door. Japanese shoppers simply ignore it.

The goods are beautifully displayed. The fully stocked shelves are neatly stacked. The computers on display are all carefully set up to show off their capabilities to maximum effect. One machine displays mind-bogglingly elaborate 3D models. Another is set up as a full-featured video-editing station, and another as a music workstation, complete with keyboards, mixers, and synthesizers. There's even a small theater with a dozen chairs where new software is demonstrated and seminars held. It's all very impressive.

The manager, Masanori Uchikawa, said more than 500 customers visit the store on weekdays, and between 700 and 1,000 on weekends. "This is the only store in Japan that can have the Apple logo displayed on the front," Uchikawa said through an interpreter. Asked if he feared Apple would encroach on his turf by opening an Apple store in Japan, he shook his head. "We would beat them if they opened a store here," he said, laughing.

The Akibahara district is the Las Vegas of electronic shopping: lots of lights, sound, and cigarette smoke. The stores range from gigantic to minuscule; some are literally holes in the wall. If it runs on electricity, it's sold here. The region claims to do more than 40 trillion yen in business annually.

Akibahara covers a square of about 10 city blocks. During the Edo period, it was home to low-status samurai, who were constantly fighting and burning it down. After a particularly destructive conflagration in 1869, a shrine to the God of Fire Protection was built, called Akiba-dai-gongen. The place soon became known as Akiba-hara, or Akiba-shrine.

After World War II, Akibahara became a black market for radio parts, thanks to an electrical engineering college nearby. American MPs regularly busted the illegal trade, but storekeepers simply retreated to a warren of passageways beneath nearby railway flyovers. Some of the original stalls still exist, but the area today is characterized by the neon-lit discount megastores. Akibahara features a number of duty-free stores where shoppers with foreign passports can buy tax-free goods.

Computer Mac Kan is one of the few stores in the area selling English-language versions of hardware and software. Most of the other stores sell only Japanese versions, and the clerks can't, or won't, speak English. Computer Mac Kan is run by Laox, a large chain of computer stores. It has a number of specialist megastores in Akibahara, including those devoted to just PCs and peripherals, networking gear, PDAs and games, and home appliances.

TEMPTING: EVERYTHING IS BEAUTIFULLY LAID OUT, THE STORE IS WELL STOCKED, AND THE STAFF IS EXTREMELY EAGER TO PLEASE. EXCEPT FOR THE CONSTANT YELLING OF "IRASSHAIMASE" (PRONOUNCED EAR-SHAI-MAH-SAY—"WELCOME"), COMPUTER MAC KAN IS A VERY ZEN PLACE TO VISIT.
CREDIT: LEANDER KAHNEY

MAC MECCA: THE COMPUTER MAC KAN STORE IS AN ALADDIN'S CAVE OF GOODIES THAT WOULD MAKE ANY MAC FANATIC DIZZY WITH EXCITEMENT.
CREDIT: LEANDER KAHNEY

THE VEGAS OF SHOPPING: TOKYO'S AKIBAHARA DISTRICT STOCKS EVERYTHING A GADGET FREAK COULD WANT, FROM LIGHTBULBS TO THE LATEST MINI-GADGETS FROM JAPAN'S EVER-INVENTIVE ELECTRONICS INDUSTRY.
CREDIT: LEANDER KAHNEY

マックを買う人たち

GOSHU TRADING: WHERE OLD MACS GO OFF TO THRIVE

In a back alley in Tokyo's famous Akihabara shopping district, a cramped used-computer store sells worthless Macintosh computers for prices high enough to make a geisha drop her soap. Goshu Trading is an obsolete-computing wonderland on the third floor of a grimy apartment building. Outside on the sidewalk, the only sign of the store above is a cracked neon sign with an Apple logo clumsily mounted on a pedestal. The sign is plastered with handwritten kanji signs and a piece of paper in English instructing customers to take the elevator to the third floor. It's not as unpromising as it sounds—the short, dirty elevator ride leads to a fluorescent-lit world of retro-computing wonder.

The store is the size of a standard U.S. hotel room, stacked floor to ceiling with neolithic Macintosh computers that couldn't be given away in the United States, much less sold. The store is one of about half a dozen shops in Akihabara selling used Macintosh equipment. No stores like them could be found selling used Windows machines.

Unlike the other used Mac stores, Goshu Trading is relatively disorganized. Where other stores are meticulously ordered, Goshu Trading is strewn with cardboard boxes spilling outmoded computer parts. But Goshu Trading contains unique treasures. In the middle of the shop floor is a Mac SE 30, but thanks to a lot of money and the guts of a modern iMac, the SE 30 has been converted to run Mac OS X, which normally runs on hardware less than a couple of years old.

Stripped of its innards, the SE 30 has been upgraded with an iMac motherboard complete with a 233 MHz G3 processor, 288MB of RAM, a 4GB hard drive, and a CD-ROM drive that sticks out the back, not the front. It also has Ethernet, two USB ports, two serial ports, a built-in modem, and a pair of audio jacks. It costs 168,000 yen (about $1,700)—almost the price of a brand new flat-screen iMac.

The conversion was done by Goshu Trading, which converts old Macs into modern machines—about one a month. It's too labor-intensive to do any more, said the store's proprietor, Yang Lee, although there's the demand. A lot of the conversions are done at the customer's behest, Lee said. "Many people have an old Mac that they want upgraded," Lee said. "They like the old Mac very much. They have the machine for 10 years. All of our customers are Apple fans."

In one corner of the store is a Macintosh 512K, the second version of the Macintosh, which was an all-in-one machine from the mid-1980s. By today's standards, the 512K Mac is so useless it's of interest only to the most dedicated collector in the United States, who might pay $10 if the machine is in good shape, and if there's no way to get it for free. But at Goshu Trading, the 512K Mac—blackened with age and covered with inky fingerprints—is on sale for 49,800 yen ($500). A Mac Plus, another dinosaur, commands 20,000 yen ($200). In the United States, these machines are landfill; people can't get rid of them.

The early all-in-one machines are coveted in Japan because they can be converted into relatively modern machines while retaining their compact shape and retro charm. The rest of the store is stacked with moth-eaten Macs that sell anywhere from $50 to $1,000.

The store also has a line on Newtons—the original PDAs pioneered by Apple that now seem so slow and clunky. A used Newton goes for 108,000 yen ($1,000). An unused one is 128,000 yen ($1,300). Goshu Trading stocks fewer than ten, a bunch of Newton accessories, and an e-Mate, an antiquated PDA-cum-subnotebook that has disappeared into the mists of computer history.

"People care about Macintosh," Lee said. "I have no Windows PC customers."

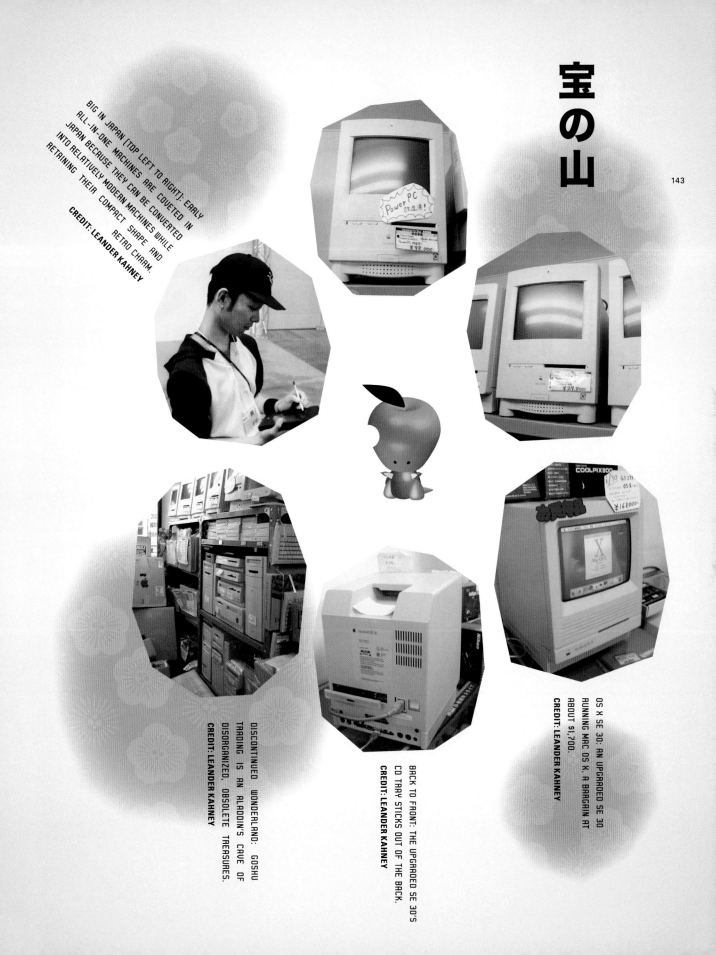

宝の山

BIG IN JAPAN (TOP LEFT TO RIGHT): EARLY ALL-IN-ONE MACHINES ARE COVETED IN JAPAN BECAUSE THEY CAN BE CONVERTED INTO RELATIVELY MODERN MACHINES WHILE RETAINING THEIR COMPACT SHAPE AND RETRO CHARM.
CREDIT: LEANDER KAHNEY

OS X SE 30: AN UPGRADED SE 30 RUNNING MAC OS X. A BARGAIN AT ABOUT $1,700.
CREDIT: LEANDER KAHNEY

BACK TO FRONT: THE UPGRADED SE 30'S CD TRAY STICKS OUT OF THE BACK.
CREDIT: LEANDER KAHNEY

DISCONTINUED WONDERLAND: GOSHU TRADING IS AN ALADDIN'S CAVE OF DISORGANIZED, OBSOLETE TREASURES.
CREDIT: LEANDER KAHNEY

PART 3: INCESSANT TINKERERS

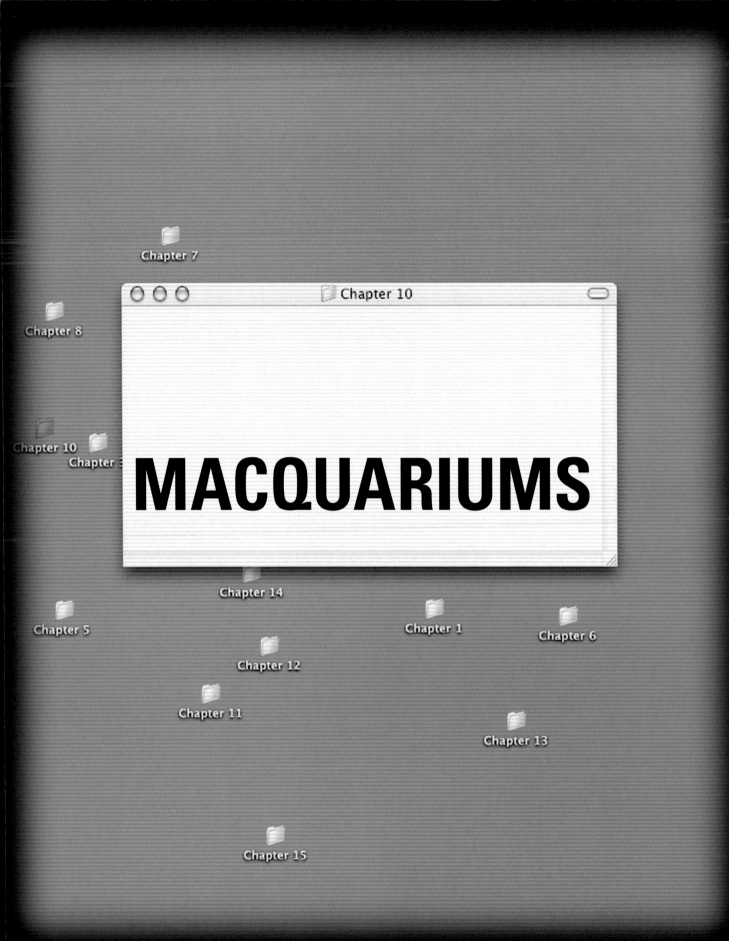

MAC AQUARIUMS

Some animal lovers stuff a beloved pet when it dies. Mac fans convert dead machines into fish tanks.

Comedian Jay Leno has an iMac aquarium. Steve Jobs reportedly has a couple of them. Timothy Leary had a Mac aquarium, and so did Abbie Hoffman. Wall Street is positively swimming in them—for some reason, they're a favorite gift among stockbrokers and bankers. Mac aquariums are as iconic as the Mac itself. Thousands reside in homes and schools across the world. Converting an old compact Mac into an aquarium is probably the obsolete machine's most common fate.

It started as a prank, but at least two companies have launched to make aquariums out of old Macs. What started as a joke has evolved into a cottage industry. The early all-in-one Macs are perfectly suited for housing fish tanks. It's a relatively simple operation to replace the electronic innards with a specially shaped glass or Perspex tank that fits snugly inside the computer's case.

No one can identify who made the first Mac aquarium, but Andy Inhatko, a veteran Mac columnist, seems to have kicked off the trend in 1992. At the time, Inhatko wrote a popular Q&A column. Someone asked him the best way to upgrade a Mac 512K, and he sarcastically suggested the best thing was to turn it into an aquarium. He received so much mail inquiring how to do it, he wrote up a 60-page plan and posted it. The document is still available on about 400 Web sites, according to Inhatko.

"The idea was kind of an old one," he said recently from his home in Boston. "But it's like asking who invented the wheel. It seems to be one of those ideas that a lot of people had simultaneously." Inhatko thinks that someone on Apple's original Mac development team made one of the first Mac aquariums. Inhatko recalled plans being published in a developer publication in 1985. The design was overly complicated, calling for 13 or 14 different pieces of glass that had to precisely conform to the inside of the case, he said.

"[Mac aquariums are] an extension of what makes the Mac so wonderful," said Inhatko. "They're very huggable, squeezable, lovable computers. When you take an old Mac and do something with it, it's a value-added upgrade. It keeps the iconic Mac design out there on shelves and in offices and schools."

However, the idea of making fish tanks out of the earliest Macs—the original 128K and 512K machines, and the Lisa—now fills him with horror, because they've become so rare. "It's like the

> *"It's a good way to keep all these Macs from the dump… We give them another ten years of life on the shelf."*

Antiques Road Show, when someone has a 17th-century piece of furniture they've ripped out to make a TV stand," he said.

Carl Blake runs MacAquarium, a Web-based business head-quartered in a warehouse in downtown Waterloo, Iowa. Blake, 38, claims to have been making Mac aquariums since 1988. He sells between 35 and 50 every month, sending them all over the world: New Zealand, Great Britain, Singapore, Mexico—even Chechnya. He sells ready-made "deluxe" models, as well as do-it-yourself kits.

The deluxe aquariums are made out of old compact Macs or iMacs. They sell for between $150 and $300—just add water and fish. The DIY kits run for $90 and up. They include an internal tank, which slots pump, filters, gravel, and instructions into the customer's empty case. Blake has made aquariums out of iMacs, the Color Classic, the Cube, and even Harman Kardon's bell jar–like subwoofer.

Blake's first aquarium was made out of an original Macintosh, the 128K. He kept two goldfish in it. They eventually grew so large their tails stuck out the top. He put them in a bigger tank. They died a week later.

"It started as a joke," he said. "My buddies laughed at me when I said it would make a good fish tank. I had a fish in it, and they just laughed and laughed." Blake has built aquariums for a number of celebrities—Jay Leno and Timothy Leary, for

example—and every year he donates one to the Los Angeles Philharmonic's charity auction. He once made 13 matching aquariums for a bar mitzvah in San Francisco.

"It's a good way to keep all these Macs from the dump," he said. "I hate to see them go away. We give them another ten years of life on the shelf."

Like Blake, Jim Lower built his fair share of fish tanks out of old Macs. Lower registered the TechQuarium Internet domain a few years ago, with the idea of launching an aquarium business like Blake's, but the living he makes as a programmer is too good. "I'm cursed with a good job," Lower said. "I could never make as much money as I do now."

Like Blake, Lower has sold Mac aquariums all over the world. But he prefers to characterize his sideline as a hobby, in case the IRS ever asks. "I guess I just had a little too much spare time," he said. "It's one of those things you do when you don't have a girlfriend."

Married now and living in Florida, Lower has also converted a lot of old Macs, including rare early models like the 128K and the Lisa. "I've gotten thousands and thousands of emails from all over the world," he said. "Most are positive. Sometimes I get a nutcase complaining that I should be preserving rather than destroying these old Macs. Someone suggested I should use my head as an aquarium."

Watery grave: Over the years, Carl Blake, founder of MacAquarium, has turned all kinds of Macs into aquariums, from the earliest all-in-ones, like the Lisa, to the latest Power Mac Cube and iMac.

New life: Carl Blake says he gives these computers another ten years of life on the shelf by rescuing them from the dump. Here his daughter takes delivery of a load of old iMacs.

(left) iAquarium: The iMac makes a particularly nice fish tank.

(right) Any Mac will do: One day, someone will lament using these classic machines as fish habitats.

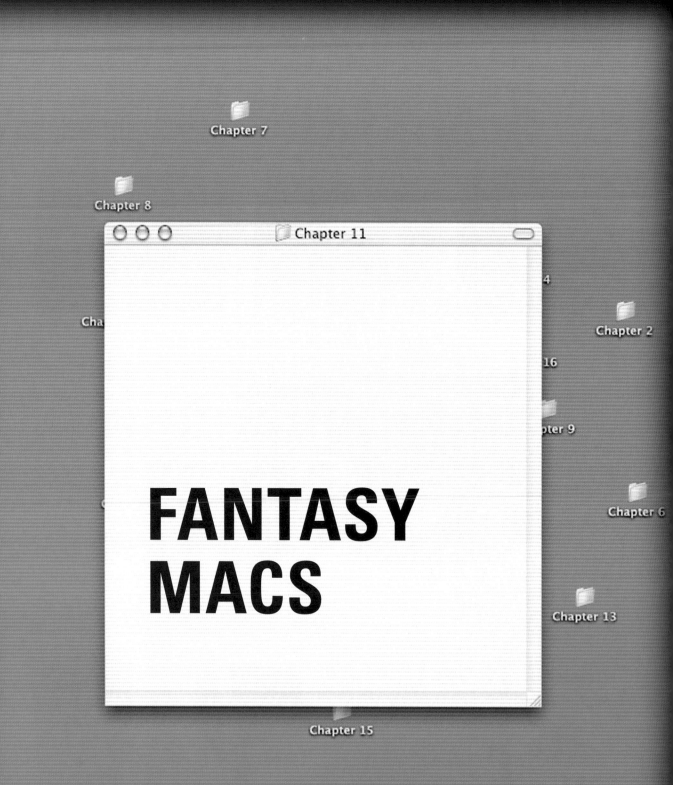

"Apple's design language is incredibly modernist and minimalist. There's such a clear design language, it is instantly recognizable as Apple's brand."

(THIS PAGE) Towering inferno: This silvery, next-generation tower Mac was mocked up by Venezuelan architect Carlos Agell, purely for the fun of it. Like a lot of other amateur Apple designers, his creation is part wishful thinking, part attention getting, and part homage.
CREDIT: CARLOS AGELL

(OPPOSITE PAGE LEFT) iLike: Venezuelan architect Carlos Agell's design for a portable music/video player, the iWalk.
CREDIT: CARLOS AGELL

(OPPOSITE PAGE RIGHT) Fooled everyone: No mock-up has attracted as much attention as the iWalk. A video purporting to show a new Apple PDA, the iWalk, appeared on Spymac's Web site in the run-up to Macworld. So convincing was the video, it was reported worldwide.
CREDIT: SPYMAC

DESIGNED and MODELED in Cinema 4D and Form•Z by Carlos Agell • http://homepage.mac.com/agell

ERSATZ DESIGNS HONOR APPLE

In the old days, Apple used to be famously leaky about future products. Before Steve Jobs returned as the company's CEO, the press and everyone else often had a good idea of what the company was working on. But these days, Jobs has made Apple obsessively secretive. Rumors still get printed, of course, but the information vacuum has fostered a strange manifestation of wishful thinking: fans have taken to designing their own "fantasy Macs."

Like fantasy baseball teams, these imaginary products are the kinds of things Mac fans would like to see from the company. They range from flat-screen iMacs to handhelds and Web pads, and they are mocked up in glorious photographic detail. Fantasy Macs are posted to the Net for others to ooh and aah over. Strangely, their fanciful hardware specifications will sometimes spark heated chat-room debates—even though they don't, and probably never will, exist.

In January 2002, Apple disappointed fans with a new line of Power Macs. Sure, everybody liked the dual 1 GHz processors, but a lot of Mac fanatics were also hoping Apple would

continue its tradition of making computers that showcase cutting-edge design. Sadly, the new machines looked just like the previous generation of silver and gray Power Macs. Given the new space-age, flat-screen iMac, fans were hoping the new Power Macs would have the kind of striking, ultramodern enclosure that makes the covers of magazines.

In the weeks before the machine's debut—the new Power Mac was widely expected—Mac fans were busy cooking up gorgeous renderings of the machine, based on what they hoped the new computer would look like. Dozens of photo-realistic concoctions of the new machine and its successor, a next-generation machine commonly referred to as the "G5," were posted to Mac-related message forums all over the Web—to be praised and picked over.

The buzz surrounding these "mock-up Macs" highlights the rapidly growing culture of designing fantasy Macintoshes, a pastime that consumes dozens, perhaps hundreds, of would-be Apple designers and thousands of armchair critics.

There are scores of message forums devoted to the discussion of mock-up Macs, including those at AppleInsider, MacAddict,

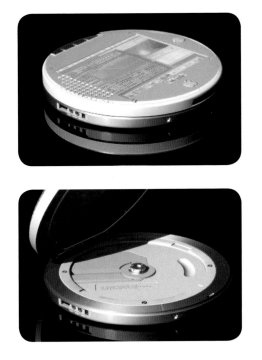

MacCentral, MacNN, and Mac OS Rumors. There is also a handful of Web sites that archive mock-up Macs, sites like David Vincent's The Apple Collection and Benjamin Van Parys' Apple Mock-ups, which between them have collected hundreds of fantastic and outrageous designs for new iMacs, PowerBooks, iPods, Web pads, and PDAs. "I like the way they are so imaginative, innovative, original, and, at the same time, realistic," explained Van Parys, who lives in Brussels, Belgium.

Fantasy Macs range from flat-screen iMacs to communicator watches. They are mocked up in glorious photographic detail using 3D software, Photoshop, and Illustrator. The best are so realistic, they could be photographs of real machines. The designs range from parody, like a computer/cooking utensil called the iWok, to the uncannily prophetic, such as Vincent Jeunejean's sketch of an outré machine that preceded the flat-screen iMac's unveiling by seven months. In between, there are scores of designs from amateur and professional designers, some of whom wish, in some secret part of their soul, that Apple will see their imaginings and summon them to a dream job in Cupertino.

Many fantasy Macs are created in the prelude to a major product announcement from Apple. Fueled by tidbits of information from Mac rumor sites, fantasy Mac designers let their imaginations run wild. At the discussion forums at Geek Culture, for example, an entire thread devoted to a mock-up Power Mac by Robert Emslie, a digital artist from France, ran to dozens of excited posts. The sleek, silvery machine, which Emslie called the "PowerSlab G5," looks like a cross between Apple's tower-shaped Power Macs and the discontinued Cube. Sporting everything from multiple processors to Bluetooth, it is a techno-fetishist's fantasy. An info-graphic at the top of the thread read, "Warning...slippery with drool!"

"Lovely design," said one post among the many commenting on the mock-up in intimate detail. The comments are generally respectful, but sometimes a machine's fanciful specifications will spark heated debate, even though the machines don't, and probably never will, exist. "Hopefully a design of yours starts a considerable flurry of comment," said Matt Weed, a graphic designer from Colorado Springs, Colorado, who has created some gorgeous images of flat-panel iMacs and other fanciful Apple hardware. "The nastier it gets, the better."

Sometimes the speculation spills over into the press. The Mac rumor sites, and occasionally the technology press, have reported mock-up Macs as leaks from inside Apple's design headquarters. In the days leading up to the January 2002 Macworld in San Francisco, German Web site Spymac received a lot of attention for a video of what purported to be an Apple PDA called the iWalk.

"The iWalk appeared to be real," said Paul Kunkel, who has written books on Apple's and Sony's design departments, "so real that it sparked days of anxious discussion on the Yahoo and Raging Bull investor chat boards."

However, it appears the iWalk video was an elaborate hoax. The Spymac site now claims to be as skeptical of the video as everyone else, having posted it for a third party. But Spymac doesn't have a very good reputation—last July the site posted a clever 3D mock-up of a similar device. Spymac didn't respond to requests for comment.

Gavin Robb, a 16-year-old high school student, also fooled a lot of people last July with a realistic 3D mock-up of a globe-shaped G5 he called the G5 Sphere. Made with Corel's Bryce 3D software, the spoof also attracted Apple's lawyers, who asked him to pull it off the Web. "I wanted to see if anyone would believe such a thing existed," Robb said. "Hence the realism."

Most mock-up Macs are created for fun. They spoof Apple, obsessed by design and secrecy, and at the same time honor the company. "This is what I would do if I had Steve Jobs' ear," said Paul Scates, 33, a graphic artist from San Diego who has made a number of nice mock-ups of flat-screen iMacs and other machines. However, Scates said he has no ambition to work in Apple's design department. "It's not something I wake up thinking about," he said. "I would like to work in their marketing department. I think they need some help with that."

The Apple Collection's David Vincent said a lot of mock-up designers are merely experimenting with 3D design tools: It's easier to create a computer than a car or a cathedral. On the other hand, Vincent said some amateur designers may have landed jobs with the help of their mock-ups. "The work they do is incredible," he said. "If you make a good picture, you are sure a lot of people will see your picture, and your name will go around."

It's important to note that none of the amateurs have produced anything as original as Apple's own design department. The new space-age, flat-screen iMac is a radical departure from anything anyone expected, with the possible exception of Vincent Jeunejean's sketch. "What's funny is that in all my mock-ups, discussions, debates, thoughts, and dreams about a new flat-panel iMac, I never once considered a design like the new iMac," Scates said.

Groovy: A translucent iMac from designer Big Rosie.
CREDIT: BIG ROSIE

"Apple leads the pack.... They care for good design, inside and out, as a philosophy. They dare to innovate; others simply follow. Without Apple to copy, the industry wouldn't know where to go."

Ethan Imboden, a senior designer with frog design, which is famously associated with Apple after helping to design various early Macintoshes, said a lot of mock-ups are emailed around the office and a lot of other design offices around the world. The most popular are the humorous ones. He recalled the first mock-up he saw: a candy-colored sex toy called the iBrator.

Imboden said a lot of things drive amateur computer designers: a surge of interest in design, greater access to sophisticated design software, and, of course, inspiration from Apple. "Apple is run by designers and creatives, and sold to designers and creatives who have the ability to express their devotion to the brand," he said. "You're sitting there at a computer being creative; why not create a computer?" Imboden said mock-up culture feeds on itself. Mock-ups may start as wishful thinking leading up to a product announcement, but they feed a self-sustaining culture, like gamers who make levels for Doom or Quake. "Why design in a vacuum when you can design and get a response?" Imboden said. "Good or bad, you're part of a community."

Imboden said he is skeptical about whether Apple's design department pays much attention to the amateurs. However, Apple is an attentive company that listens to its customers, and mock-ups are a form of visual feedback that may influence future products. "I can't think of another brand that inspires a similar culture—at least, not one that honors the company," Imboden said. "There's plenty of people out there who design fake Nikes, but that's to turn a buck."

Author Paul Kunkel said many product-based subcultures revolve around a core group of enthusiasts who design their own equipment. "Skateboarders and snowboarders often customize their gear to make it as gnarly as possible. Snowboard manufacturers like Burton observe these trends and respond with their own gnarly designs," he said in an email. "Hundreds of wanna-be car designers post their creations on the Web. And thousands more customize their cars in various ways. The custom paint jobs you see on cars and motorcycles also exist for computers, even for the Mac."

William Travis, president of Attik USA, a large design firm, thought that the level is pretty good overall, but many of the designs are too derivative of Apple. "There's not a lot of variety," he said. "A lot of them have been designed to follow a product line. They are following the stream of Apple history rather than creating something new."

Marcus Conge, who teaches 3D software at the Rochester Institute of Technology, is delighted by the amateur design community. "I think it's an incredibly positive environment that just keeps fueling creativity," he said. "I think it's wonderful."

ISAMU SANADA: MASTER MAKER OF MOCK-UP MACS

Japanese photographer Isamu Sanada fancies himself another Steve Jobs, spending weeks designing Macintosh computers. He's so good at anticipating Apple, he dreams up machines before the company does.

Sanada is prolific, popular, and adept at dreaming up designs that could easily come from Apple's own labs. His speculative designs for future Macintoshes look just like Apple's machines, though they rarely foray into truly imaginative realms. In fact, Sanada is so adept at mimicking Apple's look, he created a design for a new laptop that predicted Apple's distinctive Titanium PowerBook G4 two months before it came out.

Sanada's speculative design, which he called the PowerfulBook R2 and posted to his Applele Web site in November 2000, showed a stunningly minimalist, silvery-gray machine, shaped like a flat, wide box with hard edges. Incredibly, it looks just like the titanium-clad PowerBook Apple introduced two months later at the Macworld Expo in San Francisco. What's remarkable is that no one had seen anything like a titanium computer at the time. Apple was selling funky-looking orange and purple iBooks, but its higher-end PowerBooks were black and rounded, like most other notebooks on the market.

Sanada's mock-up is accurate down to details like the slot-loading CD/DVD drive, the location of the Apple logo, and the shape of the distinctive cooling vents, although the placement differs. Some other things are also different. Sanada gave his machine a built-in carrying handle, a feature Apple left off—although handles are built into the older iBooks.

Ethan Imboden, a senior designer with frog design, which helped Apple design various now-vintage Macintoshes, said it was incredible that Sanada had managed to preconceive the Titanium PowerBook so closely. "That's really impressive," Imboden said. "To go from the black organic PowerBook in Apple's previous design. It's prophetic, and indeed uncanny."

But as he spoke, Imboden realized that all the elements of Sanada's PowerfulBook were present in Apple's Cube, which had been released shortly before: the minimalism, the silvery-gray color, the boxy form. Imboden said it was clear that Sanada had taken those elements and applied them to a notebook, which is exactly what the company did. Imboden praised Sanada's abilities. "He's got a talent for proportion and detail, and he can certainly riff off of Apple's design language," Imboden said.

Sanada's prescient abilities are, in fact, a testament to the simplicity and consistency of Apple's designs, Imboden said. "Apple's design language is incredibly modernist and minimalist," he said. "There's such a clear design language, it is instantly recognizable as Apple's brand."

Napoleon complex: Photographer Isamu Sanada would like to be Steve Jobs. Spending his spare time making beautiful mock-ups of Macs, Sanada would like nothing more than to be noticed by Apple. Luckily he has a sense of humor (note the sock).
CREDIT: ISAMU SANADA

(TOP) Talented: Sanada's design for a flat-screen Apple desktop looks remarkably like some of the new tablet PCs, even though it preceded them by a couple of years.
CREDIT: ISAMU SANADA

(BOTTOM LEFT) Precog: Sanada has Apple's aesthetic down pat. He posted this picture of a new PowerBook two months before Apple unveiled its strikingly similar Titanium PowerBook.
CREDIT: ISAMU SANADA

(BOTTOM RIGHT) Toasty: Sanada's designs display an obvious sense of humor.
CREDIT: ISAMU SANADA

hiMac
R6

Applele
NEW SPECIES APPLE LABORATORY

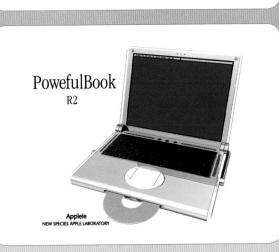

PowefulBook
R2

Applele
NEW SPECIES APPLE LABORATORY

PowerfulMac
R2

Applele
NEW SPECIES APPLE LABORATORY

iRocket.

500 MHz G3
256MB RAM
10GB HD
24X CDR/DVD
USB/Firewire
Airport
Type I (w,d,h)
2.2 pounds

(TOP) Ooh: Weed's design for an Apple subnotebook called the iRocket.
CREDIT: MATT WEED

(RIGHT) Too good to be true: Designer Matt Weed's stunning design for a new iMac. Weed became so obsessed with mocking up Macs, he neglected his business.
CREDIT: MATT WEED

iMac

Sanada calls himself the director of the New Species Apple Laboratory, which conducts "research on new Apple designs." The laboratory appears to be the crowded office of Sanada's small business, a portrait studio he owns in Toyota City, Japan, called the MarieRosa Collection.

Sanada's office is packed with Macs; he owns 16. He designs mock-up Macs in his spare time and has about 35 of those. He makes the basic forms in Shade, a 3D application from ExpressionTools, and adds detail in Adobe Photoshop. Some of them took weeks to create. "Like a lot of Mac fans, I think about ideal Mac," he said in an email interview. "Because it is pleasant, I turn ideal Mac into a picture. I made them in order to surprise my friends on the Web. I made them with the intention of a joke."

Sanada said that although his designs are popular with the Macintosh rank and file, he hasn't had any contact with Apple. He'd like to hear from the company, even though he is humble about his design abilities. "Apple's thought is more splendid than my thought," he said. But he added that he'd gladly work

for the company for a salary of $1 (the same as Jobs' annual income). "Apple created the future, and Apple continues creating the future currently," he said. "Apple shows the future."

"Sanada was one of the first to create highly polished (yet goofy) fantasy designs for future Macs," said an email from Paul Kunkel, who has written books on Apple's and Sony's design departments. "He creates timid extensions of existing products and inspired several Americans to do the same (and go much farther). Sanada takes himself (and his work) pretty seriously. He's asserted copyright protection on his designs." Sanada, however, said he has not asserted copyrights on his designs.

Swiss Web designer David Vincent, who archives a lot of mock-up Macs at The Apple Collection, said he's received a new design from Sanada almost every month for the last two years. "It is nice work he does," Vincent said. "He is hoping Apple will one day come to him and make one of his computers. He is trying to get Apple to look at him. I know this is what he wants, but Apple ignores him. It is sad."

(TOP) Drool-worthy: Weed's folding
iMac 2 and other designs have
attracted mucho traffic to his
Web site.
CREDIT: MATT WEED

(RIGHT) Detail, detail: Weed even
created close-ups of key features,
as well as mock advertising for
his mock products.
CREDIT: MATT WEED

THE PASSION FOR DESIGNING MACS

Matt Weed was so obsessed with making mock-up Macs, he neglected his graphic design business. Weed, 31, the president of Acorn Creative in Colorado Springs, Colorado, spent weeks creating elaborate designs for future Macintoshes while his small staff kept the business afloat. "Others worked on forgotten (paying) projects while the imperious leader (me) was hell-bent on creating damned fantasy Macs," Weed said in an email interview.

But Weed's neglect paid off in the end. His designs generated plenty of traffic for his company's Web site and bumped it up in Internet search engine rankings. Weed's three mock Macs—a subnotebook with a folding keyboard called the iRocket, a folding iMac 2, and a translucent flat-screen iMac—have attracted 200,000 visitors to his site, he estimated from server statistics. His designs have also been featured on other Web sites and reprinted in Macintosh magazines in Australia and Japan.

Weed creates his fantasy designs using Strata 3Dpro, a high-end rendering program used by many professional designers. "His modeling is as good as anything they create at Apple," said Paul Kunkel. "Unfortunately, he doesn't seem to care about engineering or manufacturability."

Although Weed likes his designs to be seen by a wide audience, he hasn't sent anything to Apple. "It would be offensive to them," he said. "They have a wonderful industrial design team, and they sure don't need my help."

Some of the most enthusiastic Mac mock-up artists are precocious teenagers. Eoban Binder, Gavin Robb, and Michael Matas are all still in high school and design Macs in their spare time, but two of them also run their own businesses, and the other was hired by a well-known software company. They each have at least four computers—all Macs, of course.

Binder, of Whitefish Bay, Wisconsin, started his own "little graphics company" called ePix in 1999, when he was only 12.

(TOP) Shiny: A chrome iMac
from teenager Eoban Binder.
He started his own graphics
company at age 12.
CREDIT: EOBAN BINDER

(BOTTOM) Global ambitions:
Gavin Robb's design for a
spherical Mac. He even mocked
up a detail of the machine's ports.
CREDIT: GAVIN ROBB

Chrome.
iMac2

http://www.epix3d.8m.com   Think Different

"I created a quick Web site hosted by America Online, and voilà, I was in business," he said.

Like many other designers, he uses fanciful designs, such as chrome iMacs and G5 Spheres to drive traffic to his site. "I know that a lot of people download my images, or at least view them," he said. "My gallery on my site includes my work, and for some reason people tend to upload it to a bunch of other places, too."

Robb, a 16-year-old high school junior, also runs his own graphics business. "Our company makes national ads for a large audio manufacturer and distributor," he said. Last year, Robb created a G5 Sphere that fooled many people into thinking it was real. Unlike most mock-up Macintosh designers, Robb heard from Apple—well, Apple's lawyers. He received a curt email asking him to remove the graphic from his site, which is devoted to 3D art. "Pretty soon after traffic to the site skyrocketed, I received an e-mail requesting that the site be taken down as soon as possible," he said.

Although he has obvious talent as a designer, Robb is not sure what he wants to do when he finishes school. "I guess [being a designer is] a possibility," he said.

Matas was 15 when he was hired by the Omni Group in 2002, a Seattle software developer that created the well-received OmniWeb browser for Mac OS X. He was assigned to do user interface work and tech support. He also does occasional freelance work as a graphic designer and video editor.

Matas has created a number of interesting concepts for flat-panel iMacs, and he would love to design for Apple. A caption at the top of his Web page used to read: "Steve Jobs, if you look at these and like what you see I am looking for a job so e-mail me at michael_m@mac.com."

Wobbly: Teenager Michael
Matas' whimsical design for
a flat-screen iMac.
CREDIT: MICHAEL MATAS

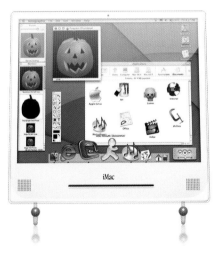

162

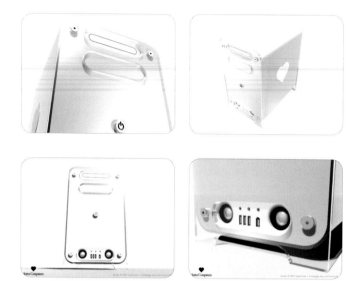

Any day now: Like a lot of Mac fans, designer Robert Emslie is eagerly awaiting Apple's next-generation machine, a G5 Power Mac. Here's a mock-up he spent many hours creating.
CREDIT: ROBERT EMSLIE

Robert Emslie, a digital artist who lives in France and Asia, noted that not only amateurs copy Apple design. "Some PC manufacturers are shamelessly selling mock-up Macs, from Compaq to Dell and eMachines, which got burned in the '90s for flat-out copying the original iMac," he said. "Microsoft made their fortune selling a mock-up of the Mac OS for years."

Emslie, 33, has been working on various mock-ups for a portable Apple Web pad since 2001. One of his designs was a winner in Geek Culture's 2002 "Design an LCD iMac" contest. Emslie was convinced Apple would unveil such a device "any day now."

"Surely they have something in the likes for future release," he said. "I, for one, sure hope so."

Emslie may have spent as long as 48 hours to create the mock-up in Corel's Bryce 3D software. He isn't sure exactly how long it took: "A lot of late-night work tends to warp time perception a bit," he said.

Designing the iPad was "simply an exercise in copying cool design," he said. "Renaissance painters learned by copying the masters of the time.... Apple leads the pack," he gushed. "They care for good design, inside and out, as a philosophy. They dare to innovate; others simply follow. Without Apple to copy, the industry wouldn't know where to go.

"Macintosh computers and their operating system create an atmosphere that kindly includes the user in an ecology of sorts that's simply nonexistent in the Wintel world. Macs ooze with coolness up to the minutest detail. I find it very hard not to enter some deep and sensual relationship with virtually every Mac

I see.... They're unobtrusive, dependable, nice to touch, snappy, practical, compact, well thought-out, long-lived," he added.

Up until January 2002, mock-up Macs looked incredibly futuristic. They were designed in weird shapes and cool colors, with flat screens and unconventional interfaces. But compared to Apple's flat-screen iMac, many now look timid and dated, strange anachronisms from a time when people imagined flat-screen computers to look like picture frames with a CD/DVD drive bolted on. "In all my mock-ups, discussions, debates, thoughts, dreams, et cetera, about a new flat-panel iMac...I never once considered a design like the new iMac," said Paul Scates, a graphic designer whose mock-ups of flat-screen iMacs drew much praise on message boards.

"When I saw the new iMac, I basically smiled and said, 'That's it...it's beautiful.' They managed to keep the iMac an all-in-one computer, but each component is kept separate and allowed to truly be the best they can be: the flat screen is really flat, and the guts are all housed horizontally.

"Of course, in hindsight, it truly is the most simple, obvious solution," Scates said. "But I was locked in to the idea that it truly had to be a one-piece design, like the old iMac of the 20th Century Anniversary Mac from several years ago. The thought of using an arm never occurred to me."

Scates said the experience of being blindsided by Apple has put him off designing concept computers. "I'll be hard-pressed to top this new iMac," he said. "I don't think I even want to try. There's nothing really for me to imagine, fantasize about, or wish for, because they've done it for me. This new iMac doused whatever I-can-design-a-cool-iMac-too fires I had burning inside me."

Say hello to iPad!

1GHz G3, 133 MHz bus, 256 MB to 1 GB RAM
38 to 80 GB hard drive, DVD/CD-R combo drive
Touch-sensitive pen-driven 14" TFT
nVidia AGPX4 graphics with 32MB
2 FireWire, 4 USB, Gigabit Ethernet
Integrated webcam and microphone
AirPort and BlueTooth included

Your home, wherever.

Fictional product design,
product names are © and ™
their respective owners.

design © 2002 flyermoney
homepage.mac.com/flyermoney/

Web pad: Designer Robert Emslie spent many an evening working on this Web pad design, which he calls the iPad. He's hoping Apple will release a similar beast "any day now."
CREDIT: ROBERT EMSLIE

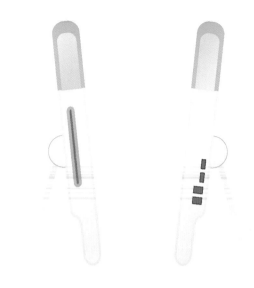

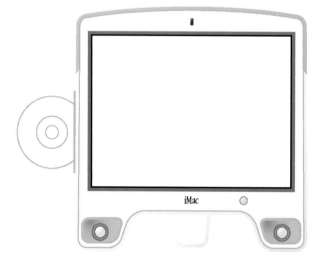

iMac

Intimidated: Paul Scates has a nice, clean eye. His designs of flat-screen iMacs, iBooks, and a new Cube are clean and elegant. But he thinks Apple does it better.
CREDIT: PAUL SCATES

(LEFT COLUMN) Apple on campus: Apple's design aesthetic is so strong, one college professor gets his students to design fantasy Macs as part of their coursework.
CREDIT: RIT/DAVID SCHAFER

(BELOW) Far out: A futuristic Apple computer designed by Yu-Chen Hsieh, a student at the Rochester Institute of Technology.
CREDIT: RIT/YU-CHEN HSIEH

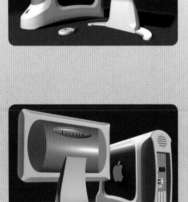

Most mock-up Macs are created for fun.

They spoof Apple, obsessed by design and secrecy, and at the same time honor the company.

LEARNING DESIGN: ABSORBING APPLE'S AESTHETIC

Apple's design aesthetic is so strong that one college professor gets his students to design new hardware specifically for Apple. Marcus Conge, who teaches 3D design at the Rochester Institute of Technology, is an unusual instructor. While most tutors get their students to design for broad product categories, like toothbrushes or refrigerators, students are rarely instructed to design for a specific company. That Conge has singled out Apple is a testament to the company's unique position in the design world.

Every semester for the last six years, Conge has assigned students the task of designing an Apple product using the 3D software he teaches—Alias|Wavefront's Studio and Maxon's Cinema 4D. The students—all trainee industrial designers—are also given the choice of designing a consumer electronic device or a common household good, but most choose the Apple assignment. "The projects keep changing, but I keep throwing the Apple stuff in there," Conge said. "The majority of the students pick the Apple stuff."

"I've never seen anyone go bonzo over vacuum cleaners like they do Macs," he added.

Ethan Imboden, a senior designer with frog design, said the exercise is a good one for trainee product designers. Apple has such a clear design "language," it shouldn't be too difficult for students to recognize the distinctive elements and reshape them into something new, but recognizably Apple. "The exercise is to make something new, but [that] looks like an Apple product," he said. "It has to communicate the brand. It's got to fit in."

Conge, however, said he encourages students to let their imaginations run really wild. "At first, a lot of the students don't want to go blue sky, to push the envelope," he said. "But I tell them they're students; now's the only time they'll be able to do that. When they go professional they won't have the freedom."

Conge said the only other area of design that inspires as much passion and enthusiasm as Macs is cars. However, he doesn't get his students to design cars. Product design and car design are like fish and fowl, Conge said; they don't mix. The premier school for would-be car designers is the Art Center College of Design in Pasadena, California.

Conge showcases some of the students' work on his 3D Toad Web site. From there, some of the Apple designs find their way onto Internet chat forums where speculative Apple designs are discussed. On a couple of occasions, the mock-ups have been reported in the media as leaks from Apple's secretive design department. Conge recalled the occasion when one particularly outrageous design showed up on a Mac rumor site, touted as a new Apple machine. "We thought that was really funny," Conge said. "We were saying, 'I doubt Apple would do something that bright green.' Even the site's readers didn't believe it. It was obviously computer-generated."

One of the students whose speculative Apple designs were popular on the Web has actually gone on to work at Apple as an interface designer. Whether or not his design caught anyone's eye at Apple isn't clear. Apple declined to set up an interview for the employee, and he didn't respond to requests for comments, thanks to Apple's policy of forbidding employees to talk to the media.

Before teaching, Conge was a digital artist and "demo god" for Alias. He has used 3D design programs on the Mac since 1984, when he picked up Swivel 3D, an early 3D program that generated simple volumetric shapes and primitives. It was running on a black-and-white Mac Plus.

Since then, Conge has been a devoted fan of the Macintosh, drawn especially to Apple's sense of style. Conge noted how influential Apple's aesthetic has been, and not just within the computer industry. "Just go down to Target and look at all the stuff in translucent colored plastic," he said. "They are the leader in the shape of their products and the materials they use. Apple inspires the students to push their designs into different directions."

Conge said that when students enroll, most of them use Windows PCs bought by their parents, although the school is filled with Macs. By the end of the course, 40 percent have switched to Macs, Conge said. "They come in as PC users and leave as Mac users," Conge said. "The parents buy them PCs because it's the standard; it's what everyone uses. But the students like the simplicity of the machines and the good design. You get what you pay for when it comes to a Mac."

But Conge has little time for fanatics. "The whole idea of an Apple religion is depressing to me," he said. "The idea that you will fight tooth and nail for an object, that's too fanatical for me."

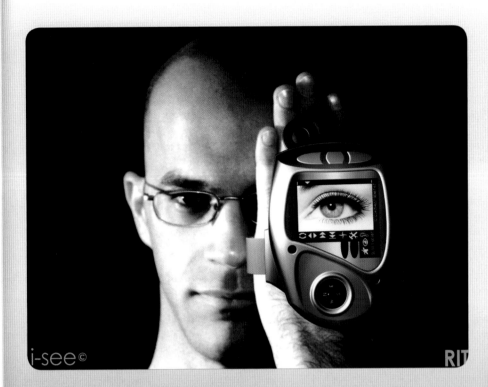

i-see©

RIT

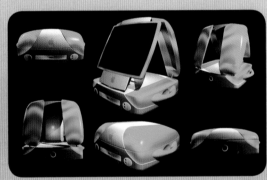

David Schafer

(TOP) Phone home: A mock-up Apple videophone called the i-see Smart Phone by RIT student Yuhay-Ray Ng.
CREDIT: RIT/YUHAY-RAY NG

(BOTTOM LEFT) PortaMac: Student Stephen Lemay's design for a fold-up PowerBook.
CREDIT: RIT/STEPHEN LEMAY

(BOTTOM MIDDLE) New iBook? This roll-up PowerBook was designed by student Michael Ienna. But where's the obligatory Apple logo?
CREDIT: RIT/MICHAEL IENNA

(BOTTOM RIGHT) Handy: A PDA design by student David Schafer. Apple has hired RIT design students whose mock-ups were popular on the Web, but it's not clear whether it was on the strength of those designs or not.
CREDIT: RIT/DAVID SCHAFER

FLAT-SCREEN iMAC DESIGNED BY AN AMATEUR?

A Belgian Web designer said he saw Apple's revolutionary flat-screen iMac design well before it debuted in January 2002, because he posted a very similar concept on the Web more than six months before. Vincent Jeunejean's sketch bears an uncanny resemblance to the funky flat-screen iMac. It has the same dome-shaped base and flat-screen display supported by a thin arm. Not only is it the same shape, details like the placement of the Apple logo and the machine's ports are strikingly similar.

"I think they copied it," said Jeunejean through a translator. "It's so similar. But I can't be sure. It's quite strange. Maybe someone on the iMac development team saw the design."

Jeunejean, a senior designer with Emakina, a new-media firm in Brussels, said he made the sketch in June 2001, shortly before Macworld Expo in New York. At the time, Apple was widely expected to introduce a redesigned iMac with a flat-panel screen. Jeunejean said he wanted to buy a new iMac and sketched out his ideal machine.

Jeunejean scanned the sketch and sent it to The Apple Collection, a Web site dedicated to Macintosh culture, which posted the image on June 30, 2001. The Apple Collection is a showcase for fanciful computer design and is popular with computer designers. The site features hundreds of designs for fantasy Macs.

The site's server logs show that Apple employees visit the site every week, said David Vincent, who runs the site from his home in Switzerland. Vincent forwarded to Wired News the original email that Jeunejean sent to The Apple Collection. The email's headers appear to confirm that it was sent last year.

The new iMac's design is so peculiar, no one besides Jeunejean seems to have predicted it. None of the other hundreds of designs at The Apple Collection resemble the new iMac.

Vincent said The Apple Collection is a popular destination for professional designers, including members of Apple's design department. "For designers who design computers, my site is a good idea for them," Vincent said. "It is the only site where you get to see all these prototypes." These imaginary machines are created by Macintosh fans to show machines they would like to see from Apple. Jeunejean said his iMac sketch was the only fantasy Mac he has created, although he had previously posted designs for some desktop pictures.

Most of the fantasy flat-panel iMac designs on the Web resemble a 1996 concept machine mocked up by frog design for Macworld magazine. frog design's conception is fairly conventional; it features a flat-screen monitor and an irregularly shaped box housing the guts of the machine. In 2001, Intel also commissioned a number of cutting-edge designs for an "Ease of Use" initiative aimed at spurring sales of funky computers to ordinary consumers. Although some are very funky indeed, none of the dozens of concept PCs look anything like the new iMac.

Jeunejean said he also sent his sketch to Apple's CEO Steve Jobs in an email, but he has no idea whether Jobs saw it because he never received a reply. "At first I was surprised, of course," he said, when he saw pictures of the flat-screen iMac for the first time. "I did not believe it. It's quite frustrating. I feel I've been copied and there's nothing in return."

Jeunejean said he dreamed up the design himself. He was not party to any of Apple's preliminary designs or prototypes, he said. "The design was logical," he said. "They made a cube and a tower. I was sure they would make something spherical. I know them too well."

But the similarity between Jeunejean's sketch and the flat-panel iMac could be a matter of coincidence. Jeunejean said he posted the sketch in June; could Apple have developed such a complex machine in such a short time? Apple claims to have been working on the machine in its current incarnation for two years, according to an article in a January edition of *Time* magazine.

Jeunejean said he would like to hear from Apple, even if it is just a coincidence. "I would like to get some feedback from Apple," he said. "I would like to get their point of view." Apple did not respond to requests for comment.

Visionary, or victim? Vincent Jeunejean is intensely curious about the similarity between the designs. He'd like to hear from Apple, just to hear what they have to say.
CREDIT: VINCENT JEUNEJEAN

Uncanny resemblance: Belgian designer Vincent Jeunejean's sketch of a new flat-screen iMac was published on the Web six months before Apple revealed its idiosyncratic design. Coincidence, or something more sinister?
CREDIT: VINCENT JEUNEJEAN

Chapter 7

Chapter 8

Chapter 10

Chapter 3

Chapter 5

Chapter 15

Chapter 12

HARDWARE MODS

er 2

pter 6

Chapter 13

CAN IT: PUTTING MACS IN UNUSUAL CASES IS POPULAR IN JAPAN. HERE'S A G3 MAC MOTHERBOARD MOUNTED INSIDE A JERRY CAN.
CREDIT: LEANDER KAHNEY

173

"I DO THIS . . . to HELP SOME PEOPLE . . . LET LOOSE AND CREAT . . ."

MAC MODDERS

Ever since the first PC rolled off an assembly line decades ago, computer owners have put their own stamp on their machines. In fact, the urge to tinker with hardware has turned into a thriving subculture called computer "modding." However, modifying Apple hardware is nowhere near as common as is modifying hardware in the Windows PC world. The obvious explanation is that PC boxes are generally ugly and utilitarian.

Since the launch of the iMac in 1998, Apple's boxes have all been high design. In contrast, with the exception of Alienware, few PC manufacturers make distinctive computers. In fact, Apple's cases are sometimes used by PC modders. Kyle Bennett put a PC motherboard inside a PowerMac G4 enclosure, which he painted maroon and black. In honor of the color scheme, he called it the Rotten Apple.

Windows PC mods can often be original and beautifully executed. Obviously influenced by Apple's Cube, Dennis Vieren made a gorgeous glowing cube out of aluminum and acrylic.

Although Mac customization is less common, some imaginative mods have been cooked up. John McDonnell, for example, shoehorned a Macintosh Quadra into a 1940s Philco radio.

McDonnell, a 34-year-old history teacher from Fontana, California, paid close attention to detail: He mounted an Apple logo on the front of the radio and carefully cut a slot for the machine's floppy drive in the side. He connected the computer's speaker jacks to the radio's original speaker. It provides "nice, rich sound," he said. To turn the computer on, McDonnell wired up the radio's original on/off switch. Turn the knob, and the machine starts up with the distinctive Mac startup chime.

McDonnell used a Macintosh Quadra 605 and a Philco Baby Grand Tombstone Radio. "The radio sat around my garage for years," McDonnell said. "I considered a number of case options, including a disco ball, a Habitrail, and an old toolbox before I remembered the radio. What I ended up with is a fully functional, Internet-ready Macintosh that would blend nicely with the decor of almost any Depression-era American home."

(LEFT) PHILCO MAC: HISTORY TEACHER JOHN MCDONNELL PUT A MAC INSIDE THIS OLD PHILCO RADIO CASE. IT'S AN INTERNET-READY MAC THAT WOULD BLEND NICELY WITH THE DECOR OF ANY DEPRESSION-ERA HOME. CREDIT: JOHN MCDONNELL

(RIGHT) RADIOHEAD: ANOTHER VIEW OF JOHN MCDONNELL'S "TOMBSTONE" MAC. CREDIT: JOHN MCDONNELL

KENT SALAS' BLUE ICE

Kent Salas had never done any modding before he embarked on one of the most ambitious Macintosh mods to date, and it wasn't even his computer. A friend loaned Salas a Power Mac G4, a machine worth thousands of dollars. He dismantled the computer, cut it up, and stripped the paint from its casing. He was so unsure of what he was doing, he labeled every component, including all the screws, to make sure he could figure out how to put it back together again. "I always end up with extra screws and parts left over," he said on his Web site.

The result is Blue Ice, a stunning, transparent G4 tower that lights up with fluorescent blue neon and has a nifty LCD screen mounted in the front panel. "I hit the power switch and boom, half my room glows electric, icy blue," Salas writes on his site.

The project cost Salas, a 38-year-old Web master from Southern California, about $300 and took a month to complete. "Not too bad considering I had to buy a drill and other minor tools," he said.

Salas bought the 5-inch LCD panel on eBay for $100. He cut a hole in the front of the G4's case and drilled a couple of holes to fasten the LCD. He added a 12-volt power supply and simply hooked the screen's RCA jacks to an extra video card that he plugged in to one of the machine's PCI slots. Thanks to the extra video card, the LCD screen can mirror the machine's desktop. Its resolution of 640 by 480 pixels is perfect for displaying music visualizations using iTunes, video clips, or system-monitoring utilities.

Salas also added a translucent power-supply cover, a five-port internal USB hub, and various fluorescent blue lamps and LEDs. To make the G4's case transparent, he stripped the paint from the side panels with alcohol.

The hardest part was making the keyboard glow. It took Salas three days to dismantle the fiendishly complex keyboard and add glowing sheets of neon light, which cost close to $200. "This was a real pain in the ass, if you know what I mean," he wrote.

"One reason I do this is to help some people, who have a Mac modder buried deep inside them, let loose and create some totally new and interesting Mac mods," he explained. "Just planting seeds of inspiration hopefully, and maybe give Apple a slight hint of what I would like to see in new hardware designs."

NICEY ICEY: KENT SALAS' BLUE ICE, A MODIFIED POWER MAC, FEATURES A LOT OF BLUE NEON. SALAS HAD TO DO A LOT OF CUTTING OF THE COMPUTER'S CASE, AND IT WASN'T EVEN HIS MACHINE.

CREDIT: KENT SALAS

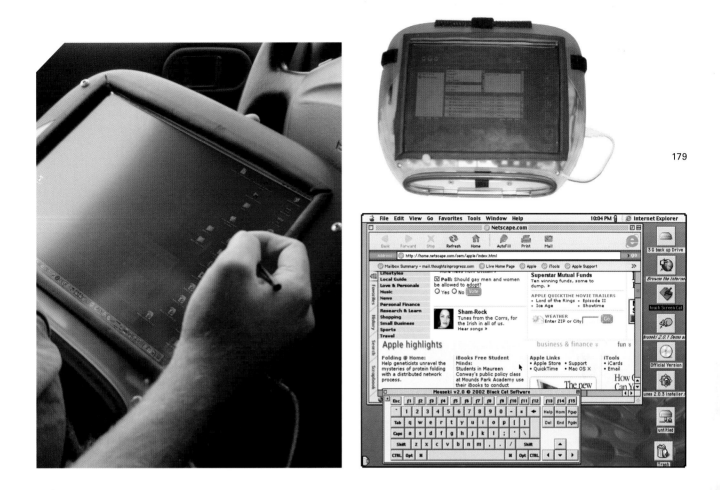

JEFF PARADISO'S WEB PAD

For a long time Jeff Paradiso wanted a Macintosh-based Web pad. But Apple doesn't make them, so he made his own. Paradiso, a graphic designer from Boston, took a touch-screen iBook (an after-market modification from Troll Touch), disassembled it, cut a screen-sized hole in its lid, and flipped the screen around so that it faces outward instead of toward the keyboard. Paradiso changed the desktop icons to large buttons and uses the operating system's built-in, onscreen keyboard to get around.

It's a bit clunky, he admits, but great for Web surfing from the couch or wandering around Boston looking for open Wi-Fi access points. "It is a lot easier than holding a laptop," Paradiso said. "One unexpected use is watching movies that I ripped from DVD."

However, the onscreen keyboard is awkward to use, and there's no handwriting recognition. Even if Paradiso loads OS X for the built-in handwriting recognition Inkwell software, it works only with Wacom's tablets.

"I loved the idea of a touch-screen device," he said. "Unfortunately, Apple discontinued the Newton. Ever since, I've wanted a Mac tablet."

(LEFT) WEB PAD PARADISO: JEFF PARADISO'S HOMEMADE MACINTOSH-BASED WEB PAD.
CREDIT: JEFF PARADISO

(RIGHT) MORE VIEWS OF PARADISO AND HIS WEB PAD. THE BOTTOM PICTURE SHOWS THE ONSCREEN KEYBOARD.
CREDIT: JEFF PARADISO

CHRISTOPHE JOBIC'S iBOOK

Christophe Jobic, a French photographer, asked a friend to customize his new iBook with a distinctive swirl of rainbow colors. The friend, a professional painter who customizes helmets for Formula One racers and mountain bike riders, sanded the inside of the computer's lid to remove the white paint. He then applied about 15 coats of different colored paint.

"I gave my friend the top cover, leaving my iBook without top protection for three weeks," Jobic wrote in an email. "He never did a computer but I trusted him. Everything has been OK."

"I did it just for the fun and to have a special iBook, just mine and no one else," he added. "It's a very cool new graphic, isn't it?"

SWIRLY: CHRISTOPHE JOBIC'S IBOOK PRINT JOB INVOLVED ABOUT 15 COATS OF DIFFERENT COLORED PRINT.
CREDIT: CHRISTOPHE JOBIC

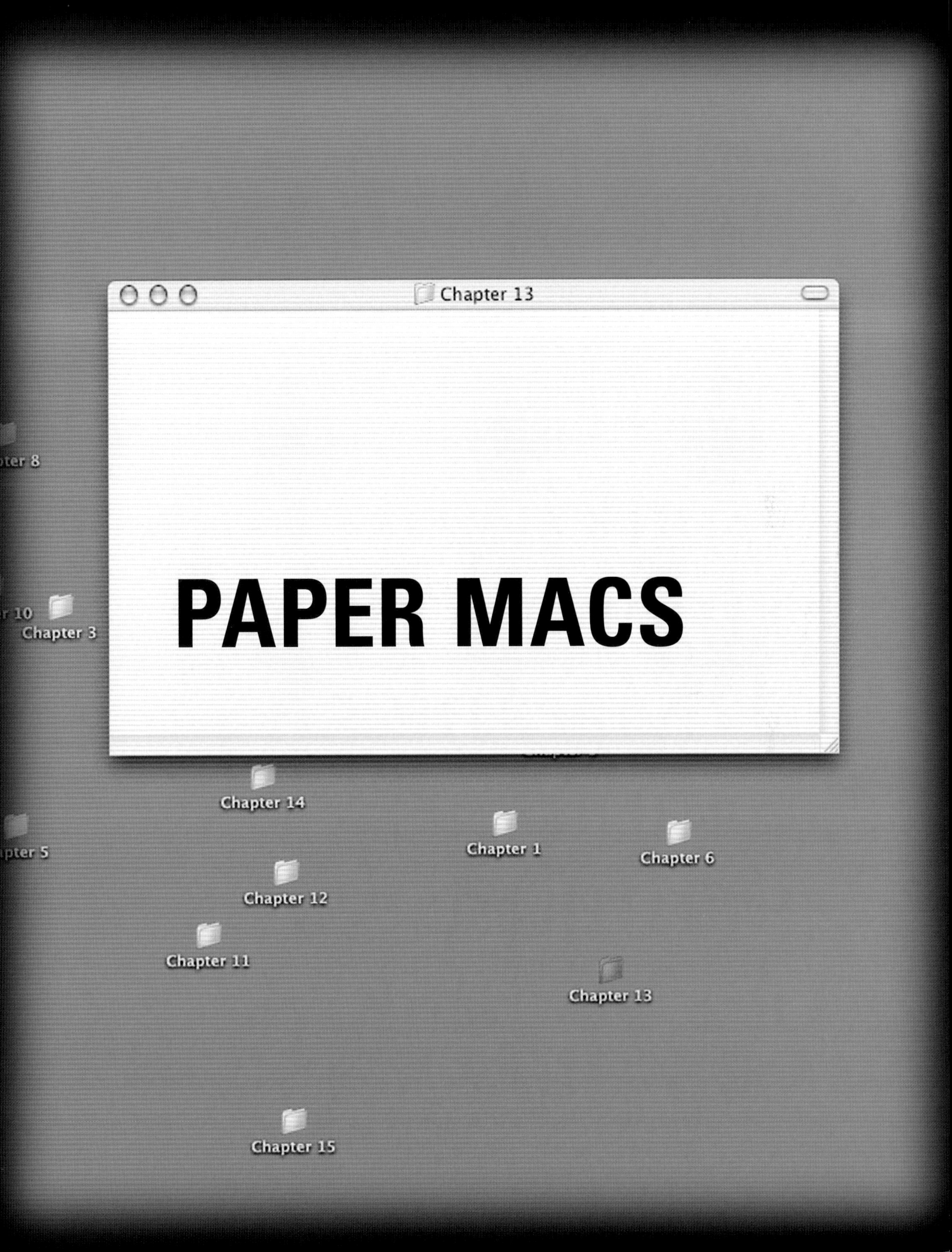

…making paper models of Macintosh computers is almost as old as the Macintosh itself.

First of many: Janis Chevalier's plans for a Mac Christmas tree ornament.
CREDIT: JANIS CHEVALIER

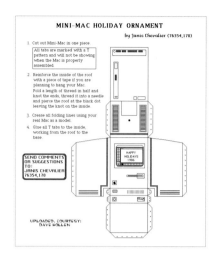

The minute Apple started selling its Power Mac G4 Cube, Mike Burgess ordered one from Apple's Web site. But he was so impatient for it to be delivered, he made a cardboard replica while he waited for the real one to arrive. "I am so excited about the new Cube that I had to see what it would look like in person!" he wrote in a note to MacAddict, where he posted plans for his cardboard Cube so that others could do the same. "I could not get it to boot up with the OS 8.6 CD, but it looks great sticking out of the top slot!" Burgess added.

Burgess made his cardboard machine from a 3D model of the computer he found on Apple's Web site. Apple posted the 3D model in QuickTime VR format to allow potential buyers to spin the Cube around in three dimensions and see it from all angles. Working with the 3D model, Burgess extracted a detailed photograph of each side of the machine. He printed them out one by one on card stock and glued them together. The results were impressive: an accurate facsimile of the silvery Cube, which he placed on his desk.

Burgess wasn't the first person to make a detailed paper model of his Macintosh. In fact, making paper models of Macintosh computers is almost as old as the Macintosh itself. The first Mac was launched in 1984; paper models of the machines appeared only a year or two later. Since then, making faux Macs from paper has flourished into a hobby all its own.

Fans have made paper models of just about every Macintosh computer ever built, dozens in all. The models range from Apple's earliest machines—Apple IIs and all-in-ones such as the Mac SE, Plus, and Color Classic—to the latest G4 desktops and iMacs. Fans have even created a model of the Pippin, Apple's doomed foray into Internet appliances.

Most are matchbox-sized miniatures that can be printed out on a color inkjet printer, cut out, and glued together. Fans can download cut-and-glue plans for most of the models from the Net in PDF format. The machines are recreated in mind-boggling detail—right down to the last screw, air vent, and microphone jack. Many model blueprints come with a miniature keyboard, complete with all the letters, numbers, and symbols on each and every key, so small they can barely be read. Many also have a miniature mouse no bigger than a thumbnail. On some, details as obscure as the mouse ball, hidden away on the bottom of the mouse, are recreated.

The first paper Macintosh was designed by Janis Chevalier as an ornament for a Christmas tree. Making homemade decorative ornaments is an American folk tradition. Chevalier uploaded plans for her model—an early all-in-one Mac—to her local user group's bulletin board in 1986. It proved to be pretty popular: She received mail from all over the country from people who wanted to decorate their trees with it. The ornament is still available from MacAddict.

The most prolific modeler of paper Macintoshes is a 34-year-old Web designer, Mitsuaki Ohashi, who has created dozens of replicas of Apple's more recent machines. He has modeled most of Apple's machines — dozens of desktops and portables in all. "I like Mac!" said Ohashi in an email. "Mac is very good tool, I think so. Mac is very intuitively operational. And good design. . . . Mac is good fellow to expand my ability."

Ohashi, who lives in Sagamihara, Japan, began making paper Macs right after Apple launched the iMac, in July 1998. "I want to buy it but I have no money," Ohashi said. "So I made it of paper!"

184

(above) **Origami Macs: Web designer Mitsuaki Ohashi's beautifully detailed paper Macs. He's created replicas of dozens of Apple's more recent machines.**
CREDIT: MITSUAKI OHASHI

(right) **Looks good on paper: This paper iBook by Mitsuaki Ohashi is about the size of a matchbook. It is perfect in every detail, right down to the screws in the bottom. The plans can be downloaded from Ohashi's site as a PDF file, printed out, and glued together.**
CREDIT: MITSUAKI OHASHI

(this page) **Mitsuaki Ohashi and more of his paper Macs.**

Ohashi's Macintosh models are popular with Mac fanatics: His site has received 130,000 page views. Ohashi owns seven Macs—three PowerBooks and three desktops, including his first machine, an LC 575.

Another keen paper modeler of Macintoshes is Dragon Tongue, a 46-year-old graphic artist and musician who lives in New Zealand and calls herself "The Creator." Dragon Tongue has recreated the entire line of the original iMac, nine fruity-colored machines, in total loving detail. "I go through periods when I become intensely interested in something, do it to the best of my ability, then move on to something else. The paper iMac [phase] was one of those periods," she said.

Dragon Tongue turned the paper iMacs into a mobile for her granddaughter's nursery. She also made a pair of Apple-themed bed ends for the baby's crib. "To make sure that Caitlin grew up with the right priorities, I created huge padded rainbow apples, the early Apple logo, to go at each end of her cot," she said. "My Mac is not a tool," Dragon Tongue said. "It is a lifestyle, a friend, a place, a home, sometimes a pain, never a 'thing.'"

Ken Forbus, a professor of Computer Science and Education at Northwestern University in Evanston, Illinois, said people create these models for many reasons, but many Mac modelers want to remember machines they loved. "These paper models serve as tangible reminders of cherished devices," he said. "That's unusual these days. People used to bond with their computers with ceremonies upon their installation and decommissioning. Now computers flow through our lives, not staying long enough to become companions. In fact, given the transient nature of today's machines, these paper versions will probably outlast the machines themselves."

There are a few models of other kinds of computers, like a Toshiba Libretto laptop, an old Commodore PET and, bizarrely, a Gateway box (not a box as in a computer, but box as in cardboard), but models of Macs are clearly the most popular. "It's obvious that there are more Macs than other computers as paper models, because Mac users like their computers and Windows users hate their systems," said Peter Visser, a paper-model designer from the Netherlands.

Michael LaFosse, an origami expert and the author of several books on paper sculpting, also wasn't surprised that people made models of Macintoshes. "It's an identity badge, it says this means a lot to me," LaFosse said. "The paper arts tend to tickle the minds of the technically adept. It's an engineering job that appeals to mathematicians, scientists. It appeals especially to people who like to do the hands-on stuff. They like to figure things out, and the first material they take it to is paper."

"Other computers are uninspiring workhorses," he added. "They're nothing I'd care to make a model of."

(above) LEGO my iMac:
Someone called iMat couldn't
afford a flat-screen iMac, so
he made one out of LEGO.
CREDIT: IMAT/ERIC PHETERSON

(right) iPaper: This paper
iPod is a lot less expensive
than the real thing. It doesn't
play MP3s, though.
CREDIT: KIERAN BAXTER

188

ANDREW DUSING'S MAC BOX FURNITURE

With innovations such as the iBook and colorful iMacs, Apple has a well-earned reputation for designing beautiful computers. But those who bother to notice the cardboard boxes the machines arrive in will also admire the artistry of the packaging. The graphic design on the shipping material is spare and elegant. The cardboard is as smooth and glossy as the snootiest magazine. The Styrofoam inside is precisely sculpted to fit the computer and its accessories as snugly as a space-age glove. No clunky, flaky inserts here.

In fact, the boxes are so attractive, they inspired one man to furnish his entire apartment with them. Andrew Dusing, a 25-year-old computer technician who lives in upstate New York, has fashioned chairs, tables, and other furniture out of dozens of Apple boxes and their Styrofoam inserts.

Dusing, who works in the graphics department of Cazenovia College, recently outfitted one of the college's computer labs with dozens of new Apple machines. When he finished setting up the computers, he couldn't bear to part with the boxes. "I really didn't want to throw them away," he said. "So I made furniture out of them. Sure, it saves money, but it's because I really like to do it. It's about thinking different. What could I make today?"

Dusing turned the boxes into a dining table, a set of chairs, and some CD racks. He even made a couch. "You can sit on it," he said, "but it's not all that comfortable."

To further show off his packing-material passion, Dusing made a pair of giant, bulky animal sculptures—a sofa-sized rhino and a giraffe that stands six feet tall. "I wanted to make some animals whose coloring reflected the pictures on the boxes," he said. "The boxes were turquoise and blue and white. I used those elements to my advantage."

Dusing made the giraffe out of packing tape and Elmer's glue; but as a result, it's starting to fall apart. The rhino is made from drywall screws and industrial-strength epoxy glue. He designed them by drawing a silhouette of the animal and dividing it into

(opposite page) Comfy:
Andrew Dusing was a bit
hard up, so he furnished his
entire flat with furniture
made from discarded Mac
boxes. Here's his couch.
CREDIT: ANDREW DUSING

(right) Put your feet up:
Andrew Dusing stretched out
on his cardboard couch.
CREDIT: ANDREW DUSING

geometric shapes—triangles, rectangles, and squares, which could be made out of cardboard.

Dusing was inspired by the huge topiary sculptures at Walt Disney World in Florida and originally planned to put the cardboard animals in his mother's front garden. "The neighbors have all these dopey ornaments on their lawns," he said. "But my mom wasn't too keen on having these giant lawn ornaments." The sculptures were exhibited at an art show at the college and received a positive response. One attendee suggested Dusing could sell them on eBay for $5,000 apiece, but he opted to keep them, despite the tight quarters in his apartment.

Dusing plans to make more animal sculptures, perhaps an elephant or a gorilla. He is also hoping to get his hands on some old Apple boxes from the 1980s that featured the rainbow-colored Apple logo. If he gets enough of the old boxes, he'll make a '57 Chevy out of them. "They're classic boxes so why not make a classic car?" he said. Dusing also wants to make more furniture. He needs a rack for his collection of videocassettes. "I'll never need to buy furniture again," he said. "Whenever a need arises, I know I can make it out of cardboard. I just wish I had more boxes."

Obviously, Dusing is a fan of the Macintosh. "I'm a big Mac fan. I'm a huge Mac fan," he said. "I use Macs every day, all day long. I hate the PC world. Mac is the only way to go. It's very sexy. It's way sleek. It's great stuff. It's all great stuff."

Dusing graduated from Cazenovia College with a degree in visual communication. The school is 30 minutes from Syracuse. "It's a sleepy little town tucked away in a small corner of the world," he said. "I've always been a dreamer," he added. "I wanted to work for Jim Henson or be on TV. Just have fun." His girlfriend thinks the sculptures are "really cool." She encourages him to make more. "She likes the fact I'm a dreamer," he said.

Dusing said he has often thought of designing an advertising campaign for Apple and sending it to the company. He'd also be delighted if the company bought one of his sculptures. "I'd love for them to maybe buy it and put it in their corporate headquarters," he said.

(opposite page) **Mac menagerie:** After furnishing his apartment, Dusing had plenty of boxes left over, so he fashioned sculptures of a rhino and a giraffe.
CREDIT: ANDREW DUSING

(this page) **Who needs IKEA?** Dusing also made a CD stand and a corner table (top left), a lamp table (bottom left), and a bookshelf (right) out of boxes.
CREDIT: ANDREW DUSING

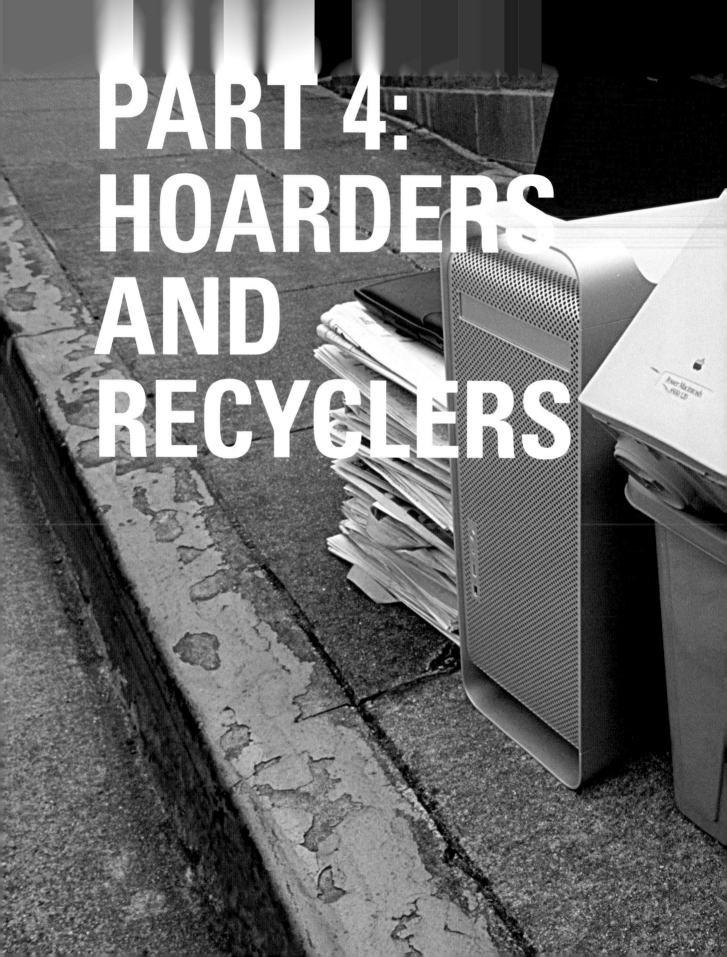

PART 4: HOARDERS AND RECYCLERS

Chapter 7

Chapter 8

apter 10

Chapter 3

Chapter 5

Chapter 14

MAC COLLECTORS AND COLLECTIBLES

Chapter 15

(36) Dealers: The staff of RedLightRunner.com, a dealer in Apple collectibles. Over the years, Apple has given out millions of branded tchotchkes. Some are now very valuable. Who knew a free promotional poster would now be worth more than $1,000?

John McKay
Co-Owner
Apple Collectible Specialist

Steven Naughton
Co-Owner
Apple Collectible Specialist

Jarrod Zeyouma
Apple Collectible Specialist

Giulio Sciorio
Photographer

CREDIT: REDLIGHTRUNNER

REDLIGHTRUNNER, SAVING COLLECTIBLES TO THE MACS

During a recent visit to the store at Apple's corporate headquarters, John McKay and Steve Naughton were shown the door. Although they'd come all the way from Arizona, the dumbstruck pair were told they weren't allowed to shop at the store, which sells a wide range of Apple souvenirs, such as watches, T-shirts, and mugs. McKay and Naughton were thrown out because they had bought some goods at the store and then resold them online, a strictly prohibited practice.

But how did Apple know? Surely someone can resell an Apple luggage tag on eBay without the company catching on? Most people can, but McKay and Naughton run a thriving business selling Apple-logo merchandise on the Web. As the founders of RedLightRunner.com, they probably have more Apple-logo goods than Apple does. How Apple recognized the pair is a mystery. Apple declined to comment.

Naughton doesn't know. "I'm not sure how they knew, but somehow they figured it out," he said. "We had 11 hours to think about it on our drive from Cupertino [California] back down to Flagstaff."

McKay, 31, and Naughton, 29, launched RedLightRunner in 1999. Based in Flagstaff, Arizona, a small city near the Grand Canyon, the company was set to do $300,000 worth of business in 2002. Sales have almost doubled every year since the company's inception. The pair sells a range of Apple collectibles, from T-shirts, mugs, and lapel pins to rare items like a $1,000 Picasso dealer display lamp.

The prices are surprisingly high. Rare posters from Apple's Think Different campaign—featuring, say, the Dalai Lama or Bob Dylan—can command more than $1,000. The posters were originally free. Many are worth $250 or more. A free tote bag from a conference is $130, an inexpensive watch is worth $200, an out-of-print book about Apple's design is $250, a lapel pin is $60, and a plastic train is $300. "Our prices are based on availability," Naughton said. "It's all supply and demand."

RedLightRunner is the biggest of about half a dozen Apple collector stores on the Web. Others include Dougintosh, inetreviews. com, and DigitalHorse. A list of sites can be found at UberMac. There is also a busy trade in Apple collectibles at eBay.

RedLightRunner claims to have 35,000 customers around the world, especially in Germany, the U.K., and Japan. "Many of these people come back over and over," Naughton said. Business

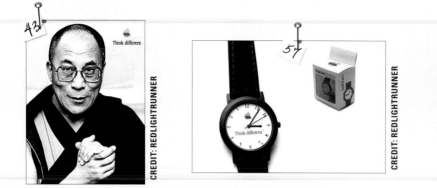

CREDIT: REDLIGHTRUNNER

CREDIT: REDLIGHTRUNNER

(43) Sticker shock: This rare Think Different poster of the Dalai Lama costs $1,000.

(57) Back in time: The hands on Apple's Think Different watch run backward.

is brisk enough for RedLightRunner to employ a programmer and a photographer. "Apple's got that collectibility," said Naughton. "It's a great company. It's a great brand. It's an icon."

"People ask me if I would ever sell Dell stuff or Microsoft, but you could never make a business out of it," he said. "It would be like trying to trade Enron stuff. There's not the same aura about it. There's something about Apple that really inspires people.... If Apple were a crappy company, we'd never get 5 cents for this stuff."

With the exception of vintage calculators, there doesn't appear to a collecting culture in computing quite like Apple's. However, Kevin Stumpf, a technology appraiser with the Ask the Appraiser online appraisal service, said RedLightRunner is evidence of a growing interest in collecting vintage computers. "It's evidence of the growing popularity of techno-collecting. If you can't techno-speak, at least you can wear a vintage techno-jacket," Stumpf said. "Techno-collecting, in general, is a pastime whose time has come.... From radios to sewing machines to earth-moving equipment to flashlights, if you can switch it on and off, it will be collected."

Dr. Tony Hyman of CBS News' What's It Worth? said brand items from hundreds of companies are collected, including Budweiser, Marlboro, Camel, Pillsbury, Wrigley, Pepsi, Moxie, numerous insurance companies, Sears, numerous auto makers, Dixie, Campbell's Soup, Jack Daniels, Green River, Nabisco, and many more. Hyman said Apple collectibles don't come close to Bud, Marlboro, or Camel. Marlboro, the leading marketer worldwide, has revenues from branded items in at least the $30 million range, Hyman estimated.

"The important question in my mind is why anyone wants to become a corporate billboard and pay for the privilege," Hyman said. "Makes absolutely no sense to me. It's bad enough that

folks want to brag that they paid too much for their clothes by wearing those emblazoned with the name of the maker. My favorite is BUM, a word that means, in various contexts, bad, shoddy, hobo, and ass."

McKay and Naughton are both enthusiastic Apple collectors, themselves. "We started RedLightRunner out of passion because we love Apple," Naughton said. "At heart I'm an Apple collector. I've got a lot of stuff. In order to buy new stuff, I have to sell old stuff. Most of the time when I sell something, I regret it." There are some things he'll never sell, like the Think Different watch he wears every day. The hands run counterclockwise.

The pair started the business after McKay had trouble finding a replacement for his favorite Apple T-shirt, which he'd worn out by wearing it every day. He eventually found one on eBay, plus a dozen more. He bought them all and quickly sold them for a profit. Eighty percent of RedLightRunner's business is one-off items: a signed Wozniak book, dealer signs, vintage Apple T-shirts, handbags, and books. The most valuable Apple collectibles are ones emblazoned with the famous old rainbow-colored Apple logo, which was discontinued in the mid-nineties in favor of a monochrome version.

Where did the RedLightRunner name come from? Naughton, who used to be a music producer before launching RedLightRunner, said he lifted it from a song by a favorite indie band, but he likes it because it is reminiscent of Apple's Think Different slogan. "It reminds you to push the envelope, to do things differently from the status quo," he said. "And it's just a good word."

Naughton paused. "All that Apple promo stuff," he mused. "There's got to be millions of pieces out there. All that stuff," he repeated, as though in a dream. "People should contact us if they have any. I'll consider buying it all."

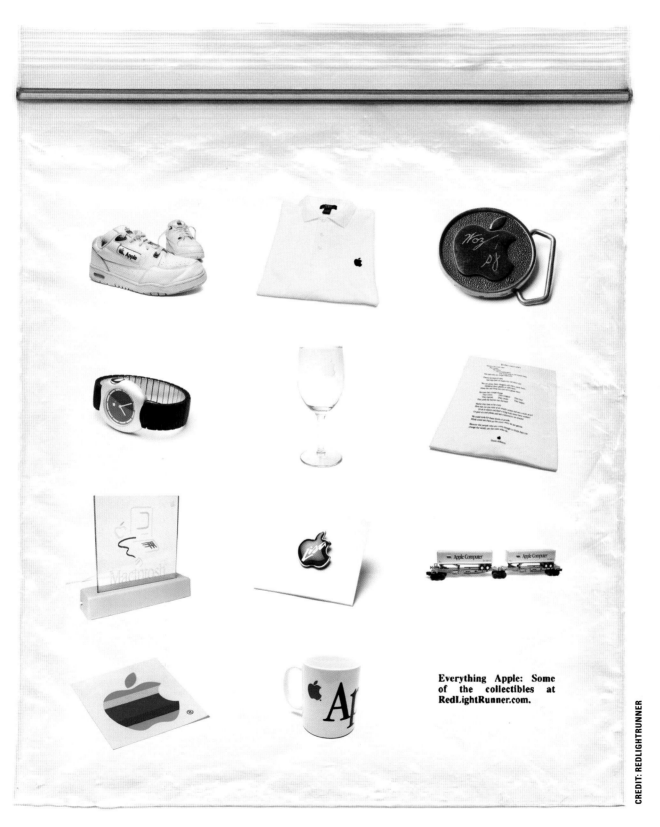

Everything Apple: Some of the collectibles at RedLightRunner.com.

THREE APPLE COLLECTORS

The Mac is more than a computer: It's a community, an identity, a church. Collecting Apple memorabilia is an important part of the Mac psyche. Psychiatrist David Levine is a dedicated collector of Apple-branded goods. He's also the kind of Mac devotee who buys extra computers just to support Apple. Levine has spent a couple of thousand dollars in the last few years on Apple-branded key chains, luggage tags, pins, watches, and posters. "I'm a Mac nut," said Levine, a lecturer in psychology at the University of Illinois College of Medicine in Rockford. "It's more emotional than an investment."

Levine's proudest possession is a suede Apple jacket adorned with some of the original Macintosh icons. He paid $400 but hasn't yet worn it outside his house. He's looking forward to the day he can wear it to Macworld Expo, which he never gets to attend because of work.

That doesn't matter, though—the Levine household is a mini-Macworld of its own. Along with his wife and two kids, the Levines have ten Macs at home: three iMacs, two older Macs, a dual-processor G4, three PowerBook portables, and an older Macintosh clone. In 2002, Levine went out and bought a dual-processor G4, which cost about $4,000, and a large flat-panel Cinema display, which cost $2,000, just to support Apple. "I don't need it," he said. "I did it to support the Mac." For the same reason, Levine also buys quite a lot of shareware. "I don't always need it," he said. "I just want to support the author. It's just worth supporting."

Like all Apple collectors, Levine identifies strongly with Mac culture—the T-shirts and luggage tags broadcast his association. "It's more than just a computer; it's a community," he said. "For many Mac people, I think it has a religious feeling to it. For a lot of people who are not comfortable with religion, it provides a community and a common heritage. I think Mac users have a certain common way of thinking, a way of doing things, a certain mindset."

"People say they are a Buddhist or a Catholic," he added. "We say we're Mac users, and that means we have similar values."

Collecting isn't always rational, and Apple collecting is no different. A few years ago, Mike Swope was given the opportunity to buy hundreds of Apple-branded items: watches, T-shirts, pens, posters, and some beach towels. He maxed out his credit card and bought the lot. Four years later, he's still trying to sell it, just so he can pay off his credit card. "I bought as much as I could," he said. "I've still got boxes of the stuff."

Swope doesn't even know what he's got. He hasn't opened some of the poster tubes. "I think I have a set [of] No. 2," he said, referring to the second series of Think Different promotional posters. "I could have a rare Bob Dylan poster, but I don't know because I've never opened it.... I'm going to have to eventually open the tubes," he added without relish.

Swope, 33, a graphic designer from Wichita, Kansas, is slowly selling his collection at inetreviews.com. He didn't really enjoy his Apple collection anyway. "I couldn't hang the posters up," he said. "I couldn't bring myself to bring them out of the tube. It might damage them. It's more valuable if it's never been taken out of the tube. It's the anal-retentive collector in me."

His wheeling and dealing has made him some money. He bought an iBook and a new iMac. Three years ago he owed $10,000 on his credit card. He now owes less than $1,000. In the first year he collected $40,000, he said, but the money has evaporated as he runs out of valuable stock. He's found it hard to find new supplies of good collectibles; RedLightRunner is tying up the market. He's also stopped selling on eBay, his most profitable outlet, because of the time and effort involved.

Like Swope, high school teacher David Ernst is an Apple collector simply because he got a chance to buy a boatload of Apple tchotchkes at fire-sale prices.

A few years ago, Ernst found an Apple dealer who was selling off hundreds of promotional items. Ernst bought it all—about 13 big boxes in all—for less than $2,000. "The dealer had an unbelievable amount of stuff," Ernst said. "I did a bit of research and saw how unbelievably high the prices were. A lot of the stuff was 10 years old and still in its original packaging." At first Ernst made a lot of money selling the items individually on eBay. "I hesitated to report it on my income tax," he said. "But I did anyway."

Then he was contacted by a collector from Japan. Ernst said the collector was a "spoiled, young rich brat" who traveled the globe buying and selling collectibles. The collector was so interested in Ernst's collection, he flew in from Japan to pick it up personally. Somehow, the brat persuaded Ernst to let him

(28) Irrational: Psychologist David Levine with his suede Apple jacket adorned with some of the original Macintosh icons. He paid $400 but hasn't yet worn it outside his house. "I'm a Mac nut," he says.

take the bulk of the collection with him back to Japan for half the agreed price. He promised to settle up later.

"Being a high school chemistry teacher, I made a very poor business decision," Ernst lamented. "He took 90 percent of my stuff and he still owes me $4,300. I'm a buffoon for trusting him."

Ernst was left with a few items. He was still selling them off in 2002. "I'm an Apple freak," he said, "but I'm not in any sense a collector."

RAINES COHEN, T-SHIRT COLLECTOR

Raines Cohen is the Imelda Marcos of Macintosh T-shirts. Over the years, Cohen has collected more than 500 T-shirts relating to Apple and the Mac. His collection is now part of Stanford University's collection of Apple artifacts. Cohen is more than a T-shirt collector, though. He is an unsung hero of the 1989 Loma Prieta earthquake.

For nearly 20 years, Cohen was at the heart of Mac culture: first as a cofounder of the Berkeley Mac User Group (BMUG) and then as a technical analyst for *MacWeek*, the seminal news weekly. Cohen spoke at numerous user-group meetings across the country, attended hundreds of company and product launches, and went to every Macworld Expo for 17 years. Along the way he collected every shirt he could lay his hands on.

T-shirts are a big part of geek culture. Every company, product, project, user group, and event is celebrated with a commemorative T-shirt, just like a concert tour. "It was the convenience of being given these things and not spending any money on the upper half of my wardrobe," Cohen said, explaining how his collection blossomed. "And identity. I'm known for wearing these things."

Cohen wore a different shirt every day. In the corridors of *MacWeek* and at events, people would ask him what shirt he had chosen that day. It took him more than six months to cycle through the collection. His closets were full of shirts. Most were stored in the basement. "Eventually I realized my wardrobe was a collection," Cohen said. "It paints quite a history."

Stanford University's library contains a voluminous collection of Apple artifacts, mostly donated by the company. The collection includes a lot of T-shirts produced by Apple, but not many associated with third-party companies or user groups.

Most of Cohen's shirts are from Mac-related companies, user groups, and events. The collection provides a kind of folksy, illustrated history of Mac culture. "Each one has a story associated with it," Cohen said.

Alex Soojung-Kim Pang, the Stanford archivist who asked Cohen for his shirts, said, "T-shirts are the pottery shards of the digital age: They don't look like much at first, but they can tell us a lot about the times that produced them. The event and user-group T-shirts in particular are vivid records of the vibrant, smart culture that grew up around the Mac—and was a truly grassroots movement, not an Apple-directed event."

Soojung-Kim Pang said he wasn't sure if or when Cohen's shirts would go on display, but said the collection is important enough to be in a museum. "Raines, himself, is one of those figures who knows everyone in the Mac world and has been involved in the Macintosh's history since the beginning," he said. "Sociologists like to talk about social networks, and how there are often a few key people who hold together communities and provide links between one group and another; Raines is one of those figures. Preserving his collection was important."

These are some of Cohen's favorite T-shirts:

THE BMUG TIE-DYE T-SHIRT: This shirt was created for the first Macworld Expo in Washington, in 1989. The event promised to be formal, and the Berkeley contingent wanted to distinguish themselves from all the suits and military uniforms. The shirt eventually became the BMUG uniform. Hundreds were sold, especially in Asia. Each was handmade by Berkeley Deadheads.

SYSTEM 7.1 SUCKS LESS: This shirt was created by an Apple programming team and sold at Boston Macworld Expo. On the back it read, "We've upped our standards—up yours!" Wearing the shirt at the Expo got Cohen banned from the Apple booth. It was eventually imitated widely. Dozens of companies inserted the name of their product. Inevitably, even Microsoft stole the idea.

MICROSOFT'S VACUUM CLEANER: Cohen is fond of a T-shirt picturing a very elaborate vacuum cleaner, which reads, "The

(62) Historic threads: Over the years, Raines Cohen's wardrobe became a historical collection. Stanford's library now has many of his T-shirts in its archive of Apple artifacts.

(73) & (75) King of collectors: Raines Cohen's historic collection of 500 or more T-shirts spans a couple of decades of Mac history.

day Microsoft makes a product that does not suck will be the day they start making vacuum cleaners."

AS THE APPLE TURNS: Cohen likes the personal touch of T-shirts sold by As the Apple Turns, an Apple fan site. Featuring the site's logo, the shirts can be personally blessed by the site's owner, Jack Miller, for an extra $10. Miller also includes a certificate of blessing and a personal thank-you note.

DEAD COMPANIES: Cohen also likes an old Apple T-shirt with a biblical riff: "The 10 Command Keys," and one commemorating Apple's long-gone online experimental community, eWorld. In fact, Cohen said he usually wears shirts only from companies that have gone out of business. This is a common practice among industry journalists. Reporters are often given shirts, but balk at giving companies free advertising. Many take pride in wearing the T-shirt only after the company goes under.

Cohen, now a database consultant and cohousing expert, said geek T-shirts are a popular and inexpensive way of "branding" a group or project. "They are something you can show off and share," he said. "It's a way of marking milestones. It gave a sense of reality to a group or project. It made it seem significant. They are inexpensive and something people would pay for. It was something you had to do."

Within Apple, the T-shirt was a big part of corporate culture. "At Apple, you couldn't talk about a product before it was released, but you could print a T-shirt with a code name to give a sense of identity within a group. It said, 'We're in this together.'"

Cohen said the quality of a shirt would often give clues about the health of a particular company, or how much they were investing in a product. The T-shirts also gave Cohen clues about what was going on inside Apple. For example, at one show in 1996, a group of programmers produced a T-shirt that made a mess of Apple's sacrosanct rainbow-colored apple logo. The fact they got away with it told Cohen the company was in disarray. At the time, of course, Apple's CEO Gilbert Amelio was being pushed out by Steve Jobs, who had just been brought back to the company.

Cohen didn't just collect shirts. In 1989, he whipped up a quick computer network for the Red Cross in the wake of the disastrous Loma Prieta earthquake. Before the dust had settled, Cohen grabbed a handful of Macs and networking equipment from BMUG and took them down to the Red Cross command post near the collapsed Cypress freeway in Oakland. In less than 24 hours, Cohen had helped create a database containing a list of more than 1,000 volunteers, their skills, the hours they had worked, and other details. It allowed Red Cross personnel to find, say, a nurse who spoke Cambodian who hadn't been working for the last 12 hours.

"The Red Cross had a minicomputer, but it hadn't been set up yet," Cohen said. "They weren't set up to respond so quickly. They hadn't taken advantage of the PC revolution. We were quick and dirty and real simple."

This, of course, was in the pre-networking era. PCs were difficult to network, but Macs, designed for schools, were relatively easy to hook up. The network had 10 terminals and about 100 volunteers working around the clock. It was used for months. It inspired the Red Cross to ditch minicomputers and mainframes for networks of PCs.

Cohen's network helped him land a job at *MacWeek* because he met one of the editors while volunteering. "Raines is a great organizer," said former *MacWeek* editor David Morgenstern. "If he were alive in the 1920s or 1930s, he would have been a great union organizer. Raines believes that people and computers can be a force for good in our society. And his sincerity brings everybody along. He's an idealistic person in an industry where only products and sales are idealized."

CREDIT: *APPLE* BY ANDY
WARHOL (COSKUN & CO. LTD.)

**Candy Apple: A pop art ren-
dition of Apple's famous
Macintosh logo was auctioned
online for $12,000.**

Andy Warhol's Apple Logo Print

In November 2000, a mysterious art connoisseur parted with more than $12,000 for a pastel-colored print of the famous Apple logo. The London-based site Sothebys.com auctioned off a signed and numbered screen print of the instantly recognizable logo by the late, great Andy Warhol. The three-foot square, pastel-hued screen print shows Apple's rainbow icon. The words "Apple" and "Macintosh" are printed above and below. The auction attracted at least two bidders and was won by someone identified only as "Paddle 50621." The bidder's identity was not revealed.

"An Apple logo selling for $12,000? It doesn't make sense," said Gul Coskun, the London dealer selling the Apple print. "It's like a joke, but that's Warhol for you."

Produced in 1985, the print is one of Warhol's Ads series, which mimicked popular advertising images of the time, including Ronald Reagan from a commercial for Van Heusen shirts, and James Dean from the poster for *Rebel Without a Cause*. "It's a typical Warhol idea," Coskun said. "It's like the [Campbell's] soup cans. It's the same idea."

The Ads prints were originally issued in portfolios of 10 images and sold as a set. There were 190 numbered portfolios issued, though there are probably about 280 in circulation when all the artist's and printer's proofs are taken into account, Coskun said. She estimated the prints initially sold for about $500 each.

Sotheby's has previously auctioned many Warhols, including several copies of the Apple Macintosh print. "Warhol prints are some of the most sought after," said Nina Del Rio, director of online auctions at Sothebys.com. "They are fun, they are easy to own, and he's widely known. He's very hot."

Del Rio said that over the years she has sold "bazillions" of copies of the Apple print. The price, she said, has fluctuated as wildly as the stock market. Over the years, Warhol prints have increased in popularity, but the economic boom of the late 1990s fueled a hike in interest and prices, Coskun said.

Still, Coskun was a little mystified by the appeal of the Apple print, one of simplest images in the portfolio and the only technology-related work. "For some reason it appeals to a lot of people," she said. "It doesn't appeal to me, I'm afraid."

CAESAR LIMA'S STUDIO MUSEUM

Like a lot of U.S. immigrants, Brazilian-born photographer Caesar Lima started from scratch when he moved to Los Angeles in 1985. Lima struggled for the first few years but now runs a thriving digital imaging studio, Caesar Photo Design, which he has turned into a shrine to the technology that helped make him successful: Apple computers.

Lima's studio is a mini Mac museum. He has 35 Macs—from the Lisa to the Cube—on display in the front foyer. He constructed the studio's reception desk from a stack of 15 working Mac Classics. "My clients love it," he said. "Everyone in this industry—art directors, designers—use Macs. They come to the studio and spend half an hour looking at my collection. They say, 'Look at this; I had one of these.'"

Lima's photography studio runs on Macs. He has nine state-of-the-art Macs—three PowerBooks, four Power Mac G4 workstations, a couple of iMacs, and an eMac, used mainly for scanning and digitally manipulating images. A Mac controls the studio's unique lighting system—a custom setup resembling a theater's lighting rig. Lima furnished an entertainment lounge next to the studio with a couple of plump sofas, a big-screen TV, and an iMac-driven sound system.

"I am a Mac freak," Lima said. "Every time I buy a new Mac system, I just could not sell the old one, so I start collecting them. It took me five or six years, and I'm still going."

Lima even tried to persuade his assistant to get an Apple tattoo for a photo shoot. She refused, opting for a temporary one instead. "She's only just been exposed [to Macs]," he said. "I think in a couple of years she will go for it."

Rovane Durso, principal of Durso Design, a design firm based in Santa Monica, California, said: "Caesar's Macintosh collection is the most intense and crazy thing I have ever seen when it comes to computers. It is almost sculptural. He's turned his studio into a museum!"

Lima, 43, abandoned a successful camera and photography business in his native Sao Paulo to move to the States. Unable to find a job even as a photographer's assistant, he worked as a clerk in a San Fernando Valley camera store. Eventually he picked up some freelance work, working out of his garage. "The only problem was my clients wanted to check out the studio," he said. "And in the summer, it was hell. It was like an oven inside. But I had to start somewhere."

These days, Lima has a long list of high-profile clients spread all over the world. Specializing in product photography, Lima has worked for Pioneer, Sebastian, Capitol Records, Yamaha, and Sony Pictures, among others. "Caesar's work created the image for our company that set us apart from any other competitor in our category," said John Amiri, an executive with Zodax, a home decor supplier. "Certain catalogs that Caesar has done for Zodax are treated almost as 'coffee table' decorative accessories."

The key to Lima's success has been developing a signature "look," which—naturally—relies on manipulating his images on the computer. Lima's photos are all tinted with a distinctive palette that looks distinctly artificial. "I don't shoot anything that looks real," he said. "I like to bend reality."

He achieves some of the effects in camera—colored lighting, multiple exposures—and finishes them off on the computer using Photoshop and other software packages. Even though the final photos are output in digital format, Lima still uses film for many shoots. "Right now I have more money in the computers than the cameras, and I'm a photographer," he said. "It's amazing. They've changed the whole business."

He added, "It is funny, I started out on a [Windows] PC. When I bought my first Mac, I felt like a kid at Christmas. Since then I am addicted to it. For sure Apple is the coolest company, an American icon."

205

(91) Welcome: The reception desk at Lima's studio is made from 15 working Mac Classics.

(97) Branded: Photographer Caesar Lima tried to persuade his assistant to get a real OS X tattoo for a photo shoot, but she opted for a temporary henna one instead. Here she is getting inked at a tattoo parlor in Venice, California.

(99) Shrine: Photographer Caesar Lima has turned his studio into a mini-museum of Macs.

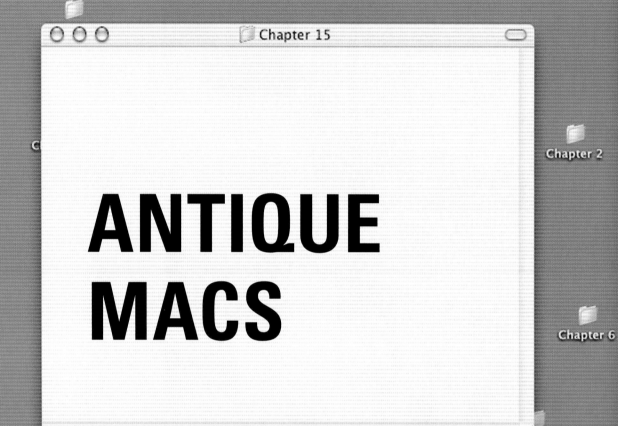

ANTIQUE MACS

Think Timeless.

think timeless

NOTHING GETS THE PULSE OF A MAC ENTHUSIAST RACING LIKE AN OLD PIECE OF APPLE HARDWARE. COLLECTING ANTIQUE MACS IS A CONSUMING PASSION FOR MANY. MUCH OF IT IS DRIVEN BY NOSTALGIA, OF COURSE, A SENTIMENT PARODIED IN THIS POSTER BY BRIAN BILLADEAU.
CREDIT: BRIAN BILLADEAU

"HAVING A STRONG COLOR CLASSIC IS LIKE OWNING A HOT ROD CAR. IT'S IMPRACTICAL, BUT IT'S COOL. THERE ARE A LOT OF PEOPLE WHO WILL PAY ANY PRICE TO HAVE ONE."

(RIGHT) A CLASSIC: ONE OF THE MOST SOUGHT-AFTER VINTAGE MACS IS THE COLOR CLASSIC, WHICH CAN BE UPDATED—AT GREAT EXPENSE—BY SWAPPING ITS INSIDES FOR THOSE OF AN iMAC.
CREDIT: UNKNOWN

(FAR RIGHT RIGHT) NEW AGAIN: DAVID VOGLER AND HIS UPGRADED COLOR CLASSIC RUNNING OS X.
CREDIT: DAVID VOGLER

THE INCREDIBLE DEVOTION TO THE COLOR CLASSIC

The iMac is the most popular computer ever made. Apple sold six million of the machines, which far outstrips sales of any other model of personal computer. But for some Apple enthusiasts, the company will never improve on the iMac's progenitor, the Color Classic.

The Color Classic was introduced in the early nineties. By today's standards, it is a dinosaur. Yet the Color Classic is eagerly sought after. So much so, it is hard to find one, especially in Asia. If you are lucky enough to stumble across a prehistoric Color Classic, it could set you back over $600, which is much more than the cost of a second-hand iMac.

The Color Classic is desirable because of its size. It is still one of the smallest, most compact computers ever made. To bring these aging, painfully slow machines up to speed, Classic fans have figured out some clever ways to upgrade its internal components. Some, in fact, will go to absurd lengths to update these ancient sloths. But so successful are the upgraders, for a short while in the winter of 2000, a Color Classic was the fastest Macintosh on the planet. Thanks to a brand-new 500 MHz G3 daughter card from an upgrade manufacturer, which hadn't yet made it into Apple's production line, it was faster than any brand-new Mac from Apple, and more than 50 times faster than the original machine.

The Color Classic was launched in 1993 and discontinued a year later. It is still one of the most miniature machines ever produced. Measuring less than one foot in any direction and weighing only 20 pounds, it is about half the size of the iMac.

The diminutive, all-in-one computer was the last in a long line of compact computers from Apple. The "toaster" Macs, as they were known, include the Mac SE/30 and the Mac Plus. They all featured a built-in monitor and a carrying handle built in to the top. But unlike its predecessors, the Color Classic didn't have a boring black-and-white display: It was the first to have a glorious color screen.

Because of its built-in color monitor, the Color Classic became, well, an instant classic. It was popular with students because it didn't take up much space in a dorm room, and it was portable. At a time when notebooks were scarce, the Color Classic could be lugged fairly easily to and from college. The burgeoning desktop publishing industry also took a shine to the Color Classic's crisp, clear 9-inch color screen.

But to keep size and costs to a minimum, Apple handicapped the Color Classic with a number of crippling limitations. It was based on an aging motherboard architecture and had an unbearably slow 16 MHz processor, which was a snail even in its day. And it couldn't be upgraded. The processor was soldered to the motherboard. Apple also limited the Color Classic's maximum memory to only 10MB. At the time, RAM was expensive, but 10MB of RAM isn't enough to do anything now. The average Web browser demands twice as much memory just to get up and running.

By today's standards, the Color Classic is way too underpowered for tasks like Web browsing, let alone for running power-hungry applications like graphics or games. Today, the Color Classic is good only for rudimentary word processing or email. And you'd better turn on the television or open a newspaper if you plan to run a computationally demanding task like a spelling checker. It is so limited, the Low End Mac Web site (http://www.lowendmac.com) has designated it a "Road Apple"—one of the worst machines Apple has ever made.

But across the world, scores of enterprising fans of the undersized machine have found some innovative workarounds. "It's a brilliant machine, but it's so painfully slow," says Rev. Stuart Bell, a church minister in England who maintains a Web site about upgrading Color Classics. "Nothing quite matches its compact look and portability. It's the definitive Mac."

Rev. Bell is a local parish priest in rural Sussex. Before becoming a man of the cloth, Bell trained as an electrical engineer. He upgraded his Color Classic with a 275 MHz G3 chip, which makes it faster than the original iMacs.

To install the new chip, Rev. Bell first had to install a new motherboard. He used a board from an old Mac LC 575, which accepts plug-in daughter cards containing the central processor. Rev. Bell chose a daughter card with a 275 MHz 603e RISC processor, which boosts his little Color Classic to 20 times the speed it originally operated at. To make room for the new motherboard and add an extra power supply, Rev. Bell had to hack away huge chunks of the computer's interior casing. It cost him a couple of hundred dollars and about 20 hours of work. He fried three Color Classics figuring out how to do it. His two kids now use it for games and homework.

Upgrading Color Classics has become so popular that in some parts of the world, prices on the old models have been driven up, and they are almost impossible to find. In parts of Asia, buyers will pay in excess of $600, compared to about $100 in the United States, reports Patrick Ng, who created a Web site documenting his strange obsession with the machine, which he calls his "Color Classic Fixation Syndrome."

"I now see the uncompromising beauty and elegance from [the] Color Classic even more obviously; it simply shines," Ng writes. "As this mystic discovery continues, my super-ego seems to warn me [of] the danger of the game, the emotional attachment to a physical object."

In Japan, there is a club devoted entirely to upgrading the Color Classic, called the Club for Creating the Strongest Color Classic. The club boasts more than 300 members who have figured out ways to install the fastest chips, the biggest hard drives, stereo sound, slot-loading CD-ROM drives, and expansion slots for things like the latest 3D video acceleration cards. "We want to use [the Color Classic] forever with high performance," explained Mikio Kobayashi, a member of the club who has upgraded her machine with a G3 chip. "We like this shape and concept of compact Mac. This has a nice Trinitron cathode-ray tube and small size."

Tom Owad, who runs Applefritter, a site dedicated to Mac modifications, suggests that the cramped living quarters of many Japanese apartments lends the diminutive Classic its air of desirability. "The land shortage has a lot to do with it," he said. There is also the "cuteness" factor. The iMac may be cool, but the Color Classic is infinitely "cuter."

The strongest machine in the club belongs to Mr. Misutiku, who installed a 500 MHz G3 chip and a TV tuner with a remote control. For a while, Mr. Misutiku's Color Classic was the fastest Macintosh available anywhere. Somehow, Mr. Misutiku managed to procure one of the first 500 MHz chips off the assembly line at Motorola. He even beat Apple, which didn't start selling its first 500 MHz Power Macintoshes until six months later.

The Club for Creating the Strongest Color Classic was founded by Takashi Imai, a writer for a Japanese Macintosh magazine, and Makoto Akizuki. Between them, the pair pioneered numerous ways of slicing and dicing motherboards from later machines to make them fit inside the Color Classic's cramped casing. Last year, Imai and Akizuki published a detailed how-to book with instructions for upgrading the Color Classic's internal components. The instructions are available on the club's Web site (http://kanchan.hn.org/).

(LEFT) THOU SHALT UPGRADE:
REV. STUART BELL AND HIS
UPGRADED COLOR CLASSIC.
CREDIT: REV. STUART BELL

(BELOW) JOHN STOCKER
UPGRADED HIS COLOR CLASSIC
WITH A 500 MHZ G3 CHIP AND
A 60GB HARD DRIVE.
CREDIT: JOHN STOCKER

```
▣▤▤▤▤▤▤▤▤▤▤▤▤▤▤▤▤▤color classic facts▤▤▤▤▤▤▤▤▤▤▤▤▤▤▤▤▤▤
```

The smiling icon that appears during the Mac startup sequence is a Color Classic.

The case was designed by Daniele Deluliis at Apple. He carved the floppy disk slot to resemble a drooping mouth. The side vents were made to look like gills, suggesting the machine breathed. And its plastic feet were fashioned to resemble the legs of a baby elephant.

The most popular method is to take a motherboard from a Power Macintosh 5000 or 6000 series machine, which can be found for about $100 on sites like eBay. Then the Color Classic's video needs to be fixed. Its standard monitor resolution is 560 by 384 pixels, which isn't big enough to run modern software applications like Web browsers. To upgrade the resolution to 640 by 480 pixels, the video-scanning voltage needs to be upped from 60 to 84 volts. The operation requires the cutting of one internal wire on the video circuit board and the soldering of another.

But fiddling around inside a Color Classic can be extremely dangerous. Its cathode-ray tube can deliver a potentially fatal shock. Instead of dicing with death, Classic fans can order an already upgraded Color Classic from specialists like Maxus Computer in Japan (http://www.maxuscomputer.com). In 2001, the company offered customers the guts of an iMac, shoehorned into an old Color Classic for $2,600, more than the price of two brand-new iMacs at the time. But when it was done, the little machine boasted a 333 MHz G3 chip and a 4GB hard drive.

In Canada, Japanese engineer Ball Chai has spent a lot of time and money in his quest to upgrade his machine to a 500 MHz G3 and an LCD touch screen. He's ruined four Color Classics and cannibalized a similar number of Power Macs.

Chai owns Tangal Communication, a Canadian Linux distributor. "I need to make a living to support my interests," he jokes.

"Having a strong Color Classic is like owning a hot rod car. It's impractical, but it's cool. There are a lot of people who will pay any price to have one." In 2001, Chai was hoping to upgrade the machine to a G4 chip, which Apple boasted capable of 1 billion operations a second, or a gigaflop.

"When you see the form and the shape, you know it is classic Apple," Chai says. "I like to keep it living." Chai also owns an extremely rare Color Classic with a clear case. It is one of only three in existence, built by Apple engineers as prototypes.

John Stocker, a Web designer, has converted three Color Classics with the guts of Power Mac 6500s. He upgraded one of his machines with a 225 MHz chip, 12GB hard drive, 128MB of RAM, Ethernet networking, video input and output including S-Video, two PCI expansion slots, and a Voodoo III video card. "All this computing goodness is crammed into a space the size of a lunch box," he writes on his Web page, which is entitled "My Exercise In Absurdity" (http://glowsoft.com/sfs/pcc/).

"This was no small task," he continues. "In fact, it took me four months of grueling work to complete." Stocker says he had to make major structural changes to the insides of the Color Classic to fit it all in. "Cooling fans needed to be added, voltage regulators needed to be made, and plastic needed cutting, filing, and drilling," he says. "It's amazing how much you can learn about computers by digging around inside one. That alone is justification to do this."

$500 FOR AN EMPTY BOX

A lot of seemingly worthless junk is auctioned on eBay every day. But perhaps taking the phenomenon to new heights, an empty cardboard box was auctioned for more than $500. The box dates from 1984 and contained an original Macintosh, the 128K. It was sold in March 2002—without the computer.

The box attracted 18 bids from about 9 different bidders. At first, the bidding remained relatively low—less than $60—but in the closing days of the auction, the price jumped in increments of about $50 as four bidders competed for it. The winning bid was $536.

"What started out as kind of silly became somewhat amazing," wrote the seller, David Hastings, in an email. "I understand collecting, but I was somewhat mystified at the high price for the box." Hastings said he expected to get maybe $40. It was the first thing he'd sold on eBay.

The box was slightly yellowed and discolored on the top and sides. But it did include all the original packaging materials: the Styrofoam inserts, and the boxes and plastic sleeves for the keyboard and mouse. Hastings said the box had been sitting in his attic for 18 years and that the Mac was long gone—he sold it to an aspiring writer in the late 1980s.

Ironically, the box is worth far more than the computer it contained. An original Macintosh is worthless, according to EveryMac, a site that lists used Macintosh prices: it has a resale value of zero. The Low End Mac Web site estimates the machine's value at $10, unless it includes the box, manuals, software disks, and assuming an interested collector can be found. Chris Lawson, a columnist for Low End Mac, said a spotless Macintosh 128K with original packaging and documentation might go for about $300, which is still $200 short of the price of the empty box. "A mint one with full packaging, manuals, and whatnot went for $300 or so a year back on eBay," he said.

Presumably, the buyer of the empty box was interested in putting together such a package. Unfortunately the winning bidder couldn't be contacted for an explanation. However, Hastings forwarded an email from one of the bidders, who discussed the box's appeal with Hastings. "You had three or more bidders that really wanted this because it will complete their Mac 128-K system," the correspondent wrote. "If you do not collect anything, it is a little hard to understand, but take it from a seasoned collector, seeing something nice as what you had there is pure bliss."

The correspondent said he was most impressed with the plastic slipcovers for the keyboard and mouse, which are extremely hard to come by. "As an Apple collector for over 15 years now, you had something that was in very good condition, and is very rare, I may add. Most people threw them away, or used them as moving boxes, wrote on them—you get the picture.... Remember: Beauty is in the eye of the beholder."

BOX OF GOLD: FIRST-TIME EBAY SELLER DAVID HASTINGS HIT THE JACKPOT WITH THIS EMPTY CARDBOARD BOX FOR THE FIRST MAC, THE 128K. HE THOUGHT HE'D GET $40, BUT THE BIDDING WENT CRAZY, AND HE ENDED UP WITH $500.
CREDIT: DAVID HASTINGS

"I UNDERSTAND COLLECTING, BUT I WAS SOMEWHAT MYSTIFIED AT THE HIGH PRICE FOR THE BOX."

THE MOST COLLECTIBLE APPLE I

Computer technician Vince Briel is planning to resurrect the Apple I, the hand-built machine that launched Apple Computer. The Apple I is one of the hottest machines on the vintage computer market, but with less than 50 still in circulation, they are extremely hard to come by. An Apple I can cost anywhere between $15,000 and $50,000, depending on its condition, history, and, of course, the economy. Briel is betting there's a market for replica machines capable of running original Apple I software without breaking the bank.

Briel has designed, built, and is currently testing a replica of the Apple I. If all goes well, he hopes to go into production by next spring. "There is a growing market for collecting rare and hard-to-find models," Briel wrote in an email. "The Apple I is king of the hill. Realizing I could never afford one, I decided to design a replica." Appropriately, Briel will build the replicas in his garage. The original Apple I's were hand-built by Apple's cofounders, Steve Wozniak and Steve Jobs, plus a handful of others, in Jobs' parents' garage. Priced at $666.66—a figure that got the fledgling company into trouble with Christian fundamentalists—only 200 were made.

Briel plans to build his replicas to order and to charge between $150 and $200. "There is probably as big a market for a replica as there was for the original," said Briel. "My intent is only to get more people involved in the history of personal computers, not make a profit—circuits are in my blood."

(ABOVE LEFT) VINCE BRIEL AND AN APPLE I REPLICA, WHICH HE HOPES TO BEGIN SELLING NEXT YEAR FROM HIS GARAGE— JUST LIKE STEVE WOZNIAK AND STEVE JOBS DID IN THE LATE '70S.
CREDIT: VINCE BRIEL

(ABOVE RIGHT) VINCE BRIEL'S PROTOTYPE REPLICA OF AN APPLE I COMPUTER, KEYBOARD, AND WIRING DIAGRAM. JUST LIKE THE ORIGINAL, THIS ONE COMES WITHOUT A CASE.
CREDIT: VINCE BRIEL

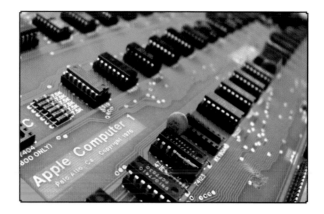

THE APPLE I MOTHERBOARD
HAS BECOME ONE OF THE
MOST COLLECTIBLE VINTAGE
COMPUTERS ON THE MARKET,
THANKS TO ITS RARITY AND
ITS PLACE IN HISTORY AT
THE CENTER OF THE APPLE-
FOUNDING MYTH.
CREDIT: UNKNOWN

There is renewed interest in retro computing. As well as Briel's Apple I, the Fischer-Freitas Company is building a limited supply of the classic IMSAI 8080, an early personal computer made famous by Matthew Broderick in the movie *WarGames*.

Briel still has a couple of technical and legal hurdles to overcome. His prototype has a couple of hardware glitches that need to be ironed out, and his plan hasn't yet been cleared with Apple or Woz. Apple likely holds copyrights on the machine's design. And although Briel redesigned the motherboard because some of the chips are hard to find, he may still need to license the ROM—a set of hard-wired instructions necessary to run original Apple I software. Apple didn't respond to requests for comment.

If Briel gets Apple's consent, the replica will be the first Apple clone since the company killed clone licenses in 1998. Although it was not the first personal computer, the Apple I is widely considered the touchstone of the personal computer revolution.

The machines were barely more than motherboards. Customers had to add their own case and keyboard and wire the machine directly to the guts of a monitor, which in those days lacked video jacks. Customers programmed the machine themselves. A tape drive for storing programs was available as an option.

Compared with other early personal computers, though, the Apple I was vastly more user friendly. The MITS Altair 880, for example, had no keyboard, monitor, or programming language. Programs were entered by hand in binary machine code via a front panel of switches and lights. "The Apple I was an important step," said Steve Wozniak in an email. "It took the step of saying that the low-cost computer would have a QWERTY keyboard and no front panel, and would have a programming language. These were brave steps."

For some, the historic computer exerts a mystical attraction. One owner, who asked to remain anonymous, described seeing his Apple I for the first time: "I slowly opened the box, looked at this pitiful little circuit board, and thought about a church I once visited in Italy," the owner said. "Inside the church…is a splinter from the True Cross…. Looking at that tiny wood fragment gave me a chill. The Apple I gave me a similar chill."

These days, the Apple I is rarely offered for sale. "From a collector's viewpoint, the Apple I is certainly the most desirable computer Apple ever made," said Tom Owad, an Apple historian who runs the Applefritter Web site. It is unknown how many Apple Is are still in circulation. Sellam Ismail, organizer of the Vintage Computer Festival and a classic computer broker, estimated there are fewer than 50. "I know of 25 in existence," he said. "I'm estimating that there may be as many as 35 to 50 total still around."

Rising prices for the Apple I in the late 1990s—one machine sold for $50,000—raised the specter of forged Apple Is. Many of the Apple I chips are still available to knowledgeable forgers, although some are extremely rare. If a forger could get a hold of the parts, passing it off as an original would be relatively easy. Sales were never documented. There's no paper trail to prove or disprove authenticity.

To protect against a sudden flood of fake Apple Is, at least one owner has sealed his machine in a storage box along with several packets of moisture-reducing pellets. "I don't want anyone to confuse my authentic Apple I with replicas that may appear in the coming years," said the owner, who requested anonymity. "I can always say that my Apple I was sealed and put into storage before the replicas began to appear."

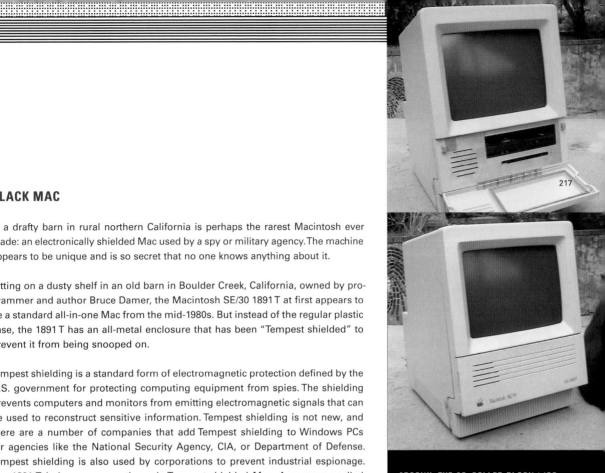

BLACK MAC

In a drafty barn in rural northern California is perhaps the rarest Macintosh ever made: an electronically shielded Mac used by a spy or military agency. The machine appears to be unique and is so secret that no one knows anything about it.

Sitting on a dusty shelf in an old barn in Boulder Creek, California, owned by programmer and author Bruce Damer, the Macintosh SE/30 1891 T at first appears to be a standard all-in-one Mac from the mid-1980s. But instead of the regular plastic case, the 1891 T has an all-metal enclosure that has been "Tempest shielded" to prevent it from being snooped on.

Tempest shielding is a standard form of electromagnetic protection defined by the U.S. government for protecting computing equipment from spies. The shielding prevents computers and monitors from emitting electromagnetic signals that can be used to reconstruct sensitive information. Tempest shielding is not new, and there are a number of companies that add Tempest shielding to Windows PCs for agencies like the National Security Agency, CIA, or Department of Defense. Tempest shielding is also used by corporations to prevent industrial espionage. The 1891 T is by no means the only Tempest-shielded Mac. A company called TechMatics Technologies used to sell a Tempest-shielded Mac Plus. But the 1891 T does appear to be the only Tempest-shielded Mac made by Apple, and Damer appears to have the only one.

"It's a Black Mac," said Damer, in reference to the black helicopters used by shady government agencies. "We don't know who used it—the CIA, the Department of Defense—or where it came from."

The Mac's innocent-looking beige metal case is in fact a Faraday cage—a metal mesh that stops the computer from radiating electromagnetic signals. It has a flip-down panel on the front for a Bernoulli drive—a removable drive common at the time. "The operative could take everything with him at all times," Damer explained. The opening for the drive is also protected by an emissions-busting ring of copper coils. Unfortunately, the motherboard of the Black Mac has been removed. So has the panel at the back housing shielded connectors for keyboard, mouse, and network ports.

Damer displays the Black Mac in his private computer museum, the DigiBarn Computer Museum, which opened in July 2002. As far as Damer knows, the Black Mac is undocumented. There's no record of it anywhere. Apart from the model number on the front, there are no identifying markings or serial numbers. Damer, who is well connected in Silicon Valley, has made extensive inquiries about the Black Mac, to no avail. "It's the rarest Mac in the world," Damer said. "This is the only one known. There's no evidence of any other existing machines out there. There's no record of it at Apple. But it's a real Apple machine—it wasn't made or adapted by another company—so it must have been a classified project."

SPOOKY: THE SO-CALLED BLACK MAC FROM BRUCE DAMER'S DIGIBARN, A PRIVATE COMPUTER MUSEUM NEAR SILICON VALLEY.
CREDIT: BRUCE DAMER

DIGIBARNSTORMER: PROGRAMMER BRUCE DAMER OWNS PERHAPS THE RAREST MAC IN CIRCULATION, A TEMPEST-SHIELDED MACINTOSH SE/30, LIKELY BUILT FOR ESPIONAGE WORK.
CREDIT: BRUCE DAMER

In fact, Damer's Mac was most likely made by Candes Systems of Harleysville, Pennsylvania, as an after-market modification. Apparently Apple was so pleased with the shielded cases made by Candes, it allowed the company to use the Apple logo, the only time a third party has been allowed to do so. "CSI bought the Apple products and remanufactured them to meet the National Security Agency's strict Tempest guidelines for secure computers," explained Jason Signore, Candes head of sales and marketing. "Apple was so pleased with the final design—they retained the look and feel of an off-the-shelf Mac—CSI was allowed to use Apple's rainbow logo on our products."

Signore said the 1891 T was one of many Tempest-shielded Macs made by CSI. He also has a Mac IIci, IIcx, IIfx, and Quadra 700. He plans to donate a couple of working systems to the DigiBarn. "I managed to save a few of these models from the trash heap a year or two ago," he said.

In the early '90s, Candes was shipping hundreds of Tempest Macs every week to different agencies, Signore said, including NASA, the Drug Enforcement Agency, the CIA, and the NSA. He thought most of the Tempest Macs were used for mapping or battlefield imaging applications. But Signore was unable, or unwilling, to elaborate. "A lot of the time, the agencies we sell them to aren't the ones that use them," he said. "In the end, we don't know who we are selling it to, or what they're using it for." Signore said he saw some Tempest Macs on TV during the Gulf War. "There they were in the desert in these tents," he said. "What they were doing with them, I couldn't tell you."

Signore also has a Tempest-shielded Mac Plus with two floppy drives (it originally came with only one) and an on/off switch just for the screen on the front. Signore said the switch was to protect the screen from prying eyes. He recalled visiting a government facility where 40 or 50 operatives sat at similarly equipped workstations. Before he entered the room, warning lights spun and everyone switched off their screens. The operatives waited patiently until he walked through, the lights spun again, and everyone went back to work.

GAMER: ALLAN LUNDELL, AN EX-EDITOR
OF *BYTE MAGAZINE*, IS DISTRACTED FROM
THE GAME HE'S ENGROSSED IN. THE OLD
SYSTEMS STORED AT THE DIGIBARN SOME-
TIMES INDUCE MISTY TEARS OF NOSTALGIA.
CREDIT: LEANDER KAHNEY

BRUCE DAMER, CURATOR OF THE DIGIBARN
AND A MAC CHIMNEY. THE AFTER-MARKET
ACCESSORY, MADE OF CARDBOARD, HELPED
COOL EARLY MACS, WHICH STEVE JOBS
INSISTED HAVE NO COOLING FANS.
CREDIT: LEANDER KAHNEY

BRUCE DAMER'S DIGIBARN

In addition to the Black Mac, Damer's DigiBarn features a collection of vintage Macs, including one of the first Macs ever shipped, complete with all its shipping materials and documentation. He also has an Apple II GS "Woz Edition"—the last of the Apple IIs, specially designed by Apple cofounder Steve Wozniak and adorned with his nickname. Damer popped the lid to reveal the GS's motherboard. "It's a classic Woz design," Damer explained. "Few chips. Lots of slots. Open."

He gestured to the original Macintosh, the brainchild of Steve Jobs, sitting on a bench nearby. "The Mac is from the same time but is the total opposite," he said. "Jobs closed it up. You need a special screwdriver to open the case. No slots. Closed and proprietary. There's the two cultures of Apple right there. One open, one closed."

Damer's museum houses a number of Mac oddities, like a Ouija board game called Gypsy by Magnum Software. Instead of gathering around an upturned wine glass, everyone puts their finger on the computer's mouse. The letters of the Ouija board are displayed on the computer's screen. "It combines the illogic of the spirit world with the logic of computers," said Damer. "It's a great idea for a game."

The pride of Damer's collection is a Cray 1A Supercomputer, a giant, multimillion-dollar dinosaur from the Cold War used to simulate nuclear weapons. These days, its computing power is roughly equivalent to a 300 MHz Pentium PC.

The DigiBarn also showcases about 3,000 nerdy T-shirts donated by Taylor Barcroft, who collected them over the course of attending a decade's worth of trade shows. And there are lots of original documents, like the first issue of *Byte Magazine*.

Damer is working hard to get most of his machines operating with original software so that people can relive the early days of computing. "Every time you bring a nerd to the computer museum, their faces light up with memories," said Galen Brandt, Damer's partner. "You see grown men crying when they see some of these systems."

THE NEWTON

When Jonathan Wise's Handspring Visor organizer died, he decided to get a different handheld. After shopping around, he found a machine that did it all: Web, email, calendar, and address book. Was it the latest sleek Clié from Sony, or a skunkworks Pocket PC yet to hit the market? No, was the granddaddy of them all: Apple's Newton, which is still going strong despite being discontinued by Apple in 1998.

The Newton should have gone away, but amazingly, it has kept current, in both hardware and software, thanks to the efforts of Newton enthusiasts. The Newton community is holding steady. It may even be growing. "The handwriting recognition is unbelievable," Wise said. "But the best thing about owning a Newton has to be the community. In the time it takes to get put on hold by a Handspring tech support agent, you can have 15 different solutions for your problem from Newton users world-wide…. I'd much rather have an out-of-warranty product with this community behind me than a brand-new product backed by Hewlett-Packard or Palm."

Released in 1993, the Newton was one of the first PDAs (personal digital assistants) on the market. Early models were bulky, expensive, and bug-ridden. Apple marketed the Newton poorly, and it was widely ridiculed; a memorable Doonesbury strip by Garry Trudeau effectively doomed the device.

Later models were vastly improved, but the Newton never took off. Palm stepped in and quickly dominated the handheld market with the wildly popular PalmPilots, which were smaller, cheaper, and easier to use. In 1997, Palm had a 66 percent market share, Windows CE had 20 percent, and Newton just 6 percent, according to market research firm Dataquest. At the height of its popularity, only an estimated 200,000 Newtons were in use.

Apple finally killed the Newton in February 1998 after Steve Jobs returned to the company, even though fans demonstrated in the parking lot of Apple's Cupertino campus. Apple officials gave them coffee and cookies but refused to resurrect the device. Fans still take their Newtons to Jobs' keynote speeches at Macworld and wave them in the air in silent protest.

It doesn't seem to matter, though. Without any help from Apple, Newton users have kept the platform current with technological changes through a series of software hacks and hardware fixes, most of which are freely available. "There's a lot of sentimentality for the hardware," said aficionado Victor Rehorst, a grad student and programmer from Toronto who maintains the popular NewtonTalk mailing list. "People try to keep it going as long as they can."

Wireless networks like Wi-Fi (802.11b), GSM, and GPRS all emerged after the Newton was killed, but Newton hackers have released software to support them all. There's also an MP3 player for the Newton called Mad Max, adapted for the Newton by Eckhart Köppen. Eric Schneck wrote an iTunes plug-in that syncs a Newton with Apple's digital jukebox.

Sure, the Newton's limited processing power (160 MHz processor) and memory (average 4MB) limits storage to a handful of songs at a fairly low bit rate, but it saves Newton users $300 on an iPod. The Newton also has no headphone jack, although one can be fashioned with an inexpensive homemade dongle.

The biggest problem with a Newton is its size: It's as big as a brick. "People make fun of your Newt," Wise said. "My boss once asked me if it was actually a flatbed scanner."

Despite the drawbacks of the aging hardware, fans will argue the Newton's merits over newer devices. The handwriting recognition—arguably the best ever—big screen, and superb networking capabilities are still better than newer, competing devices, they argue. "The Newton was always the Ferrari to the Palm's Yugo," said Peter Markel, Ideacast's producer for PlanetNewton.com. "Hardware-wise, Newton could, and mostly still does, run rings around the Palm platform."

The hardware has allure, but most users are attracted to the community. Plus, the Newton is no longer Apple's device. It belongs to the users. "It's the open-source spirit," Schneck said. "I write for the Newton because it's a community to which I can make a visible contribution." Markel estimated that 20,000 day-to-day Newton users remain, and the community may even be growing. Rehorst's NewtonTalk mailing list has grown by 300 subscribers in the past year alone. Three new user groups were launched last year, in Los Angeles, Washington, and Toronto. There are about 20 active user groups worldwide, concentrated in the United States, Japan, Korea, France, and Denmark. "The Newton community is great, friendly, and very competent," said Marco Polenta, an Italian Newton fan. "Newton developers are still continuing to work on Newton projects, and most of their software is shareware or freeware. I think this is very cool."

Rehorst maintains a comprehensive archive of Newton software. He's collected about 1,400 titles, and new ones are added every week, he said. There's all kinds of software, from Telnet clients to biorhythm calculators.

Albert Muniz, a consumer behaviorist at DePaul University in Chicago, is studying the Newton community. He said Newton users provide each other invaluable technical and social support. Without it, many would abandon the platform. "People stick with the Newton because the community is so strong," Muniz said. "If they have a problem, they turn to the collective genius of the group to get an answer."

As well as software and help, the community maintains many good Newton Web sites, such as Newton Reference, which has hundreds of Newton-related links. The Newton Hall of Fame provides interesting background, and This Old Newt, a Newton Weblog, tracks new software and other items of interest. Maintenance can be a problem, but there's a steady trade of Newtons on eBay. Top-of-the-line models that originally cost more than $1,000 can be picked up for about $150. Most users own two or more models, cannibalizing the spares for parts. Sun Remarketing has lots of spares; there's even a 220 MHz upgrade for later models.

But as users continue to develop the Newton, Apple is leaving it further and further behind. For example, Apple hasn't provided software to sync with its new operating system, Mac OS X, except through the clunky Classic compatibility environment (there is a third-party utility). Ironically, the Windows version still works with Microsoft's latest operating systems, 2000 or XP.

(BELOW LEFT) NEWTONOPHILE: MARCO POLENTA, AN ITALIAN CARTOONIST AND GRAPHIC DESIGNER, COULDN'T BE MORE DELIGHTED WITH HIS NEWTON. THANKS TO THE NEWTON COMMUNITY, PLENTY OF NEW SOFTWARE AND HARDWARE UPGRADES ARE STILL RELEASED FOR THE AGING HANDHELD. CREDIT: MARCO POLENTA

(BELOW RIGHT) DIEHARDS: DESPITE ITS SIZE, THE NEWTON STILL HAS A STRONG FAN BASE. CREDIT: GEEK CULTURE

The Newton community is so unique, it is the subject of a detailed academic study. Albert Muniz, an assistant professor in the marketing department at Chicago's DePaul University, and Hope Schau, an assistant professor of marketing at Philadelphia's Temple University, have been studying the Newton community for more than a year. The researchers are interested in self-sustaining "brand communities," or groups of people devoted to a particular brand, a hot topic in consumer behavior research.

Despite being discontinued in 1998, the Newton is still in wide use and has been kept pretty current through software and hardware developed by its users. But the Newton community is locked in a paradox. On the one hand, the Newton is very much alive; it's a usable, technologically sophisticated device that continues to develop through the efforts of its fans. On the other hand, the Newton is on life support. Every year it gets more and more outdated, and the supply of usable machines is always dwindling. In light of this, how do Newton fans justify their choice of handheld? There are, after all, plenty of others to choose from.

Muniz and Schau argue that rumors of the Newton's return—in one form or another—allow the Newton community to answer this question in a number of ways. According to the researchers, rumors of the Newton's resurrection have surfaced at least nine times since 1998, when Apple discontinued the device. The most recent recurrence was the iWalk hoax on the Spymac Web site in January 2002, which generated volumes of discussion in both the Mac and Newton communities, Muniz and Schau said.

"There's this large storytelling myth thing going on," Muniz said. "It's an act of self-defense." First, the rebirth of the Newton validates the platform's technical superiority. If it's good enough to be reintroduced, it's good enough to keep using, fans reason. Discussion of the rumor then provides group cohesion and consensus. For a group that thrives on collective problem solving, a new rumor is a juicy problem to be solved. Members enjoy coming to a consensus about the meaning and likelihood of the rumor. The rumor fuels optimism: The current crop of Newtons may eventually clap out, but while there's a chance Apple will make replacement machines, it's worth hanging on. The rumor also gives power to the powerless: Newton users

can't reintroduce the Newton themselves, but they can proclaim its technological superiority, complain about its cancellation, identify those responsible, or express resistance to consumer forces compelling them to get newer devices. These are never-ending topics of discussion in the Newton community, Muniz and Schau note.

The researchers marveled at the amount of time Newton fans spend discussing, disseminating, and elaborating on the relaunch rumor. The rumor discussions are revealing of the group's collective hopes, fears, and beliefs, Muniz and Schau said. During rumor debates, participants take on clearly defined roles to an almost "ritualistic" degree, Muniz and Schau said: the believer, the guarded believer, the skeptic. Regardless of their role, all wanted more details. The authors likened the attitude to fans of *The X-Files*, who are guardedly skeptical about aliens but desperately want to believe. The researchers note how unrelated events are made germane to the rumor, like a sudden glut of Newtons on eBay, which has been cited as evidence that people were getting ready for a new device. Muniz and Schau conclude that the rumormongering is an essential process in the creation of the Newton "ideoculture," a group identity with clearly defined knowledge, beliefs, behaviors, and customs.

The researchers also identify other factors contributing to the group's identity, like the need to tinker. Muniz and Schau were impressed by the pride Newton users took in mastering a discontinued device. "Even in the beginning, the Newton was technologically challenging," Muniz said. "It was designed for the technologically savvy. They enjoy the challenge."

Muniz and Schau note Newton users' joy of being contrary, or being perceived as an underdog. There is also a strong resistance to the disposability of technology. "They resist the planned and rapid obsolescence of technological products," Muniz said. "It's a form of consumer resistance. It's a rejection of the rapid obsolescence and the need to design these products to the lowest common denominator."

But Muniz and Schau also note the relaunch rumor is bittersweet: Some fans wonder if a new Newton would kill the community because ownership of the device would shift from the community back to Apple.

ONE MAN'S RETRO MAC REVIVAL

Devan Simunovich is a one-man Macintosh retro revivalist. The 24-year-old San Francisco designer is an avid collector of old all-in-one Macs. He has about 50 Mac Classics, Mac SEs, and Mac SE/30s. But he's not keeping his passion to himself. He often lugs carloads of his machines to raves and other events, setting up vintage gaming lounges or video walls made from compact Macs stacked atop each other. Over the last couple of years, Simunovich has set up his c-trl lounge installations at numerous parties, raves, gallery openings, fund-raisers, and the occasional corporate shindig.

Simunovich is part of a thriving Mac underground obsessed with retro machines. He and thousands like him lovingly maintain Macs that should have been landfill decades ago.

When setting up an installation, Simunovich loads up his compact Honda Civic with a couple dozen machines, which fit snugly because of their boxy shape. When creating a game lounge, he sets up the beige computers back-to-back on tables and networks them via LocalTalk. The game lounges are reminiscent of the rows and rows of computers Apple set up at Macworld trade shows—circa 1986.

Simunovich has collected between 200 and 300 vintage Mac games, including classics like Tetris, Tank Bolo, Star Wars, and Lemmings. A selection is loaded onto each machine. Gamers can play networked games like Tank Bolo or Bus'd Out, though most don't realize they're on a network.

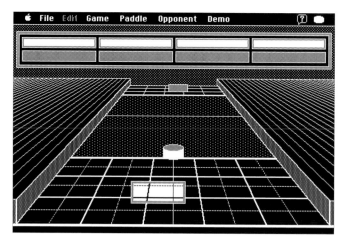

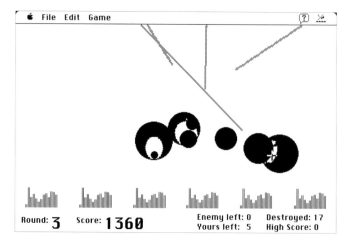

OLD SCHOOL: SOME OF
THE GAMES LOADED ON
SIMUNOVICH'S MACHINES
INCLUDE CLASSICS LIKE
AIR HOCKEY (TOP LEFT),
DR MAC (TOP RIGHT),
TETRIS 2 (BOTTOM RIGHT),
AND MISSILE COMMAND.
CREDIT: DEVAN SIMUNOVICH

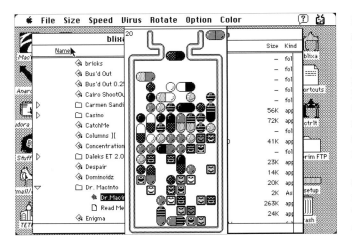

For many people, the sight of a machine they haven't used since their high school days, running a game they haven't seen in decades, is powerfully nostalgic. "A lot of people say, 'Wow, I haven't played this game in 15 years,'" said Simunovich. But he gets just as many admiring comments from people who were just kids when the machines came out and have never seen them in action before. "They are amazed when I tell them it has an 8 MHz processor and was made 15 years ago," Simunovich said. "A lot of people are astonished that these machines still run at all."

Surprisingly, Simunovich belongs to this group himself. He'd never seen a compact Mac until he spotted one a couple of years ago at a San Francisco thrift store. "I never had one," he said. "I'd never seen one before in my life. I thought, 'This is really cool. I've got to try it out.' It was a blast. It's not so much nostalgia for me as technological acrobatics."

Simunovich continued to buy compact Macs at thrift stores for $15 to $20 apiece until he'd collected about a dozen. He then went out and bought a pallet-load for $500 at a local wholesaler, boosting his collection to about 50 machines. He stores them at a friend's warehouse-cum-performance space.

Simunovich owned an old IBM as a teenager and played a lot of DOS games, which were like Atari's first console games in sophistication: The graphics were relatively simple and clunky. Old Macs, by comparison, are much more sophisticated. Although the graphics are black-and-white, they can sometimes achieve a level of photo-realism, and they are much better at creating gaming staples like simple 3D.

Impressed by these capabilities, Simunovich has also created a number of video walls made from stacked compact Macs. The most ambitious was built from 25 machines arranged in a five-by-five grid, which was displayed at a recent fund-raiser for the upcoming Transcinema festival.

Simunovich's video wall has also been shown at San Francisco's Museum of Modern Art and various other galleries around California. Simunovich created a number of black-and-white movies to play on the wall, consisting of random imagery, bits of movies found on the Net, abstract textures, and black-and-white Webcam footage taken at the event.

To play a single video across 25 separate screens, Simunovich devised a clever way to split them up. He created a filter in After Effects that breaks his movies into segments corresponding to the grids of the video wall. Each segment is loaded into a screensaver program on the corresponding machine's hard drive. The screensaver is configured to play the movies in a loop on startup. To synchronize the machines, he plugs them all into the same power strip. Flick the switch, and they all boot up simultaneously. There's always a difference of a few seconds between each, but that just adds to the exhibit's charm.

Simunovich is part of an enduring subculture of people fascinated by retro Macs. There are numerous Web sites dedicated to old machines, like Dan Knight's Low End Mac, Tom Owad's Applefritter, and System 6 Heaven. There are also a number of software emulators that allow modern machines to run old software, including vMac, which emulates a Mac Plus, and its offshoot, Mini vMac, which runs on Mac OS X. There are also Mac emulators for Windows and Linux, including Basilisk II, SoftMac, and Fusion PC.

Philip Cummins, the 24-year-old programmer who leads the vMac project, said the software has earned a steady following since its release in 1997. "People use [vMac] to run classic games and get that whole System 6 experience," Cummins said from his home in Perth, Australia. "It's getting back to the basics, before things got too complicated. It's a way of holding on to the past for a little bit longer."

Simunovich said he's seen a steady resurgence in interest in compact Macs. It dovetails the trend of taking old Atari consoles and Commodores to raves, where they are set up in gaming lounges. Running old games is the driving force behind the retro craze, he said. Simunovich runs a popular Hotline server full of software for black-and-white machines, mostly classic games. Interestingly, the server is an old SE/30 with an upgraded 2GB internal hard drive and an external 4GB drive. For such an old machine, it runs well as long as there are not more than 10 or 15 people logged on.

"A lot of people are dragging old machines out of closets and getting them running again," Simunovich said. "I was continually amazed by the steady flow of people coming through and grabbing stuff so they could get that old Mac in the closet working again. In the end, I guess it's that sort of technological resuscitation that makes this really interesting to me."

He's run into plenty of collectors, especially through the Hotline server, he said, but he's the only person he knows who has a Mac gaming lounge. "There's an element of technological nostalgia," he said of the movement, "but it's also the will to resuscitate obsolete technology, to make old things work again, to breathe new life into an old piece of junk."

DEVAN SIMUNOVICH WAS TOO YOUNG TO GROW UP ON MAC CLASSICS, BUT IT HASN'T STOPPED HIM AMASSING A SIZABLE COLLECTION, WHICH HE HOOKS INTO RETRO GAMING LOUNGES AT RAVES. CREDIT: DEVAN SIMUNOVICH

WEB REVIVAL FOR OLD MAC INTERFACE

System 6, the Macintosh operating system circa 1989, is long gone. Or is it? On the Web, a number of Web site designers have used its spare, clean look as inspiration for good design.

Shelby Cinca's The Mind Control site (http://www.themindcontrol. com) was inspired by the old Mac interface, as was Bill Jagitsch's Jags' House (http://www.jagshouse.com/), a site devoted to old Macs, and Josh Koppel's design site (http://www.joshkoppel. com). One of the most faithful is Christopher Murphy's design for the independent record label Bremsstrahlung Recordings.

Bremsstrahlung specializes in "lowercase sound," a genre of electronica so extremely minimalist, it is almost silent. So when Josh Russell, who runs the label, decided to have his label's Web site redesigned, he chose a look based on the bare-bones, black-and-white interface of System 6. Bremsstrahlung Recordings' Web site looks just like the desktop of a 1980s compact Mac, like a Mac Plus or Mac Classic.

Clicking around the site is exactly like navigating the old System 6 desktop. Different parts of the site are represented by familiar Macintosh icons. The icon for a floppy drive links to the main index page. A printer icon goes to the reviews page. The long-forgotten icon for switching floppy disks—a pair of floppies connected by arrows—leads to a library of MP3s. And instead of advancing from page to page as in a traditional site, the Bremsstrahlung site recreates the tiling windows of the old Mac interface. Click an icon, and the page pops up as a new window stacked on top of the old one. To back up to the previous page, the user clicks in the little square box in the window's top-left corner, just like an old Mac.

Christopher Murphy, the designer, painstakingly created the entire site, pixel by pixel, in MacPaint and Photoshop. MacPaint is the black-and-white painting program that came preinstalled as one of four basic applications on old Macs. While it appears simple, the design was, in fact, incredibly demanding. Each page of the site is made of upwards of 20 Photoshop layers. "I certainly didn't take straight screenshots," Murphy said.

Murphy did some of the work on an old Mac Classic he found in a dumpster; some was done on a much newer Titanium PowerBook. "In my studio I have one of the oldest Macs sitting alongside one of the newest Macs, and they're both used equally on a daily basis," Murphy said. "Most of my work is

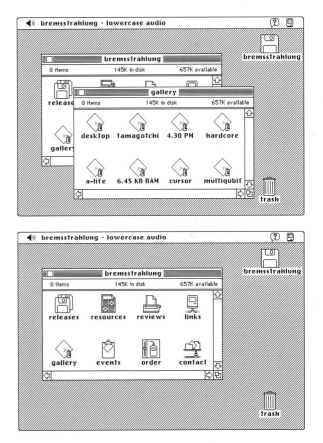

UNFUSSY: THE BREMSSTRAHLUNG RECORDINGS LABEL SPECIALIZES IN MINIMALIST RECORDINGS, SO IT IS ONLY FITTING ITS WEB SITE SHOULD BE BASED ON THE BARE-BONES LOOK OF APPLE'S SYSTEM 6.
CREDIT: CHRISTOPHER MURPHY

MACHEAD: DESIGNER
CHRISTOPHER MURPHY WITH
THE CLASSIC MAC THAT
INSPIRED HIS SYSTEM 6-STYLE
WEB SITE DESIGN. HE ACTUALLY
BUILT THE SITE ON THE
MACHINE, PIXEL BY PIXEL.
CREDIT: CHRISTOPHER MURPHY

pixel-based, and the Classic is incredibly fast because the software footprints are so, so small."

Murphy runs Fällt, an independent record label, design shop, and publishing house in Belfast, Ireland. Coincidentally, just before he found the Mac Classic, he had tried to buy one a few days earlier on eBay. "On my way home one day, I noticed a pristine Classic in a dumpster," he said. "I couldn't believe my luck."

Murphy has also painted a series of oil-on-canvas pixel paintings, also inspired by the Classic. Measuring just 32 by 32 pixels—about the size of a computer icon—the paintings have

been exhibited in a gallery in Belfast. "The point was to take the subject matter from one medium—the clean, digital perfection of the screen—to another—the less precise world of traditional drawing and painting," he said.

Murphy beat out different designers for the Bremsstrahlung Web site redesign because Russell liked Murphy's sense of stripped-down design. "It's clean and minimal and goes with the music," Russell said. "It has similar aesthetics to lower-case sound. It works with very little and gets something of substance out of it. It's a very elegant design, and for a lot of people, it's nostalgic."

> # "PEOPLE KEEP USING IT, AND PEOPLE KEEP BUYING IT OFF THE APPLE WEB SITE. THE ONLY PEOPLE THAT ARE NOT BEHIND IT ARE APPLE [EXECUTIVES] RIGHT NOW."

HYPERCARD: FORGOTTEN BUT NOT GONE

Apple's multimedia programming environment, HyperCard, still has a fiercely dedicated following despite no meaningful update in about 15 years. First released in 1987, HyperCard is a simple programming environment so powerful yet simple it is used by professionals and children alike. Fans claim it is one of the greatest pieces of software Apple ever produced and are incensed it is slowly dying because the company can't figure out how to sell it or whom to sell it to. "It was and still is the most significant tool I've ever used," said Richard Wanderman, a technology consultant and, at one time, a leading HyperCard advocate.

The HyperCard torch is carried by the International HyperCard User Group (iHug), which has 300 or 400 active members. Two or three times a year, iHug collects several thousand dollars in donations to set up booths at Macworld Expo and promote HyperCard on Apple's behalf. "People send [money] in because they like HyperCard so much," said iHug president Michael Mays.

"When people see what you can do with it, they say, 'Wow. I never knew you could do that so easily with a computer.'"

iHug runs an active mailing list and publishes a line of promotional CDs with sample HyperCard stacks and applications. iHug wants to see HyperCard ported to run on Mac OS X, and the incorporation of overdue features, like fully integrated color. HyperCard is still, at heart, black and white.

iHug campaigned vigorously for several years, with little luck. Its efforts culminated in a meeting with Phil Schiller, Apple's head of worldwide marketing, who reportedly ended up asking them, "But how do we sell it?" Clearly, Schiller wasn't convinced by iHug's answers. But Mays said, "People keep using it, and people keep buying it off the Apple Web site. The only people that are not behind it are Apple [executives] right now."

Because it can be used to create custom applications in minutes, HyperCard is still used by many academic researchers and small businesses. Some companies run HyperCard applications, written years ago on a Mac Plus, on the latest dual-processor G4 Power Macs. Renault, the French auto giant, reportedly uses HyperCard for its inventory system. The software runs part of the lighting system for the tallest buildings in the world, the Petronas Towers in Kuala Lumpur, Malaysia. HyperCard is used widely in schools to teach programming concepts and for creating interactive learning materials or class reports.

It's hard to estimate the number of people who still use HyperCard. In July 1999, MacCentral published an article about HyperCard, which attracted a huge response, leading the author to conclude HyperCard was used widely. iHug estimates there are perhaps 10,000 HyperCard users worldwide. Apple continues to sell the software for $99, but hasn't updated it since 1998. Apple didn't respond to requests for information.

The software's power lies in its ease of use: Information is stored in a series of "cards" arranged into "stacks." Cards can be linked to each other, just like hypertext links on the Web. A built-in, plain-English programming language, HyperTalk, executes commands. The result is both simple and powerful. Fifth graders get to grips with HyperCard in minutes, building databases of their Pokemon cards. Cyan, the game publisher, used it to create fiendishly complex games like Myst and Riven. It allowed ordinary people, such as Jacqueline Landman Gay—who had hardly touched a computer before—to start a successful software company.

Before HyperCard, programming was more or less the exclusive domain of professional programmers. HyperCard was the brainchild of programming genius Bill Atkinson, who wanted a programming tool "for the rest of us." When it was released, the *Wall Street Journal* described HyperCard as "a major development in the industry, changing the way information is organized and used."

HyperCard was originally free but became so popular Apple started charging $250. In the mid-1990s, it was spun off with Apple's Claris software division. Then it was brought back to Apple and finally put on ice when Steve Jobs returned to Apple in 1997.

HyperCard has been highly influential—it has been cited as helping shape Java and the Web. It had the potential to be the first Web browser. Many programming tools these days have HyperCard-like graphic interfaces, including Microsoft's Visual Studio. It has been superseded by a number of Mac-only and cross-platform successors, including SuperCard, MetaCard, and Revolution, which are either too expensive or complex for casual users, HyperCard advocates say.

There have been calls to release the source code to the open source programming community. "It's something people can use to begin programming with right away, without having to understand all the nuts and bolts of the operating system," said iHug's Mays. "There's a one-to-one correspondence between a task and the programming environment," he said. "Even simple databases are more complicated."

Mays, who owns two Dallas fast-food franchises, said a pair of professional programmers toiled for weeks to build a system that would report all the orders coming through his restaurants' registers. Fearing they would never finish, Mays sat down and in a few hours created an application himself in HyperCard, which he still uses. "In one afternoon I did what it took two professionals two or three weeks to do," he said. "If you need something and you don't have several thousand dollars to hire a developer, HyperCard fills a niche."

David Neale, who uses HyperCard to publish a number of Elvis Presley–related Web sites, said he fears for the software's future and has started experimenting with alternatives, including RealBasic, Perl, and FileMaker, without much success. "I have yet to find anything with such a simple interface hiding a friendly script language, whose apparent simplicity can be so superbly extended with external functions and commands," he said. "How such a forward-thinking company can allow such a clearly superb piece of software to stagnate is quite simply astonishing," he added. "Given the right push under Mac OS X, HyperCard could still be a great product, way ahead of anything else in the field."

HYPERCARD: WHAT COULD HAVE BEEN

Bill Atkinson is the programming genius behind HyperCard, MacPaint, and much of the original Macintosh operating system, but these days he's wistful about what HyperCard could have been. Like, for example, the first Internet browser.

Atkinson, now a successful nature photographer, created a string of groundbreaking applications during a long career at Apple, but he feels that one of his greatest achievements, the HyperCard multimedia programming system, failed to live up to its potential.

The software has been phenomenally successful and highly influential, but Atkinson feels that if only he'd realized separate cards and stacks could be linked on different people's machines through the Net—instead of just cards and stacks on a particular machine—he would have created the first Internet browser.

"I have realized over time that I missed the mark with HyperCard," he said from his studio in Menlo Park, California. "I grew up in a box-centric culture at Apple. If I'd grown up in a network-centric culture, like Sun, HyperCard might have been the first Web browser. My blind spot at Apple prevented me from making HyperCard the first Web browser."

HyperCard was conceived and created in the 1980s, almost a decade before the explosion of the Internet. "I thought [having] everyone connected was a pipe dream," he said. "Boy, was I wrong. I missed that one."

Atkinson recalled engineers at Apple drawing network schematics in the form of a bunch of boxes linked together. Sun engineers, however, first drew the network's backbone and then hung boxes off of it. It's a critical difference, and he feels it hindered him. "If I thought more globally, I would have envisioned [HyperCard] in that way," he said. "You don't transfer someone's Web site to your hard drive to look at it. You browse it piecemeal…. It's much more powerful than a stack of cards on your hard drive. "With a hundred-year perspective, the real value of the personal computer is not spreadsheets, word processors, or even desktop publishing," he added. "It's the Web."

Atkinson worked at Apple for 12 years. When he joined the company, there were 30 people working there, and there were 15,000 when he left. "I witnessed and participated in a huge explosion," he said.

Atkinson still uses HyperCard every day. His address book is a big HyperCard stack, and he has written a number of custom programs to help him with his photography and to maintain his Web site. His wife, Sioux, whom he met at Apple, created a HyperCard application that does all the business inventory and accounting, tracking which galleries have his pictures, the clients, and accounts payable. "This company is run on a giant HyperCard stack," Atkinson said.

PART 5: NEW FRONTIERS

TECHNOLOGY IS GOOD.
PIRACY IS BAD.

MUSIC TO HACKERS' EARS

Over time, Apple has transformed the iPod from an audio player into a general-purpose digital assistant, capable of storing contacts and calendars, as well as gigabytes of music. It's possible that Apple had planned from the start to make the iPod into a kind of PDA, but it's likely the company took its lead from iPod hackers, who were busy figuring out clever ways to make the iPod do more than just play music almost from the minute it hit store shelves.

In the first few weeks after the iPod's debut, hackers figured out clever ways to store not only names and addresses on the iPod but calendar items, news stories, song lyrics, and phrases in foreign languages. One enterprising teen even worked out a way to steal software using his iPod. The iPod was also persuaded to work with Windows. Although Apple eventually released a Windows-compatible version of the iPod, at first it was supposed to be Mac-only. But Joe Masters, a Massachusetts college student, wrote a free program called EphPod to connect iPods to Windows machines.

It took Apple six months to catch up with the hackers. Half a year after its initial release, Apple updated the iPod's software to let it store contacts. The Windows version of the iPod didn't appear for another six months, but by that time iPod hackers had moved on.

Companies like Griffin Technology, for example, developed the PodMate, a small infrared unit for turning an iPod into a TV remote control. Griffin planned to sell it, but withdrew it from the market at Apple's request. The company went on to develop other iPod add-ons, including an FM transmitter called the iTrip.

Jean-Olivier Lanctôt-David, a 14-year-old hacker from Canada, figured out a way to display online news headlines on the iPod. Lanctôt-David whipped up PodNews, a program that fetches headlines from the Web in XML format and displays them on the iPod's small screen. It's quite an achievement, especially for a young teen.

Apple's software for the iPod now has the ability to download thousands of contacts from applications such as Microsoft Entourage, Palm Desktop, and the Mac OS X Address Book. But hackers figured out how to do this first, and also make it work with other contact databases, including Yahoo's online address book.

After Apple added contacts, iPod hackers turned to calendar functions. A French hacker created K-Lendar, which displays calendar events, such as a list of meetings, as an iPod playlist. Events can be set by time, category, comments, or description.

Michael Zapp, an instructor at the University of Manitoba in Canada, created a pair of AppleScript applications to take data from Microsoft Entourage (the Macintosh version of Outlook) and transform it into vCard file format, which can be displayed using the iPod's new contacts feature. One of Zapp's scripts extracts events, allowing the iPod to display schedules; the other extracts text notes, which can display any kind of information. "I've had people say that they may just retire their Palm since they can now do everything they use it for with the iPod and my apps," said Zapp. "I think people are tired of carrying around lots of gadgets and are looking for anything that can reduce the load." The only problem, Zapp said, is that information can't be entered when the iPod is away from a Mac—all data has to be typed into a Mac and transferred manually.

Joe Masters, a senior at Williams College in Williamstown, Massachusetts, who wrote EphPod, said the iPod had great potential as an organizer, especially because it's much easier to program than Palm devices. "It's got so much space and it's very easy to hack," he said. "Apple's done a great job. It's very simple. Synchronizing it is very easy. It's just a hard drive. You just copy files over. There are no weird synchronization protocols like the Palm. And you don't have to worry about space, like on a Palm. It's enormous. Who cares how much space you use?"

Masters said he'd like to see Apple add support for text, the same way it added support for contacts in vCard format. That way the iPod could display everything from memos to books, newspapers, and, of course, email. Masters would also like Apple to publish details of the iPod's firmware, which would make it possible to add games and other programs. The iPod's

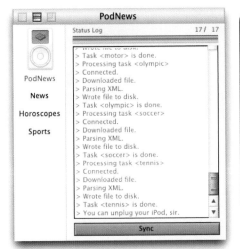

```
PodNews                    17 / 17
Status Log
> Wrote file to disk.
> Task <motor> is done.
> Processing task <olympic>
> Connected.
> Downloaded file.
> Parsing XML.
> Wrote file to disk.
> Task <olympic> is done.
> Processing task <soccer>
> Connected.
> Downloaded file.
> Parsing XML.
> Wrote file to disk.
> Task <soccer> is done.
> Processing task <tennis>
> Connected.
> Downloaded file.
> Parsing XML.
> Wrote file to disk.
> Task <tennis> is done.
> You can unplug your iPod, sir.

          Sync

PodNews
News
Horoscopes
Sports
```

Pod person: Jean-Olivier Lanctôt-David, a 14-year-old hacker from Canada, and a screenshot of his PodNews program, which fetches headlines from the Web in XML format and displays them on the iPod's small screen.

237

iPod nut: Joe Masters (left) and his college buddies enjoy some doughnuts. Masters wrote EphPod, which connects iPods to Windows machines. The EphPod window is shown below.

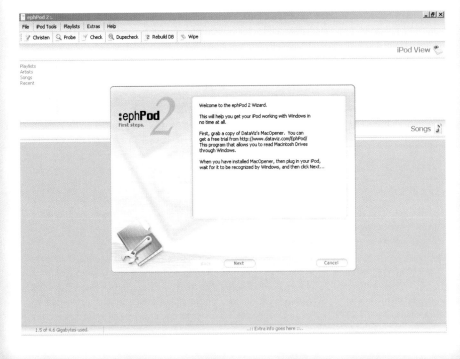

```
ephPod 2
File  iPod Tools  Playlists  Extras  Help
 Christen   Probe   Check   Dupecheck   Rebuild DB   Wipe
                                                        iPod View

Playlists
Artists
Songs
Recent
                                                        Songs
:ephPod 2
First steps.

Welcome to the ephPod 2 Wizard.
This will help you get your iPod working with Windows in
no time at all.

First, grab a copy of DataViz's MacOpener.  You can
get a free trial from http://www.dataviz.com/EphPod/
This program that allows you to read Macintosh Drives
through Windows.

When you have installed MacOpener, then plug in your iPod,
wait for it to be recognized by Windows, and then click Next...

                Next              Cancel

1.5 of 4.6 Gigabytes used.           ...:: Extra info goes here ::...
```

238

scroll wheel, he said, would be great for games like Tetris. "If Apple opened the firmware, that would blow it open," he said. "That would change everything. That would be phenomenal."

iPod hackers also figured out all kinds of undocumented tips and tricks, including a diagnostic mode that checks the iPod's internal hard drive, among other things.

The hacks provide clues to the future direction of the iPod. VersionTracker, a popular software-download Web site, lists more than several dozen different hacks for the iPod. "No doubt Apple is taking its cue from some of these hacks," said Blake Patterson, who runs the iPodHacks Web site. "Apple is seeing that a lot of users want these kind of organizer functions." Apple didn't respond to requests for comments.

iPOD PIRACY (HAVE iPOD, WILL SECRETLY BOOTLEG)

When Apple introduced the iPod, the company was aware that people might use it to rip off music from the Net or friends' machines. Each new iPod, in fact, is emblazoned with a sticker that warns, "Don't Steal Music." But it is unlikely that Apple imagined people would walk into computer stores, plug their iPod into display computers, and use it to copy software off the hard drives. This is exactly the scenario witnessed in early 2002,

just a few months after Apple first introduced the iPod, by Kevin Webb at a Dallas CompUSA store.

Webb, a computer consultant from Dallas, was browsing his local CompUSA when he saw a young man walk toward him listening to an iPod. Webb recognized the iPod's distinctive ear buds. The teenager stopped at a nearby display Macintosh, pulled the iPod from his pocket, and plugged it into the machine with a FireWire cable. Intrigued, Webb peeked over the kid's shoulder to see him copying Microsoft's Office v. X suite, which retailed for $500.

When the iPod is plugged into a Macintosh, its icon automatically pops up on the desktop (if it's set up as an external hard drive, which is easily done). To copy software, all the kid had to do was drag and drop files onto the iPod's icon. Office v. X is about 200MB, but it copies to the iPod's hard drive in less than a minute. "Watching him, it dawned on me that this was something that was very easy to do," Webb said. "In the Mac world it's pretty easy to plug in and copy things. It's a lot easier than stealing the box."

Webb watched the teenager copy a couple of other applications. He left the kid to find a CompUSA employee. "I went over and told a CompUSA guy, but he looked at me like I was clueless," Webb said. Unsure whether the kid was a thief or an out-of-uniform employee, Webb watched as he left the store. "I thought

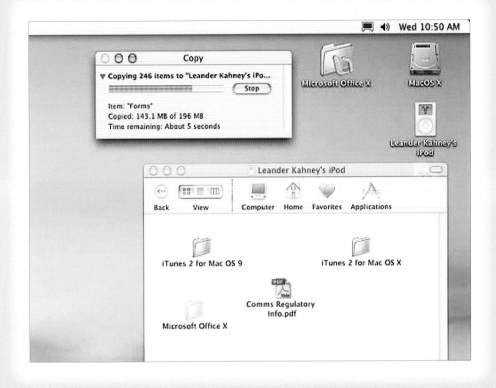

there's no point in getting any more involved in this imbroglio," Webb said. "Besides, this is Texas. You never know what he might have been carrying."

The iPod's FireWire interface—one of its most important but undersold features—allows huge files to be copied in seconds. The iPod doesn't even have to leave the user's pocket. And while the iPod has a built-in anti-piracy mechanism that prevents music files from being copied from one computer to another, it has no such protection for software.

Ironically, Microsoft pioneered an easy-to-use installation scheme on the Mac that makes its Mac software relatively easy to pilfer. When installing Office, users simply drag and drop the Office folder onto their hard drive. Everything is packaged together, including a self-repair mechanism that replaces critical files in the system folder. By contrast, a lot of software on the Windows platform relies on a bunch of system files that are only installed during an installation process. Simply copying an application from one machine to another will not work.

"This is the first we have heard of this form of piracy," said Erik Ryan, a Microsoft product manager. "And while this is a possibility, people should be reminded that this is considered theft."

While the iPod may be ideal for a software-stealing spree, there are a number of other devices on the market that could also be used by virtual shoplifters, including any number of external FireWire drives and tiny USB keychain drives. However, except for those with new USB 2 ports, most keychain drives are a lot slower than FireWire, requiring the virtual shoplifter to hang around while the ill-gotten gains are transferring.

CompUSA and other computer stores could take a few simple steps to prevent software from being copied, said Mac expert Dave Horrigan, who writes a syndicated Macintosh column. Any Mac can easily be configured to allow changes only by administrators, he said. Also, a system profile tool logs all peripheral equipment, but it must be running to log an iPod. For Macs running OS X, a locked dummy file in an application's package will protect the entire file from being copied without a password.

Dennis Lloyd, publisher of iPod fan site iPodlounge, said he was shocked to hear of an iPod put to such use. "I can see how easy it would be to do," he said. "It's a shame someone has stooped this low to bring bad press to the insanely great iPod."

OTHER FORMS OF THEFT

It's not just Apple's iPod that can be used to sneakily copy software from machines at computer stores; there are dozens of tawdry ways involving built-in CD burners, digital cameras, and even the Internet, which was used to send software from inside an Apple store. It's long been known that the built-in CD burners of demonstration machines are great for making pirate copies of software.

One Mac user, who asked to remain anonymous, told how a not-too-bright CompUSA employee actually copied some software for him when he asked to test an iMac's built-in CD burner. "The CompUSA employee gladly complied," the anonymous user said. "Why be covert, when the employees are happy to help?" Anon said he later destroyed the disc.

"This sort of stuff goes on all the time in school environments," wrote J. R. Griffith, multimedia chair of a high school in Houston. "We catch students all the time either trying to burn to the CD-R or copy to their [Iomega] Zip drives or Jaz drives." Some Mac users said using FireWire hard drives like the iPod harkens back to the old days, when software was copied from stores using floppy disks. "I did this same sort of in-store piracy with floppy disks when I was 18 years old," said Darin Adler. "I even brought floppies with my own copying program to circumvent copy protection."

Another Mac user, who also asked to remain anonymous, described how a "friend" used his digital camera to copy software from a Los Angeles Kinko's. "I know of someone who got software from Kinko's in this way," he said. "They had two 64MB memory cards. One can also put in a program like Aladdin Systems' StuffIt Deluxe, execute it on the target computer, and pack things down quite a bit.... A couple of minutes of relative privacy is all it takes." The use of a digital camera is particularly sneaky. People often take cameras to stores to test their compatibility before buying a new computer.

Perhaps the cleverest method of snagging some ill-gotten software was described by Machacker, who claims to have sent himself software over the Internet from inside an Apple retail store. "I was at the mall with some friends on the way to an Underoath concert," he said. "We stopped off at the store, and I did it for kicks."

The machine had a high-speed connection to the Internet. Although it was protected from intrusion from outside the store's firewall, there was nothing to stop Machacker from sending stuff from the inside. All he needed was the Internet Protocol (IP) address of his machine at home, which had a fast, persistent connection to the Net. Using the File Transfer Protocol (FTP) server built in to Mac OS X, Machacker sent himself a copy of Macromedia's FreeHand 10, an illustration program that costs $400. Apple encourages shoppers to play around with the demo equipment, and he was pretty much left alone. "The staff and shoppers had no idea what I was doing," he said. "It was pretty simple."

Bob Kruger, vice president of enforcement at the Business Software Alliance, a Washington, D.C. trade association, said he'd never before heard of people stealing software by copying it inside a store with a digital device. "It's awful," he said. "It means that people have no sense that they're doing anything wrong or that they have to conceal what they're doing. It's not as obvious as shoplifting, but it's still a very blatant act. It's an indication of how much work still needs to be done educating people why piracy is wrong."

Kruger said his organization estimates the software industry loses a whopping third of its potential income to piracy, or $12 billion annually. But Kruger added that the kind of one-off piracy described above is just a drop in the bucket compared with piracy in the workplace, over the Net, and by professional counterfeiters. Most piracy is performed by companies that don't buy licenses for all the software installed on employees' machines, Kruger said. Corporate piracy accounts for perhaps 60 percent of lost revenues, Kruger estimated, followed by Internet file trading and large professional counterfeiting operations, many of which now sell their wares through online auction sites.

Ironically, Kruger said software piracy is on the decline, despite technologies that make it easy. Twelve years ago, Kruger said, as much as half the software in use was unauthorized. Today it's about one in three programs. "It's not a problem of the technology," he said. "It's a problem of people using the technology. Technology is good. Piracy is bad."

ANDREW ANDREW (THEY WALK ALIKE, THEY DJ ALIKE)

Andrew Andrew, a pair of New York DJs, was among the first club DJs to swap bulky boxes of records for Apple's svelte iPods. Instead of a box of records, the pair totes a pair of iPods to gigs at galleries, parties, and clubs all over town. They host a regular Tuesday-night spot, the iParty, at Apt., a trendy nightclub in the Meatpacking District.

Even by New York standards, Andrew Andrew is eccentric. The two dress identically, have the same haircut, and wear the same glasses. They eat the same food, read the same books. They carry identical iPods, cell phones, Palm handhelds, and wallets. They look like twins but are, in fact, business partners. Their company, Andrew Andrew, is a registered partnership with a diverse line of products. They DJ, play in a band, and have created a line in fashion labels, cakes, and house furnishings. As they walk through a large bar in the East Village, every head turns. They attract intense curiosity. Once, someone actually got mad, accusing them of impersonating twins.

For attention seekers, they are quite reserved, almost shy. They refuse to divulge any distinguishing information—last names, birthdays, backgrounds. They always wear the same outfits. Their haircuts are cropped short. They drink the same vodka tonics and when they smoke, Andrew lights two cigarettes. Like twins, they finish each other's sentences. "When you're with someone a lot, you start to talk alike," explained one of the Andrews.

Andrew Andrew live together in an apartment in Queens that doubles as their office. Their wardrobe contains two of everything, arranged by color. They've discarded everything that doesn't match. Their toiletries are paired. Their library contains two of each book, which they read in synchrony. They have the same tattoo of Mario on their right arms. They eat the same food. "In seven years we'll be chemically exact," the other Andrew said.

The pair met at Disneyland about three years ago. Andrew approached Andrew and asked him, "Mac or IBM?" "It's the pivotal question of our time," Andrew said.

They are both Mac guys, although they now think IBM, at least the old IBM, is cooler. "IBM is retro computing," said Andrew. "It's DOS, green screens." The same aesthetic is applied to their home furnishing "division," called Advanced Settings. They sell a dust cover for the original iMac, which has become dated. Made of canvas with a Toile print (very hot in the design world, Andrew said), the cover shields the iMac, keyboard, and mouse when not in use.

"When you first got the iMac it was cool," Andrew said. "But it's become dated, a parody of itself." "In 10 years you can take [the cover] off when the iMac becomes cool again," said the other.

They've designed a similar cover for the new VW Beetle.

The two serve as DJs at art galleries and nightclubs about once a month. Dressed as mad scientists in white lab coats to match the iPods, they play an eccentric set. They choose a word—"sex," "work," or "world," for example—and play songs containing the word in the artist's name, song title, or lyrics. It makes for a diverse mix: opera, pop, rockabilly, techno, and dozens of other styles. It doesn't always go down too well.

(BELOW TOP) Listen up: Andrew Andrew is a pair of New York DJs that spins tunes with Apple iPods instead of vinyl. The pair not only has matching iPods, the two dress alike, eat alike, and read the same books—simultaneously. When they met, the first question Andrew asked Andrew was, "Mac or IBM?"
CREDIT: ANDREW ANDREW

(BELOW BOTTOM) Mad Mad: When iPod DJing, Andrew Andrew often dress as mad scientists. The white lab coats match the iPods.
CREDIT: ANDREW ANDREW

In fact, this brand of DJing goes down best at art galleries, where the arty crowds are tolerant of eccentricity. At one nightclub gig, they were asked to leave after just 30 minutes. But as they became better known, people started to catch on.

Naturally, their iPods contain the same songs. (Their Palms are also synchronized to the same files.) Before the iPods, they DJed with 15 to 20 preburned CDs and a handwritten set list. The iPods have vastly simplified the process. "We've been DJing differently to other DJs from the get-go," said Andrew. "So for us, the iPod is perfect. A lot of people don't like the songs, but for the DJ, it's perfect."

Andrew Andrew's bakery division is similarly unique: They sell just one cake, printed with a photo in food dye of the two standing on either side of Madame Tussaud's wax Napoleon. For a while, one of the cakes was displayed in a Manhattan bakery. The pair took great delight in hanging around, watching people do a double take.

"It's about making people do a double take," said Andrew. "Everything we do is about awareness," said the other. "It's high-minded, but it's so capitalist."

iPOD DJING (WITH AN iPOD, WHO NEEDS A TURNTABLE?)

Yesterday it was jukeboxes. Today, it's the iPod. An upscale New York nightclub has a unique DJ setup, complete with a pair of iPods. The difference—patrons are invited to be the DJs.

(LEFT) What a pair: DJs Andrew Andrew and their matching tattoos and gadgets at an East Village bar.
CREDIT: LEANDER KAHNEY

(ABOVE) Team Pod: New York's trendy Apt. bar allows patrons to be the DJ. The nightclub has set up a pair of iPods through a standard mixing desk. Patrons take a ticket, deli style, and when their number comes up they get seven minutes of dance floor fame.
CREDIT: APT.

The club is called Apt. (pronounced A-P-T), a trendy lounge in Manhattan's Meatpacking District. Next to the bar is the DJ table. The setup is based on a standard mixer, which allows the DJ to fade between two music sources. But instead of two turntables, there's a pair of iPods. Everyone gets to play. Would-be DJs take a numberaed ticket from a deli-style dispenser. Printouts of all 3,000 songs are available to help DJs prepare a set list. "Playing of any heavy metal ballads will result in immediate expulsion from the premises," the printout warns. With 3,000 songs to choose from, patrons play everything from Black Sabbath to Basement Jaxx. Sets last seven minutes; the time is counted down on a giant digital clock.

The iPod setup provides hours of boozy, gregarious fun. Half the bar crowds around the mixing desk, offering advice or criticism or just dancing away. "It gets pretty crazy," said Sai Blount, the lounge's music promoter. "We have people yelling. Some people boo. A couple of girls came in here three or four weeks in a row. They got really good. They were like professional."

Matt Maland, a 27-year-old part-time DJ, is a semi-regular. He's even figured out how to make the iPods scratch. By hitting the center button twice in quick succession, the music backs up a fraction. "It's fun," he said. "It's different. It's a challenge. You have to think what songs go together more than vinyl because you can't beat-match."

The iPod DJing has become a major attraction. The fun runs until 3 or 4 a.m. every night of the week. On Tuesdays, the bar hosts iParty, overseen by New York's preeminent iPod DJs, Andrew Andrew.

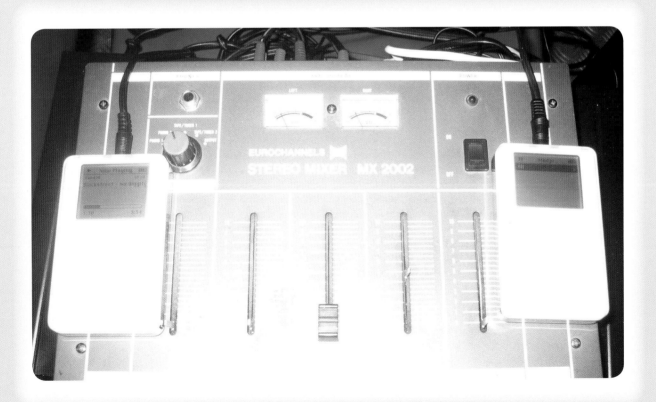

The gallery features pictures of iPods in front of bombed-out palaces in Afghanistan, on jungle expeditions in Peru, and in Mick Jagger's garden in London.

There are dogs, dogs on motorbikes, lovers, statues, and a nearly naked cowboy.

There are snaps of people with iPods riding a roller coaster in Orlando, Florida, sunbathing in Greece, and giving birth in New York.

iPods have been captured on top of mountains, 825 feet below the Earth's surface, and inside a Parisian fridge.
ALL PICTURES COURTESY OF iPODLOUNGE

iPODS AROUND THE WORLD

Apple's iPod is the subject of a unique homage: hundreds of photos from all over the world showing iPods in exotic locales. The iPods Around the World gallery, part of the iPodlounge Web site, has collected more than 1,000 pictures of iPods in settings all over the globe, from far-flung travel destinations to their owners' own backyards.

The gallery features pictures of iPods in front of bombed-out palaces in Afghanistan, on jungle expeditions in Peru, and in Mick Jagger's garden in London. iPods have been captured on top of mountains, 825 feet below the Earth's surface, and inside a Parisian fridge. There are snaps of people with iPods riding a roller coaster in Orlando, Florida, sunbathing in Greece, and giving birth in New York. There are dogs, dogs on motorbikes, lovers, statues, and a nearly naked cowboy. Pictures have been sent from nearly 60 countries, including Vietnam, Turkey, Russia, and Iceland.

The gallery was the idea of Dennis Lloyd, publisher of iPodlounge. "I'm surprised that it's been so successful," he said. "But I had a feeling the iPod would take the MP3 world by storm." The gallery is reminiscent of the kidnapped gnome phenomenon—featured in the movie *Amélie*—wherein globetrotters borrow a neighbor's garden gnome and send back picture postcards documenting the gnome's travels. "I think some of the best pictures have been those that were from very remote areas or areas that had been recently in current news," Lloyd said.

The collection has grown so large, Lloyd is categorizing the pictures and plans to launch a dynamic gallery with a searchable database. The gallery has even inspired a couple of imitators: Newtons Around the World and a Sony CLIÉ gallery that is now defunct.

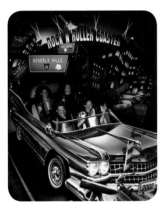

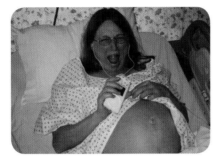

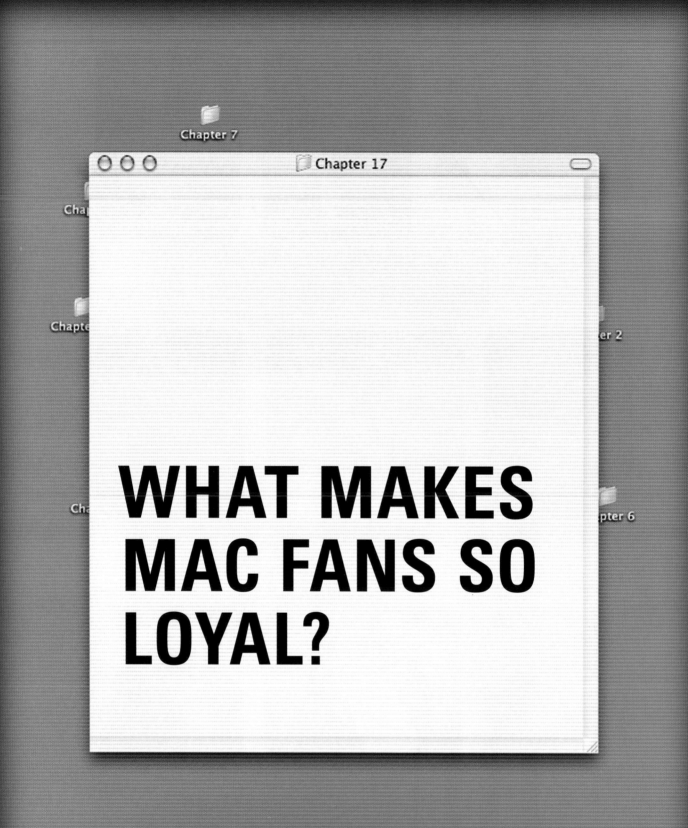

Apple represents creativity and individuality; Microsoft represents business and conformity. Apple is the scrappy underdog; Microsoft is the big, predatory monopoly.

One of the defining characteristics of the Mac community is its loyalty to Apple. Through thick and thin, Apple's customers stick by the company. In the summer of 2002, Apple upset the Mac community by suddenly announcing a $100 annual subscription fee for its .Mac online services, which were formerly free. On top of this, an upgrade for OS X—the kind of upgrade users usually don't pay for—would cost $130. The new pricing policies prompted howls of protest. Web sites, online forums, and news stories were full of acrimonious kvetching about "gouging" and "bait-and-switch." Longtime users launched petitions and fired off angry letters, and for the first time in years, there were lots of threats to leave the Mac platform altogether. But despite the howling, there's been no mass exodus to Windows. The opposite, in fact, seems to be true. Anecdotal evidence points to more and more people switching to the Mac.

Could other companies get away with this? Probably not. Yahoo and Hotmail, which provide free online email, have started charging for extra services, but they supply basic service for nothing. Likewise, Microsoft's latest update for Windows XP is free. Andrew Lackey, a visiting professor of business and economics journalism at Boston University, said Apple's monopoly in the Mac business allows it to get away with things companies in a competitive market can't. "With Apple you're a captive, and to some extent they abuse that privilege," Lackey said. "I would have thought Apple would be all folksy, like a Ben & Jerry's kind of company. But in my experience, PC companies are much more responsive."

The loyalty to Apple has led some to describe the Mac community as masochistic, the "punish me harder" brigade in the words of the Register. "They eat it up," said Matthew Rothenberg, an editor at Ziff Davis and a longtime Apple watcher. "It's like a B&D [bondage and dominance] relationship. There needs to a psychosexual analysis of the Mac community."

Customer loyalty was the only thing that saved Apple during the late 1990s, when the company was in danger of going out of business, according to Gil Amelio, the CEO in charge at the time. "It's the cult," Amelio told *Computerworld*. "It's what's kept the damn thing afloat through some of the most incredibly bad business decisions I've ever seen anywhere."

During this time, psychologist Ross Goldstein was commissioned by a rival computer manufacturer to figure out how to appeal to marooned Apple customers if the company went under. Goldstein, a clinical psychologist with the B/R/S Group, a market research firm, recruited a number of Apple users for a focus group. To qualify, they had to agree they would consider migrating to Windows if Apple went out of business. But as soon as the session started, they all reversed themselves and said they'd never consider switching.

"They were steadfast in their resistance to moving over," Goldstein said. "It was humorous. They were picked because they might switch, but they all said, 'I'll be an Apple user until my dying keystrokes.' The degree of loyalty to the platform, and everything it represented, was so profound. It was fascinating." Goldstein said participants' left brain, the logical side, was telling them they might have to switch if Apple went under. But the right brain, the emotional attachment to Apple, rejected it. There was a profound sense that Apple was one of them—

counterculture, grassroots, human, approachable, Goldstein said. "Apple really appeals to the humanistic side of people," Goldstein said. "The image of the brand, the heritage, the experience. It really spoke to who they were."

By contrast, Microsoft was the dark enemy. "It was almost as though they were prisoners of war," Goldstein said. "Microsoft had taken over the computer world, and they might have to go over, but they would not do so willingly." As Goldstein discovered, for a lot of Mac fans, one of the major appeals of Apple is that it's not Microsoft.

To Mac users, Apple represents everything that Microsoft isn't. Apple innovates; Microsoft copies. Apple puts out solid products; Microsoft puts out buggy ones. Apple represents creativity and individuality; Microsoft represents business and conformity. Apple is the scrappy underdog; Microsoft is the big, predatory monopoly.

Such is Mac users' derision, Microsoft is commonly referred to as Micro$oft, Microshaft, or Microshit. Bill Gates, of course, is the Antichrist. There's the common perception that Gates is in business for every penny he can get, while Apple exists to create great technology—to change the world, in Steve Jobs' words. For Apple, turning a profit is secondary.

"There's a lot of ill will toward Microsoft for a lot of reasons," said Steve Manning, cofounder of Igor, a brand consultancy in San Francisco, California. "Microsoft crams a bad system down peoples' throats. It's the evil empire, Big Brother, a monolithic corporation. Apple has done a lot of things right in the way they position themselves and the way they speak to the world."

Manning said that while he's obliged to use a Windows machine at work, he went out and bought several Macs for his home. Like a lot of Mac fans, he enjoys the feeling that he's in control of his computer, rather than Microsoft. "At home, it's nice to use a machine that the corporation can't force you to use," he said. "It's mine. It's personal. This is mine and you can't taint it."

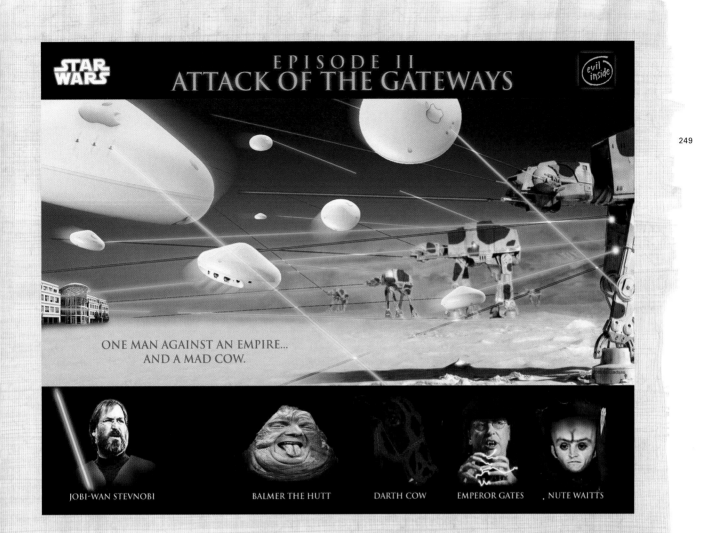

EPISODE II
ATTACK OF THE GATEWAYS

evil inside

ONE MAN AGAINST AN EMPIRE...
AND A MAD COW.

JOBI-WAN STEVNOBI   BALMER THE HUTT   DARTH COW   EMPEROR GATES   NUTE WAITTS

ewingsquadron

(left) Use the Mac, Luke: In the Mac universe, Apple is the scrappy underdog, epitomized by Luke Skywalker. Microsoft, of course, is the big, bad empire.
CREDIT: EWINGPILOT

(above) To Mac users, Apple represents everything that Microsoft isn't. Apple innovates; Microsoft copies. Apple puts out solid products; Microsoft puts out buggy ones.
CREDIT: BRIAN BILLADEAU

"Without the brand, Apple would be dead.... The brand is all they've got. The power of their branding is all that keeps them alive. It's got nothing to do with products."

Dark and bubbly: Apple is one of the leading branding companies in the world. Marketing experts like Marc Gobé argue that Apple's brand is the key to the company's success. It's got nothing to do with products like the iMac or iPod.

CREDIT: ROBERLAN BORGES

APPLE: IT'S ALL ABOUT THE BRAND

Ask marketers and advertising experts why Mac users are so loyal, and they all cite the same reason: Apple's brand. It's no coincidence that during the late 1980s and early 1990s it was a marketing executive from Pepsi, John Sculley, who turned Apple into the biggest single computer company in the world, with $11 billion in annual sales. Sculley marketed Apple like crazy, boosting the advertising budget from $15 million to $100 million. "People talk about technology, but Apple was a marketing company," Sculley told the *Guardian* newspaper in 1997. "It was the marketing company of the decade."

The current CEO, Steve Jobs, spent $100 million marketing the iMac, which was a runaway hit. Apple continues to spend lots of money on high-profile ads like the Switch campaign, and it shows.

"It's a really powerful brand," said Robin Rusch, editor of brandchannel.com, which awarded Apple "Brand of the Year" in 2001. "The overwhelming presence of Apple comes through in everything they do."

Marketer Marc Gobé, author of *Emotional Branding* and principal of d/g worldwide, said Apple's brand is the key to its survival. It's got nothing to do with innovative products like the iMac or the iPod. "Without the brand, Apple would be dead," he said. "Absolutely. Completely. The brand is all they've got. The power of their branding is all that keeps them alive. It's got nothing to do with products."

Gobé, who hails from France, formulated this view while researching his book, in which he tells how brands have established deep, lasting bonds with their customers. Apple, of course, is the archetypal emotional brand. It's not just intimate

Marketer Marc Gobé, author of *Emotional Branding*,
said Apple's brand is the key to its survival.
CREDIT: MARC GOBÉ

with its customers; it is loved. Other examples are automaker Lexus, retailer Target, and outdoor clothing line Patagonia. "Apple is about imagination, design, and innovation," Gobé said from his office in New York. "It goes beyond commerce. This business should have been dead 10 years ago, but people said we've got to support it."

Gobé is, of course, referring to Apple's financial tailspin during the mid-1990s, when the company looked in danger of going out of business. At the time, its products were lackluster, its branding a mess. "Before Steve Jobs came back, the brand was pretty much gone," he said. "That's one of the reasons Apple has been rebranded—to rejuvenate the brand." Apple abandoned the old rainbow-hued Apple logo in favor of a minimalist monochrome one, gave its computers a funky, colorful look, and streamlined the messages in its advertising. It's done wonders, Gobé said.

Gobé argued that, in some cases, branding has become as powerful as religion. "People's connections with brands transcend commerce," he said. Gobé cited Nike, which sparked customers' ire when it was revealed the company's products were assembled in sweatshops. "They were not pissed about the products," Gobé said. "It's about the company's ethics. It's interesting how emotionally involved people are."

According to Gobé, emotional brands have three things in common:

THE COMPANY PROJECTS A HUMANISTIC CORPORATE CULTURE AND A STRONG CORPORATE ETHIC, CHARACTERIZED BY VOLUNTEERISM, SUPPORT OF GOOD CAUSES, OR INVOLVEMENT IN THE COMMUNITY: Nike blundered here. Apple, on the other hand, comes across as profoundly humanist. Its founding ethos was power to the people through technology, and it remains committed to computers in education. "It's always about people," Gobé said.

THE COMPANY HAS A UNIQUE VISUAL AND VERBAL VOCABULARY, EXPRESSED IN PRODUCT DESIGN AND ADVERTISING: This is true of Apple. Its products and advertising are clearly recognizable. (So is Target's, or even Wal-Mart's, Gobé said.)

THE COMPANY HAS ESTABLISHED A "HEARTFELT CONNECTION" WITH ITS CUSTOMERS. THIS CAN TAKE SEVERAL FORMS, FROM BUILDING TRUST TO ESTABLISHING A COMMUNITY AROUND A PRODUCT. IN APPLE'S CASE, ITS PRODUCTS ARE DESIGNED AROUND PEOPLE: "Take the iPod; it brings an emotional, sensory experience to computing," Gobé said. "Apple's design is people driven."

Gobé noted that Apple has always projected a human touch—from the charisma of Steve Jobs to the notion that its products are sold for a love of technology. "It's like having a good friend," Gobé said. "That's what's interesting about this brand. Somewhere they have created this really humanistic, beyond-business relationship with users, and created a cult-like relationship with their brand. It's a big tribe—everyone is one of them. You're part of the brand."

The human touch is also expressed in product design, Gobé said. Apple's flat-screen iMac, for example, was marketed as though it were created personally by Steve Jobs and Jonathan Ive, not by factory workers in Asia. "People are anxious and confused," Gobé said. "Technology is accelerating faster and faster than we can keep up with. People need to find some grounding, that human touch, the leading hand. There's a need to recreate tribes that give people a grounding."

Writer Naomi Klein is a leading critic of branding, especially Apple's. Klein, author of *No Logo*, argues that companies like Apple are no longer selling products. They are selling brands, which evoke a subtle mix of people's hopes, dreams, and aspirations. Klein notes how Benetton used images of racial harmony to sell clothes, while Apple used great leaders—Cesar Chavez, Gandhi, and the Dalai Lama—to persuade people that a Macintosh might also allow them to "Think Different."

"People are drawn to these brands because they are selling their own ideas back to them, they are selling the most powerful ideas that we have in our culture, such as transcendence and community—even democracy itself, these are all brand meanings now," she told the *Guardian* newspaper.

Klein's analysis of branding finds a receptive audience in the marketing community. Jean-Marie Dru, described by *Adbusters* as the "ad industry's current wonderkid," also believes that brands thrive or perish based on the ideals they espouse. "Apple expresses liberty regained; Pepsi, youthfulness; Oil of Olay, timeless beauty; Saturn, the American competitive spirit; and AT&T, the promises of the future," he wrote in his book *Disruption.* To Dru, brands are more important than products. Products have limited life cycles, but brands—if managed well—last forever. "The battle of brands and products will be, above all, a battle of ideas," he wrote.

Ryan Bigge, writing in *Adbusters,* said: "Our dreams and desires for a better world are no longer articulated by JFKs nor generated through personal epiphanies—they are now the intellectual currency of Pepsi and Diesel. We used to have movements for change—now we have products. Brands may befriend us, console us and inspire us, but the relationship comes at the highest price imaginable—the loss of self."

Apple's famous "1984" Super Bowl ad, for example, was expressly political: Its message was, give power to the masses. The power, of course, was computing power. "Macintosh was always bigger than the product," Steve Hayden, the ad's copywriter, told *Adweek.* "We thought of it as an ideology, a value set. It was a way of letting the whole world access the power of computing and letting them talk to one another. The democratization of technology—the computer for the rest of us."

The "1984" ad began a branding campaign that portrayed Apple as a symbol of counterculture—rebellious, free-thinking, and creative. According to Charles Pillar, a columnist for the *Los Angeles Times,* this image is a calculated marketing ploy to sell expensive computers. "Expressions of almost spiritual faithfulness to the Mac, although heartfelt, weren't a purely spontaneous response to a sublime creation," he wrote. "They were a response to a calculated marketing ploy to sell computers that cost much more than competing brands.

"I'm not making this up. Members of the Mac's original engineering and marketing team told me all about it. They did it by building a sense of belonging to an elite club by portraying the Mac as embodying the values of righteous outsiderism and rebellion against injustice. It started in the early '80s with the famous '1984' TV commercial that launched the Mac, and continued with 'The computer for the rest of us' slogan and several ad campaigns playing on a revolutionary theme."

Steve Manning, cofounder of Igor, a brand consultancy in San Francisco, California, said even a seasoned professional like himself is seduced. "Even though I understand this stuff, I've bought into it," he said. "I own four Macs. They're more expensive, but the advertising and marketing works."

FOR MAC USERS, IT TAKES A VILLAGE

Consumer behaviorists like Tom O'Guinn think the key to Apple's customers' loyalty is the Mac community itself. Apple users are not loyal to Apple per se. They are loyal to Apple and to each other. "It's not just about the relationship to the marketer," said O'Guinn. "It's a triad between marketer, customer, and customer."

O'Guinn said that's why there's a storm of protest about Apple's treatment of its customers, but few defections to other computer platforms. "You may get mad at the company, but the bond with the community means you don't really have a

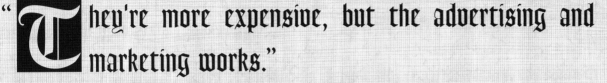

"They're more expensive, but the advertising and marketing works."

choice," he said. "You may complain, but you're not going to leave. In a cohesive community, the marketer can get away with all kinds of stuff because the cohesion is so strong."

O'Guinn, a professor at the University of Illinois's College of Advertising, is a leading expert in "brand communities," of which the Mac community is a prime example. In March 2001, O'Guinn coauthored a paper with Albert Muniz of DePaul University in Chicago introducing the idea of brand communities—a community that has developed around a brand, instead of, say, a neighborhood, church, pastime, or profession. "This is about brands," the authors wrote. "This is the tie that binds."

Published in the *Journal of Consumer Research,* the paper was the fruit of five years of research, O'Guinn said. According to Muniz and O'Guinn, research into consumer behavior has traditionally focused on the relationship between a marketer and an individual consumer. Despite the centrality of community to modern social thought, it is rarely applied to groups devoted to particular brands. The paper explored three brand communities loyal to the Macintosh, Saab, and the Ford Bronco.

The authors argued that these communities are real communities, not ad hoc coalitions of like-minded people. Nor are they "homogenous lifestyle segments" or "consumption constellations." They are real communities, bound by a brand, that display three central characteristics of all communities:

SHARED CONSCIOUSNESS: A shared consciousness, or "consciousness of kind," is the most important element, the authors note. It is a sense of "we-ness." The authors argued that it doesn't matter that the Mac community is mediated by mass media: magazines, books, and the Internet. Although members are spread all over the globe, they easily imagine they are alike because they assume they share common values. "Members feel that they 'sort of know each other' at some level, even if they have never met," the authors wrote.

RITUALS AND TRADITIONS: Members of brand communities engage in certain rituals and traditions. Saab drivers wave to each other as they pass on the road. Mac users often share stories about the brand—the Mac's relative immunity to viruses, for example. There's the communal use of logos. Mac users are

well known for their predilection for Apple stickers, T-shirts, and Web banners, the authors wrote. They also show a keen interest in the history of Apple. A lot of Mac users know the date January 24, 1984—the day the Mac was introduced.

MORAL RESPONSIBILITY: Members have a sense of moral responsibility to the community as a whole and to each other. People look out for each another, help repair products, solve problems, and share information, like where to get the best deals. This information is often more useful than information provided by the marketer because it's untainted by self-interest, the authors wrote.

In conclusion, Muniz and O'Guinn said brand communities perform several important functions on behalf of the brand: recruiting new members, perpetuating the history and culture of the brand, and providing free help and information. The community also exerts a lot of pressure on members to remain loyal. Of the three, the Mac community is the most cohesive, the authors noted.

On the downside, brand communities can be a pain in the neck for a secretive marketer like Apple. "Brand communities, particularly those operating within computer-mediated environments, could pose enormous rumor control problems," the authors wrote.

Muniz and O'Guinn noted that social critics often blame contemporary commerce for the destruction of communities. From Kant and Marx onward, many theorists have argued that modern industrialization has destroyed traditional, largely agrarian communities, bringing dislocation, isolation, and the profound discontent of the modern soul. But Muniz and O'Guinn see positive benefits of brand communities: They give consumers a greater voice, provide an important information resource, and grant wider social benefits through communal interaction.

"The intersection of brand—a defining entity of consumer culture—and community—a core sociological notion—is an important one," the authors wrote. "We believe brand communities to be real, significant and generally a good thing, a democratic thing and evidence of the persistence of community in consumer culture."

"**People say they are a Buddhist or a Catholic. We say we're Mac users, and that means we have similar values.**"

iProphet: The Mac community reveres Steve Jobs as a deity. Only he has the power to create or destroy products. Jobs has been portrayed as Apple's savior and a technology prophet. His life story, in fact, closely adheres to Joseph Campbell's classic hero myths.
CREDIT: CARLOS AGELL

WORSHIPPING AT THE ALTAR OF MAC

Umberto Eco, the Italian semiologist, once famously compared Macs and PCs to the two main branches of the Christian faith: Catholics and Protestants. The Mac is Catholic, he wrote in his back-page column of the Italian news weekly, *L'Espresso,* in September 1994. It is "cheerful, friendly, conciliatory, it tells the faithful how they must proceed step by step to reach—if not the Kingdom of Heaven—the moment in which their document is printed." The Windows PC, on the other hand, is Protestant. It demands "difficult personal decisions, imposes a subtle hermeneutics upon the user, and takes for granted the idea that not all can reach salvation. To make the system work you need to interpret the program yourself: A long way from the baroque community of revelers, the user is closed within the loneliness of his own inner torment."

Eco was joking, but, as some experts have noted, the Mac community does in fact resemble a religion. As do Mac users themselves. "For many Mac people, I think [the Mac community] has a religious feeling to it," said psychologist David

Levine, a self-confessed Mac nut. "For a lot of people who are not comfortable with religion, it provides a community and a common heritage. I think Mac users have a certain common way of thinking, a way of doing things, a certain mindset."

"People say they are a Buddhist or a Catholic," he added. "We say we're Mac users, and that means we have similar values."

Russell Belk, a consumer behaviorist at the University of Utah, goes further. He argues that the Mac community is quasi-religious. Belk has been studying the Mac community for a couple of years and has produced a video monograph called *The Cult of Macintosh* based on a series of interviews with Mac users. It was shown in public for the first time in October 2002 at a marketing conference in Atlanta.

"The Mac and its fans constitute the equivalent of a religion," Belk wrote in the video's abstract. "This religion is based on an origin myth for Apple Computer, heroic and savior legends surrounding its cofounder and current CEO Steve Jobs, the devout faith of its follower congregation, their belief in

The Mac community is the equivalent of a new-age religion, according to Russell Belk, a consumer behaviorist. Belk argues Mac religion is based on myths surrounding the origin of Apple, the savior status of Steve Jobs, and the devout faith of the Mac congregation.

CREDIT: KEVIN STACY

the righteousness of the Macintosh, the existence of one or more Satanic opponents, Mac believers proselytizing and converting nonbelievers, and the hope among cult members that salvation can be achieved by transcending corporate capitalism." Religion, Belk said, is a belief structure that helps people make sense of the world. The "cult of Mac" is a set of beliefs about Apple and the Mac that make sense of the world of technology. It also imparts the community with a quasi-religious character.

In the monograph, Belk argues that Steve Jobs is revered as a deity with the power to create or destroy. Apple's "corporate mythology" portrays him as a "savior." Jobs' life story, in fact, adheres closely to the classic heroic adventure myths delineated by Joseph Campbell, Belk noted. Just like the legends of Odysseus, Jason, Krishna, or Christ, the Jobs' mythology contains the same key elements:

Think Different

THE CALL TO ADVENTURE: joining the Homebrew Computer Club

A HELPER: Steve Wozniak

A WONDROUS JOURNEY: the explosive growth of the early PC industry

TRIALS: competition from IBM, and failures like the Lisa and Apple III

MORE HELPERS: the engineers and artists who created the first Mac

APOTHEOSIS: Jobs is anointed as the technology industry's seer, a prophet

FLIGHT: the expulsion from Apple and a decade in the wilderness at NeXT Computer

RESURRECTION: the return to Apple

THE BOON THAT RESTORES THE WORLD: the iMac and subsequent hit products

Belk noted that Jobs is often portrayed as saintly and ascetic: He draws no salary, and he is a nonsmoking vegan. Belk said Mac users have a love-hate relationship with Jobs. He can be a visionary or a despotic tyrant.

While conducting the interviews for the video, Belk said he noticed how Mac users frequently referred to the community as religious in character. Mac users talk about "evangelizing" the platform, being "persecuted" for using a Mac in a Windows-dominated world, and the "sacrifices" they make for their choice of computer. "It was an analogy that occurred to them before," he said. "It really strikes a chord.... They're in a minority and they're suffering for their beliefs. There's a feeling of martyrdom that has been cultivated."

Belk said Mac users often invoke moral reasons for their choice of machine. To some, it's nothing less than good versus evil. Bill Gates and Microsoft are satanic, the "evil empire," motivated solely by profit. Apple, on the other hand, is driven to create innovative technology. "I'd rather follow a cause that has a noble undertaking than one that is mercenary," one interviewee told Belk.

Apple's marketing department works hard to foster the devotion of its followers, Belk said. The corporate myth of the company's founding—two guys in a garage—resonates with biblical overtones. "It's a miraculous birth in humble surroundings," Belk said. The Apple logo is another biblical reference, Belk said. Apple employed a chief evangelist, Guy Kawasaki, whose job was to bring "good news" to the Mac congregation via the EvangeList mailing list. At one point, Kawasaki attended Billy Graham's school of evangelism.

Belk said some Mac users were more extreme than others, and many projected their own "closet fanaticism," in Belk's words, onto others perceived as more zealous. However, Belk said all the interviewees repeated the same ideas, which told Belk they shared common beliefs.

The Mac community may resemble a congregation, but is it a cult, full of zombie-like fans, slavishly devoted to Apple and all its works? Would Mac fans quaff poisoned Kool-Aid if Steve Jobs commanded it? The press certainly thinks so. Apple is constantly referred to as a "cult brand," and Mac users as the "cult of Mac."

Author Douglas Rushkoff says the Mac community has all the hallmarks of a cult. He devoted a chapter to the cult of Macintosh in a recent book, *Coercion: Why We Listen to What "They" Say*. According to Rushkoff, Mac users perceive themselves as a persecuted minority, a telltale cult trait. And the line between self-image and the Apple brand is often blurred. Mac users work on Macs, their friends work on Macs, they wear Apple-logo shirts, and they drive cars sporting Apple stickers.

"The Mac, like any cult product, is seen as a way for a person to become more who they are," Rushkoff wrote in an email. "Like a Harley helps identify a biker more than any of the 'rice-eaters' that the majority ride, a Mac helps a person create a sense of individuation. At least in image, if not in reality."

For Rushkoff, the clearest sign is the donation of time and energy to sell computers on Apple's behalf. Rushkoff was amazed to discover that Mac enthusiasts went to computer stores to act as volunteer salespeople in the hope of converting nonbelievers.

Even Mac users describe the community as a cult. Rodney Lain, a popular online columnist, noted the Mac community is insular, polarized, elitist, and preoccupied with recruiting new members. "The Mac community—some of us, anyway—exhibits characteristics of cult behavior," he wrote. "Read some of the Mac-related mailing lists. Sometimes, you'll cringe at the fanaticism. Keep in mind that I am a Mac fanatic myself. I should know one when I see one."

Dave Arnott, author of *Corporate Cults,* said the Mac community shows signs of cultlike devotion: Mac users are completely dedicated to the platform, they are isolated from the mainstream, and, in Steve Jobs, they have a charismatic leader. "Some [Mac users] seem to have made an irrational decision to stay with the system when perhaps they should have not," he said. "That's cultlike devotion." Arnott noted that many cult members feel besieged, and that external pressure leads to greater group cohesion. This is true of Mac users, who feel under constant threat from Microsoft.

But Arnott said the Mac is certainly not a cult. Devotion to the Mac is no different than devotion to a car, or a hobby like rollerblading. "We are all culted to some extent," he said. "But how culted are we? It's a question of commitment. I'm committed to my car. But I would give it up. It depends on the depth of the commitment."

Steve Hassan, a clinical psychologist, author, and cult expert, agreed. "There's definitely a cult of Mac out there," he said. "I guess I could be called a member of that group. I'm also a member of the cult of bicycles, scuba diving, and a few other things I care about. As long as it's not destructive, it's a healthy affiliation."

But Hassan, a member of the Moonies during the 1970s who has deprogrammed members of destructive cults, was quick to point out that true cults—like David Koresh's Branch Davidians—are authoritarian, have a pyramid structure, and practice behavior modification and mind control. "There is a vast difference between the Mac cult and a destructive cult," Hassan said. "There's a continuum from healthy to destructive. If everyone needed to dress like Steve Jobs, talk like Steve Jobs, and think like Steve Jobs, you'd have a cult."

(left) Cult expert Steve Hassan said there is a cultlike mentality surrounding the Mac, but it's nothing like the Moonies.
CREDIT: STEVE HASSAN

(below) MacElangelo: And on the eighth day, God created Apple.
CREDIT: MOSZ

BABY, FRIEND, PET: THAT'S MY MAC

For some psychologists and anthropologists, human social instincts are key to Mac loyalty. Just as animal lovers anthropomorphize their pets, Macs users associate human characteristics with their machines.

Geoffrey Miller, an evolutionary psychologist at the University of New Mexico, said the flat-panel iMac, for example, triggers a fostering response because it resembles an infant. In psych talk, it's neotenous. It has childlike features, like the big-eyed characters in Japanese anime. "The new iMac has the essential features of a baby that needs nurturing," he explained. "A big head with a frail neck and body. These are all the cues a healthy human infant might give. It says, 'I've got a big brain so I'm worth taking care of, but I've got a little neck so I need nurturing. Don't abandon me for a Dell PC.' It taps into a response the same way a healthy but needy infant does."

Macs are also generally viewed as "warm" and "friendly," and because of this people enter into social relationships with them, Miller said. "People don't rank their friends objectively or scrutinize their good and bad traits; they simply accept them, faults and all," he said. "Apple isn't judged by performance dimensions because it's a social relationship [users] have with their computer. It's a friendship."

Miller also said Macs are more feminine than Windows PCs. As a result, women feel like their Macs are friends or confidantes.

For their part, men aren't threatened by Macs because they're not sexual rivals. They're more of a female helper. "For men, it feels like a courtship with the computer," Miller said. "They are gentlemanly, protective. The [Windows] PC is a masculine device. Why do I want a sexual rival on my desktop, rather than a feminine servant?"

Miller is the author of *The Mating Mind: How Sexual Choice Shaped the Evolution of Human Nature,* and he is researching the impact of evolutionary psychology on marketing and consumer behavior.

Clinical psychologist Ross Goldstein said Macs are unconsciously perceived as something like an older brother—a little bit nerdy perhaps, but also cool, friendly, and intuitive. Microsoft, on the other hand, is more paternal: a rigid, cold father figure. "[Apple] introduced a sense of play to computing," Goldstein said. "Microsoft is demanding, disciplined, and also fucked up. It gives the experience of being under the thumb. There's this relationship with the two brands."

Goldstein said an element of "imprinting" may also be present in people's relationships with their Macs. Discovered by animal behaviorist Konrad Lorenz, imprinting happens when newborn animals associate their mother with the first thing they see. Ducklings, for example, imprint on a stuffed fox if that's what they encounter on hatching. Likewise, Goldstein said, computer neophytes imprint on Macs if that's their first machine.

Cute: Some psychologists claim that the flat-panel iMacs trigger a nurturing response from their owners. With a head too big for its small neck, a round bottom, and a bright, shining screen, the computer appeals to the user in similar ways as infants do.

CREDIT: LEANDER KAHNEY/APPLE COMPUTER

Brigitte Jordan, a corporate anthropologist at the Palo Alto Research Center, said Mac users were devoted to their machines because of their unique design and the "playful, cheerful" interface. But she noted that PC users can be just as dedicated to their machines. Jordan said people are attached to their computers for two reasons: Computers are storehouses of owners' identities, and they are interactive.

"Computers are now central to our lives," she said. "People cannot operate without them. I would be absolutely sunk without all the information on my computer. When a system goes down, it feels like a part of ourselves is cut off. They function as part of your memory. You don't have to remember things because the machine does it for you."

The interactivity of computers also triggers a deep psychological attraction. "The computer is the one machine that responds to us more than any other thing we have invented," she said. "Children are inherently attracted to something that's responsive, things that move, cats, mobiles, wind-up toys.... It's something that we're hardwired for. It underlies human sociability. It plays into our evolutionary heritage. We learn practically everything by social interaction. The computer is important because it enters into the process. It's that basic abil-

ity, hardwired into us, that underlies our fascination with computers."

Of course, all of this sounds like psychobabble to Mac users. Does anyone buy a Mac because it brings out their parenting instincts, grants membership to a new-age cult, or makes them feel like Gandhi? "No one likes to have their rationality challenged," said Raines Cohen, one of the cofounders of BMUG, a pioneering Mac user group based in Berkeley, California. Ask any Mac user why they use a Mac, and they will extol the virtues of the machine—its ease of use, its striking design, its innovative approach to technology. Many of the dozens more reasons are exhaustively documented by both Apple and scores of Mac-advocacy sites.

"I use the Mac for only one reason," said Martin Joseph. "It's the best personal computer available." Joseph takes exception to calling Mac users cultists, zealots, or "radical extremist fundamentalist Macheads." Joseph contends that calling the Mac a cult brand labels Mac users as irrational.

"Portraying Mac people as zealots is a way to minimize the fact that the Mac is a more advanced system," he said. "Actually, looking at the software and hardware combinations available, one realizes that people are dedicated to Macintosh because it just works."

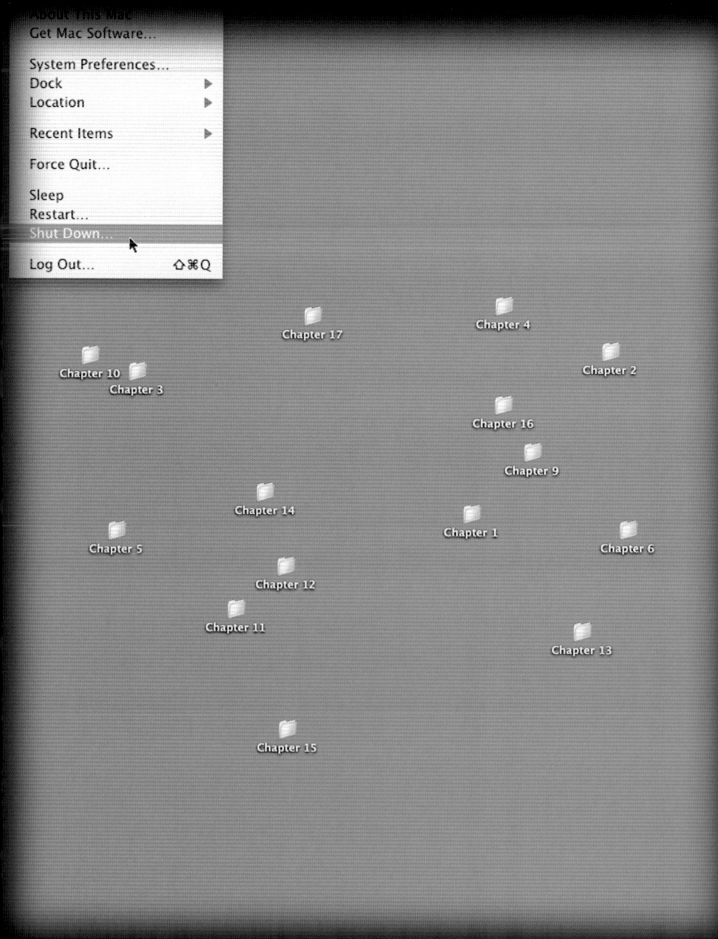

About This Mac
Get Mac Software...

System Preferences...
Dock ▶
Location ▶

Recent Items ▶

Force Quit...

Sleep
Restart...
Shut Down...

Log Out...   ⇧⌘Q

Chapter 17

Chapter 4

Chapter 10
Chapter 3

Chapter 2

Chapter 16

Chapter 9

Chapter 14

Chapter 5

Chapter 1

Chapter 6

Chapter 12

Chapter 11

Chapter 13

Chapter 15

INDEX